Springer Series in Optical Sciences   Volume 27

Springer Series in Optical Sciences

Edited by David L. MacAdam

Editorial Board: J. M. Enoch   D. L. MacAdam   A. L. Schawlow   T. Tamir

D.L. MacAdam

Color Measurement
Theme and Variations

With 92 Figures and 4 Colorplates

Springer-Verlag Berlin Heidelberg New York 1981

6569-8988

ISBN 3-540-10773-8 Springer-Verlag Berlin Heidelberg New York
ISBN 0-387-10773-8 Springer-Verlag New York Heidelberg Berlin

Library of Congress Cataloging in Publication Data. MacAdam, David L., 1910-. Color measurement. (Springer series in optical sciences; v. 27). Bibliography: p. Includes index. 1. Colorimetry. I. Title. II. Series. QC495.M2 535.6'028 81-8802 AACR2

Typesetting: K + V Fotosatz, Beerfelden.
Offset printing: Beltz Offsetdruck, Hemsbach/Bergstr. Bookbinding: J. Schäffer oHG, Grünstadt.
2153/3130-543210

This book is dedicated to the memory of
Arthur Cobb Hardy

Arthur Cobb Hardy (1895 – 1977)

Inventor of recording spectrophotometer
Inspiration and teacher of pioneers in applied colorimetry
Professor of Optics and Photography at Massachusetts Institute of Technology
Teacher of leaders of renaissance of optics
Co-author of *Principles of Optics* (McGraw-Hill, New York, London 1932)
Founder of MIT Color Measurement Laboratory
Coauthor of *Handbook of Colorimetry*
Chief of Camouflage Section of NDRC – Research on visibility and influence of color on perception of distant objects
President of Optical Society of America and Secretary for 17 years
Recipient of Ives Medal, Longstreth Medal of Franklin Institute, Modern Pioneer Award of National Association of Manufacturers, and Progress Medal of Society of Motion Picture and Television Engineers
Honorary D.Sc. (St. Lawrence University)
Honorary LL.D. (University of California)
In gratitude for inspiration and guidance, and
In tribute to his unique contributions to applied optics and colorimetry

Preface

Color is attractive and interesting to everyone. Consequently, control of color is important to all producers, buyers, sellers, and users of colored materials. In various ways, color is an indication of freshness, quality, or other desirable (or undesirable) characteristics of goods. To assure acceptability, saleability, and favorable price − especially in contracts and monitoring of conformance to specifications − numerical expression of color is greatly superior to verbal descriptions. Disagreements concerning words or visual comparisons with samples are all too likely and frequent. Such disagreements underlie much unpleasantness and loss in commerce in consumer goods. Such loss of money and good will must amount to billions of dollars per year, world wide.

Persistent efforts to substitute measurements of color for visual judgment have marked the twentieth century. Because visual perception of small color differences is so acute, the requirements for accuracy and world-wide reproducibility of color measurements have been severe. Only during the last half century have practical spectrophotometers with adequate accuracy been available.

The characteristics of color vision differ even among persons with normal color vision. If different laboratories or countries used different visual data for interpretation of the significance of measurements obtained from spectrophotometers, the need for interchangeably reproducible color specifications would be subverted. To forestall that danger, the International Commission on Illumination (CIE) recommended data that characterize a standard observer for colorimetry. Related to those data, a coordinate system for maplike representation of the results of color measurements was recommended at the same time (1931) by the CIE. Methods for using the CIE data and coordinate system constitute the subject of colorimetry.

The earliest and still most successful exposition of colorimetry was the MIT *Handbook of Colorimetry* (1936). It was written for newcomers because there were then very few cognoscenti. It effectively introduced colorimetry and the CIE standards to industry.

The first three chapters and the first three sections of each of Chapters 4 and 5 of this book consist of revisions and abridgments of the *Handbook of Colorimetry*. The revisions conform to current agreements on terminology by the CIE and other international organizations.

The later sections of Chapters 4 and 5 begin the variations on themes introduced by the *Handbook of Colorimetry* that are promised by the subtitle of this book. They deal with some alternate methods and with some implications of colorimetry.

The remainder of the book presents further variations on the theme of colorimetry. Chapters 6 and 7 discuss applications to two important kinds of problems, colors of light and objects, respectively. Daylight and light from man-made sources are subjects of Chapter 6. Colorant mixtures are discussed in Chapter 7.

Chapter 8 is concerned with the abilities of normal observers to see small color differences and with representation and use of such information to assess color differences evaluated by colorimetry.

Chapter 9 describes color-order systems, particularly their relations to the uniform color scales of the Optical Society of America. Those color scales are illustrated by four pages printed in color.

Chapter 10 discusses the dependence of color-matching data on the chromaticities of primaries, in terms of the CIE observer data and coordinate system. The alychne and apeiron are defined; orthogonal color-matching functions and self-conjugate primaries are discussed.

Chapter 11 is devoted to chromatic adaptation and color constancy. The important effect of color constancy is to make objects seem to retain their colors unaltered despite significant changes of spectral distributions of the light with which they are illuminated.

Readers are not expected to be acquainted with mathematics beyond high-school algebra. The only symbols that may be unfamiliar to some are Σ for summation and Δ for the difference between two quantities. Each is explained in a note, at its first occurrence. Calculus and vector and matrix algebra, which are sometimes encountered in expositions of colorimetry, are unnecessary embellishments and are omitted, without loss.

In general, useful information and formulas are given without formal derivations or proof. The major exception is the proof of Ostwald's theorem concerning the spectrophotometric curves of optimal colors. The proof is given as an example of the power and method of use of Newton's center-of-gravity principle. Ostwald offered the theorem unproved; Schrödinger's proof was very long and difficult.

To maintain continuity without interruptions or digressions, all accessory information is placed in an Appendix entitled "Notes and Sources". Those notes are numbered in sequence. A superscript number is placed at the place in the text to which each note is related. Readers to whom the material is new may ignore those numbers during their first reading. Subsequently, like readers already familiar with the subject, they may find the notes helpful. Some of the notes are merely references.

There is no pretense that the references are complete. They are given only as suggestions for sources of further information or data, or to give credit for pioneering contributions to the subject, especially to authors named in the text.

This does not purport to be a reference book. The subject matter was determined by my own experience and interests. Therefore there are no discussions of the anatomy, physiology, or psychology of color vision, or of color-vision theories, or of anomalies of color vision or color blindness. Topics in colorimetry that are obsolete or, in my opinion, obsolescent have been omitted to save space for some new topics that I think may become significant.

The newest exciting application of colorimetry that is not included is discussed in *Color Theory and Its Application in Art and Design*, by G. A. Agoston (Springer, Berlin, Heidelberg, New York 1979), Springer Series in Optical Sciences, Vol. 19, the same series to which this book belongs.

The portrait of Professor Hardy, used as a frontispiece, was furnished by the MIT Museum and Historical Collection.

Permission has been granted by the MIT Press for inclusion of revisions of text, figures, and selected tables and charts from the *Handbook of Colorimetry*. I was a co-author of that book.

Generous career-long support of my work in colorimetry by the Eastman Kodak Company is gratefully acknowledged. The most recent instance of that support is entry of the typescript of this book into the Document Processing system by Debe Jayne of the Research Laboratories, whom I sincerely thank. The figures were prepared over a period of four decades by the Photographic Service Department, with a recent burst to unify style and nomenclature.

This is to thank also my beloved wife, Muriel, who converted my atrocious handwriting into typescript during the summer of 1980 at Cape Cod.

Rochester NY, January 1981   *David L. MacAdam*

Contents

1. The Physical Basis of Color Specification

People have been conscious of color from the earliest times. Cave dwellers decorated their walls with coloring materials that they dug from the earth. Mineral colors, a few vegetable dyes, and some dyes obtained from insects and mollusks were the only materials available until the last century. The paucity of usable materials was not remedied until after Perkin's synthesis of mauve from coal tar in 1856. That discovery led to the introduction of thousands of synthetic dyes and pigments. In the ever-increasing use of color today, the lack of suitable coloring materials no longer limits the variety of attainable colors.

As frequently happens, the solution of that problem created another. The synthesis of a vast number of new dyes and pigments made it necessary to look for a new method of color specification. When the number of available materials was small, it was feasible to designate the color of a dye or pigment by reference to its origin. Such names as Tyrian purple, madder, henna, and indigo arose in this way. The modern equivalent of that identification method would be to give the chemical composition or structural formula of each new *colorant*. Such a specification would be inadequate for a number of reasons. To mention only one: dyes and pigments are generally used today in mixtures of two or more at a time. This is almost invariably a physical mixture, rather than a chemical combination. Hence, the interpretation of mixture phenomena is to be found by use of laws in the branch of physics known as optics, rather than by application of the laws of chemistry. The purpose of this volume is to indicate the physical method of color specification and to present formulas, methods, and results that facilitate this specification.

1.1 Definition of Color

The term *color* is commonly used in three distinctly different senses. The chemist employs it as a generic term for dyes, pigments, and similar materials. The physicist, on the other hand, uses the term to refer to certain phenomena in the field of optics. Hence, the physicist, when confronted with the task of measuring the color of a material, measures the relevant optical properties of the material. Physiologists and psychologists often employ the term in still another sense. They are interested primarily in understanding the nature of the visual process and use the term, on occasion, to denote sensation in the consciousness of a human observer. Color is also a household word and is commonly used indiscriminately in all three senses.

All three definitions of color are so firmly rooted in our language that it would be futile to suggest that two of the meanings be abandoned in order to satisfy the scientist's desire for a single meaning for every term. Indeed, it would be difficult to obtain any degree of unanimity concerning the single meaning that should be adopted, even among scientists. It seems inevitable that all three definitions of color will continue in use and that ambiguity can be avoided only by reference to the context. There is usually no difficulty in recognizing cases in which the chemical definition is intended. However, the distinction between the use of the objective physical definition and the subjective psychological definition is somewhat more subtle.

The distinction can best be illustrated in terms of another concept, temperature. Temperature may be defined objectively in terms of the expansion of mercury. It may also be defined subjectively in terms of sensations. This analogy suggests at once that there is no one-to-one correspondence between the objective and subjective aspects. We know, for example, that although the ocean may remain at the same temperature, as indicated objectively by a thermometer, it feels warmer on a cold day and colder on a warm day because it is contrasted with air at different temperatures. A hot or cold shower taken prior to entering the ocean has a similar effect. These phenomena have their counterparts in the field of color. The sensation that results when we look at a colored object depends to a considerable extent upon the nature of the surrounding field and the nature of the field to which the observer has previously been exposed.

This volume is concerned chiefly with a method for specifying the colors of objects or materials. A specification of this sort, which treats color as an inherent property of an object or material, must necessarily be based on objective measurements. Color, in the sense in which it is used throughout this volume, may be defined explicitly in terms of a definite set of physical operations. Indeed, every genuine definition of any concept is merely a statement of the operations by which that concept is specified. The operations described in this chapter may be regarded as a definition of color[1].

1.2 The Spectrophotometric Specification of Color

The basis of the objective method of color specification will be clear from an outline of the procedure that is followed in the solution of a specific problem. Consider an object coated with a paint that would commonly be called green. Let this sample be illuminated by a suitable source of light. Imagine, further, that a prism is placed so as to disperse the light that falls on the sample into its spectral components − violet, blue, green, yellow, orange, and red. Consider for a moment only a single component – the violet, for example. It is evident that a surface cannot reflect more violet light than falls upon it.

The ratio of the amount reflected divided by the amount incident is called the *reflectance* of the surface. Therefore, the reflectance of the surface must have a value between 0 and 1. The exact value can be determined by use of an instrument known as a *spectrophotometer*. Experiment shows that in almost all cases, the value does not depend on the intensity of the measuring beam[2]. The reflectance of a surface for violet light is one of its inherent properties. The same argument applies with equal force to all of the other components of the spectrum. As a consequence, a purely objective specification of the color of a surface can be expressed in terms of the reflectance for each spectral component. In the case of our example, the inherent color characteristics of the green paint might be indicated by:

Spectral region	Reflectance
Violet	0.11
Blue	0.28
Green	0.33
Yellow	0.17
Orange	0.12
Red	0.06

This subdivision of the visible spectrum into six broad regions is arbitrary; the color of the spectrum varies without abrupt change throughout its length. The physical difference between the various regions of the spectrum is wavelength; the wavelength varies continuously from one end of the spectrum to the other. The unit of length that is commonly employed for specifying the wavelength of visible radiation is the *nanometer* (nm) (25,400,000 nanometers equal one inch). In terms of this unit, the spectral regions mentioned above comprise approximately the following ranges of wavelength:

Violet	400 – 450 nanometers
Blue	450 – 490 nanometers
Green	490 – 560 nanometers
Yellow	560 – 590 nanometers
Orange	590 – 630 nanometers
Red	630 – 700 nanometers.

Reflectance measurements for six spectral regions, although useful as an illustration of the principle underlying spectrophotometric analysis, do not, in general, define the color of a reflecting surface with sufficient precision. Instead, the reflectance is ordinarily determined for as many wavelength regions as the nature of the problem requires; the results are often exhibited in the form of a chart like Fig. 1.1. Such a curve is called a spectrophotometric

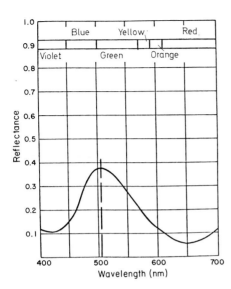

Fig. 1.1 Spectral reflectance curve of a typical green paint. The dashed vertical line indicates the dominant wavelength. In this case, the dominant wavelength is 506 nm, which is a bluish green

curve. The curve accurately defines the property of the sample that was roughly described by the data in the preceding tabulation. Every possible color can be represented on a chart of this type. For example, a perfectly white surface, which reflects completely all of the visible radiation that falls upon it, would be represented by a horizontal line at the top of the chart. Similarly, an absolutely black surface would be represented by a horizontal line at the bottom.

The spectral reflectance curve of a material constitutes a permanent record that does not require preservation of a sample of the color. Furthermore, the units in which the curve is expressed are universally understood and accepted. The wavelength of light has been adopted internationally as the fundamental standard of length, to which all other standards of length are referred. The values of reflectance are referred to a white standard whose reflectance is 1.00 for all wavelengths. Reference to such a standard is achieved by absolute methods of reflectometry[3].

Spectral reflectance curves are, at first, somewhat confusing to those who are not acquainted with them, chiefly because the curves convey so much more information than can be obtained by visual examination.

The unaided eye is incapable of analyzing light into its spectral components. For example, even such a common source as sunlight is not intuitively resolved into the various spectral colors that it contains. Those who are accustomed to mixing dyes and pigments sometimes claim to be able to see in the resulting mixture the components that they have added. This is merely a judgment based on experience, not analysis. It is of interest to note that the ear possesses the analytical power that the eye lacks. The ear is capable of analyzing as complex a stimulus as the music of a symphony orchestra into the components produced by the various instruments.

All of the information supplied by the spectrophotometric curve is essential for solution of a great many problems, notably when color matches are required that will be valid under any type of illumination, for establishment and maintenance of color standards, and for interpretation of mixture phenomena. However, there are other problems for which knowledge of the stimulation of the eye is sufficient. A typical problem is the establishment of a color language that conveys no more information than the eye can acquire by ordinary visual examination. The information supplied by a spectral reflectance curve can be used as a basis for evaluating the stimulation that results under any specified set of conditions.

1.3 Standard Illuminants

The visual stimulation that results when we look at a colored surface depends upon the character of the light with which the surface is illuminated. If all of the energy radiated by the source of light is confined within a narrow band of wavelengths in the violet end of the spectrum, the surface will reflect only violet light. Stated more generally, if a surface is illuminated by light of substantially a single wavelength, it will reflect only light of that wavelength[4].

Even though the green paint under consideration is known from the curve in Fig. 1.1 to reflect green light more effectively than light of other wavelengths, it may nevertheless be made to take on any hue of the spectrum if it is suitably illuminated. In view of this, it may be wondered how such a sample could have been identified with the green region of the spectrum before the advent of spectrophotometry. The reason is simply that daylight, which is the traditional source by which samples are examined, consists of a mixture of all of the components of the visible spectrum in nearly equal proportions. Hence, when light of daylight quality falls upon the surface whose spectral reflectance is indicated by the curve in Fig. 1.1, a preponderance of blue-green light is reflected into the eye of the observer.

The spectral reflectance curves of a few typical colors are shown in Figs. 1.2 – 6. In each case, the wavelength of the spectral region with which each color is most closely identified when illuminated by daylight is indicated by the dashed vertical line[5]. The curve for the purple (Fig. 1.6) requires special mention because it possesses two regions where its spectral reflectance is high. Purple is not a spectral color but is a combination of red light and violet light. It is impossible to find a single region of the spectrum that simulates purple; the wavelength indicated by the dashed line in Fig. 1.6 is that of the green that is complementary to it. The *complementary* color is the color that would produce a neutral gray in an additive mixture with the purple. An *additive* mixture is one in which the light from each of the components reaches the eye in an unmodified state. That is the case, for example, when the colors (lights) are combined on a projection screen. Mixtures of dyes or pigments are known

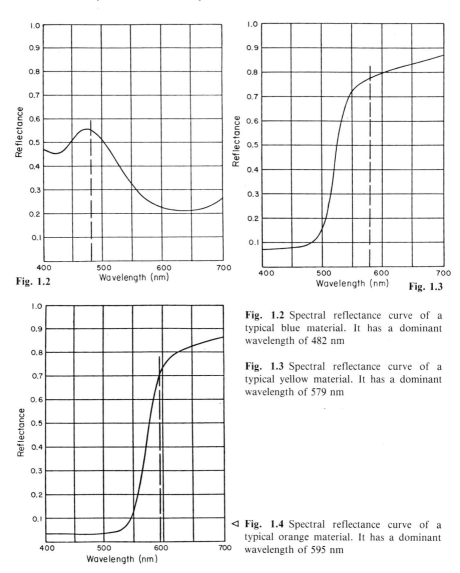

Fig. 1.2

Fig. 1.2 Spectral reflectance curve of a typical blue material. It has a dominant wavelength of 482 nm

Fig. 1.3 Spectral reflectance curve of a typical yellow material. It has a dominant wavelength of 579 nm

◁ Fig. 1.4 Spectral reflectance curve of a typical orange material. It has a dominant wavelength of 595 nm

as *subtractive* mixtures. Each of the dyes or pigments modifies the light from all of the other constituents of the mixture.

The statement that daylight consists of a mixture of all components of the spectrum in nearly equal proportions requires further elaboration. Extensive investigations into the distribution of energy in the spectrum of daylight have been made over long periods of time, in order to average the effect of the state of the weather and the altitude of the sun. Briefly, the method employed in determining the spectral distribution of energy in a source of light consists of dispersing the light into a spectrum by means of a prism. Each spectral region

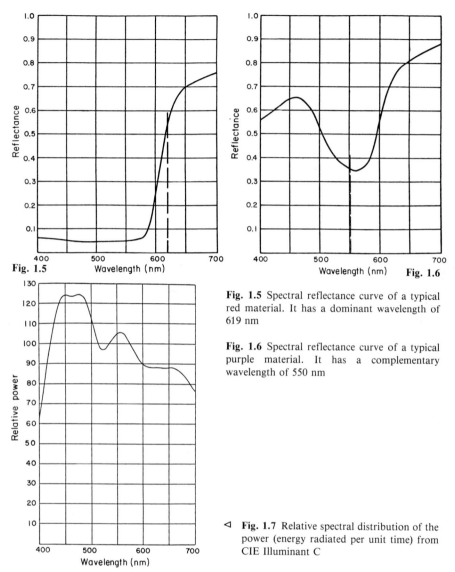

Fig. 1.5

Fig. 1.6

Fig. 1.5 Spectral reflectance curve of a typical red material. It has a dominant wavelength of 619 nm

Fig. 1.6 Spectral reflectance curve of a typical purple material. It has a complementary wavelength of 550 nm

◁ **Fig. 1.7** Relative spectral distribution of the power (energy radiated per unit time) from CIE Illuminant C

is then isolated in turn, and the amount of energy present in each region is determined. Instruments for such measurements are called *spectroradiometers*. On a clear day, daylight is a mixture of sunlight and blue light from the sky. This mixture is found to have substantially the same quality as the light from any part of the sky on an overcast day.

A filter has been prepared which, when used with a tungsten lamp operated at the proper temperature, provides a source that is a close approximation to average daylight. The spectral distribution of energy in this source is shown by the curve in Fig. 1.7. At the meeting of the International

Commission on Illumination (Commission Internationale de l'Eclairage, CIE)[6] in 1931, the representatives of the various countries adopted a source that has this distribution of energy as an international standard of illumination to be used for the purposes of colorimetry except when special conditions dictate the use of other sources. This standard is known as CIE illuminant C.

Another standard adopted at the same meeting is designated illuminant A. It represents a source that has an energy distribution similar to that of a gas-filled incandescent-tungsten lamp.

If light that has the spectral quality of illuminant C falls on the surface of green paint whose spectral reflectances are represented by the curve in Fig. 1.1, the spectral distribution of the energy reflected into the eye of an observer is obtained by multiplying, at each wavelength, the value shown in Fig. 1.7 by the corresponding value in Fig. 1.1. The result of this is shown in Fig. 1.8.

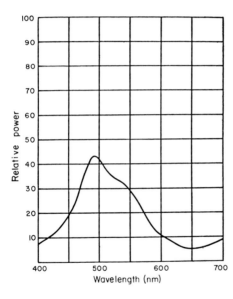

Fig. 1.8 Spectral distribution of power in the light reflected from the green paint of Fig. 1.1 when the illuminant has the spectral-power distribution of Fig. 1.7 (Illuminant C)

Because the curve in Fig. 1.7 is relatively flat, the shape of the new curve differs only slightly from that of Fig. 1.1. This is merely a special case, which serves to illustrate the principle that multiplying at each wavelength the incident energy by the reflectance of the surface gives the distribution of energy in the light reflected by the surface.

The next problem is to determine how light with a known distribution of energy stimulates the eye of an observer. No two observers respond in precisely the same manner, but the differences are small, except for about 2% of the population who demonstrably have anomalous color vision. Colorimetry is designed for the other 98%.

1.4 Color Specification in Terms of Equivalent Stimuli

No one can describe the sensation produced by light of any particular spectral quality. We can no more do this than we can describe the sensation produced by being pricked with a pin. Of course, we might say that being pricked with a pin evokes the same sensation as contact with a hot object or contact with a high-tension wire. Such a reply is not a description of the sensation. It furnishes the useful information that another stimulus evokes the same sensation. The analogy suggests the possibility of evaluating a color in terms of certain standard or primary stimuli. Indeed, it has been known for nearly two hundred years that a normal observer can duplicate the effect of any color stimulus by combining the light from three primary sources in the proper proportions. A simple experimental technique by which this may be accomplished in the majority of cases is as follows. The observer looks into an optical instrument that contains a two-part field of view. The light whose color is to be matched is introduced into one part of the field, and light from the three primary sources is combined in controlled amounts in the other part. By manipulation of the controls of those amounts, a combination can be found that produces an exact color match between the two parts of the field. Only one setting for each of the three controls produces a color match. By calibrating the controls, the amount of each primary can be recorded. The unknown color can then be specified by those amounts. These are known as the *tristimulus values;* each number represents the amount of one of the primary stimuli.

Instruments of this type, which synthesize an equivalent stimulus, are known as *colorimeters.* The tristimulus values obtained with a properly designed colorimeter constitute a color specification for a given test sample and for the observer who determines the equivalent stimulus. Another observer who performs the same experiment will also obtain a valid specification of the color, in terms of an equivalent stimulus. The two specifications may be slightly different, even though neither observer has demonstrably anomalous color vision. Consequently, for interlaboratory comparisons or for long-time color-standardization programs based on the use of colorimeters, a large group of observers would have to be employed.

The CIE recommended an alternative procedure for international use. This consisted of determining color-matching data for a large group of carefully selected observers. These basic data can be used in conjunction with spectrophotometric data to compute, for any test sample, the average tristimulus values that would have been obtained by that group of observers if they had used a colorimeter. Because the readings obtained with a spectrophotometer are independent of peculiarities of an observer's eye, this procedure provides a basis for specification of color in terms of the average chromatic properties of an internationally accepted group of observers.

The data required for computation of such a result had to be obtained by use of colorimeters. Because these data had to be determined only once, observance of the various precautions associated with colorimetry was feasible. The procedure by which the basic data were determined was substantially as follows. One half of the photometric field of a colorimeter was illuminated by a measured quantity of light of approximately a single wavelength − 400 nm, for example. An observer was then asked to determine the amount of each of three primaries required to make the two halves of the field match. Those amounts of the primaries are the tristimulus values for this quantity of light of that wavelength. The wavelength of the light was then changed, say to 410 nm. Again a color match was made and the tristimulus values were recorded. This process was continued until the entire visible spectrum was examined. In the report of the data, adjustment was made for the amount of energy of the wavelength that was used in each determination[7].

Investigations of this sort were carried out by *Maxwell*[8], by *König* and *Dieterici*[9], and by *Abney*[10]. The results were chiefly of academic interest until 1922 when the Colorimetry Committee of the Optical Society of America summarized and republished them in a convenient form[11]. The publication of the OSA data was an important event in the development of the science of colorimetry. Before 1922, spectrophotometers were used only when the nature of the problem demanded a wavelength-by-wavelength analysis; colorimeters were used when only the evaluation of an equivalent stimulus was required. After the publication of the OSA data, it became feasible to compute tristimulus specifications, i.e., the amounts of three primaries whose combination would match a specimen, from spectrophotometric data. A spectrophotometer can now be made to do the work of both instruments, and the precautions, individual differences, and uncertainties associated with colorimetry can be avoided.

However, the OSA data were based on work that had been done when the experimental facilities were barely adequate. About 1928, *Wright*[12] and *Guild*[13] in England independently redetermined the fundamental data, each employing a number of carefully selected observers. When their results were reduced to a comparable basis, their data were found to be in good agreement with each other and in fairly good agreement with the OSA data. Because the subject had assumed considerable importance, the International Commission on Illumination (CIE) in 1931 recommended international agreement on them[14].

Although supplementary data, based on extensive redeterminations by *Stiles* and *Burch*[15] (in England) and Speranskaya (USSR)[16] were recommended (in 1964) by the CIE[17] for optional use with samples that subtend 4° or larger visual fields, the 1931 CIE data are, half a century later, still recommended and generally used.

In the experiments by Wright, the primaries employed were spectrum colors whose wavelengths were 650, 530, and 460 nm. In Guild's experiments, on the other hand, the primaries were produced by passing light from an incandescent lamp through red, green, and blue filters. Each investigator determined the tristimulus values for the various spectrum colors in terms of the set of primaries that he had adopted. Because Wright and Guild used different primaries, they obtained different tristimulus values. For the purposes of colorimetry, however, either set of data is adequate; the primaries are employed merely as intermediates in terms of which two colors can be compared. Any well-defined set of primaries is adequate; the advantage of one set over any other set reduces merely to a matter of convenience.

There is one complication common to the primaries used by both Wright and Guild. When matching the various spectrum colors, both investigators found it necessary to use negative amounts of at least one of the primaries. A negative amount of a primary is obtained, in effect, by diverting the light from one primary to the side of the field opposite that illuminated by the other two primaries. There it is combined with the radiation whose tristimulus values are being determined, in order to produce a mixture that can be matched by the other two primaries. Because of the presence of both positive and negative values, the results are in an inconvenient form for use in computation. It will be clear later that no set of real primaries can be found that will match all colors (including the spectrum colors) without employing negative amounts of at least one of the primaries. If negative tristimulus values are to be avoided, the primaries must be chosen outside the realm of real colors. Fortunately this is no hardship because, when the basic data have been determined for one set of primaries, the results that would have been obtained with any other set, real or imagined, can easily be calculated by a simple linear transformation,

$$r' = k_1 r + k_2 g + k_3 b, \quad g' = k_4 r + k_5 g + k_6 b, \quad b' = k_7 r + k_8 g + k_9 b,$$

where r, g, and b are tristimulus values based on one set of primaries, r', g', b' are tristimulus values based on another set of primaries, and k_1, $k_2 \ldots k_9$ are the tristimulus values of the first primaries on the basis of the second set of primaries. The transformation is called linear because r, g, and b are used, not any functions of them, such as powers or logarithms.

The tristimulus values that were adopted by the International Commission on Illumination for the various spectrum colors are given in abridged form in Table 1.1 and are represented graphically in Fig. 1.9. The values of $\bar{x}$, $\bar{y}$, $\bar{z}$ in Table 1.1 indicate the amount of each of the CIE primaries that is required to match the color of one watt of radiant power of the indicated wavelengths. That none of these values is negative results from linear transformation of the data of both Wright and Guild to a set of primaries that lie outside the gamut of real colors. Although, as mentioned before, the choice of primaries is essentially immaterial, it may assist the reader in the interpretation of CIE tristimulus values to have in mind some idea of the characters of those primaries. The value of X (which is conventionally designated $\bar{x}$ in the case of

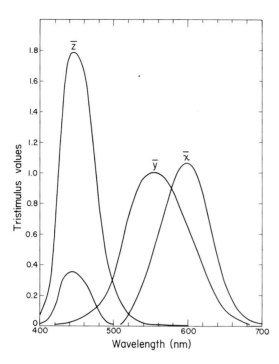

Fig. 1.9 Tristimulus values per watt of indicated wavelengths, for CIE 1931 standard observer. These values for the spectrum are the CIE 1931 color-matching data

spectrum colors) represents the amount of a reddish primary that has higher saturation than any obtainable red. The value of Y (or $\bar{y}$ for a spectrum color) represents the amount of a green primary that is considerably more saturated but of the same hue as the spectrum color whose wavelength is 520 nm. The value of Z (or $\bar{z}$) represents the amount of a blue primary that is considerably more saturated than, but of the same hue as, the spectrum color whose wavelength is 477 nm. [18]

We now have the data necessary to evaluate the stimulus that is equivalent to the sample of green paint when the latter is illuminated with light that has the spectral quality of illuminant C and when the sample is viewed by the standard CIE 1931 observer. The details of the procedure by which this result is computed will be discussed and illustrated by examples in Chap. 5. In simplest form, the method consists of dividing the visible spectrum into a suitable number of equal wavelength intervals, determining the contribution to the tristimulus values made by the light within each interval, and summing the results. In the case of the green paint selected for illustration, the tristimulus values that result from that computational procedure are $X = 15.50$, $Y = 24.19$, and $Z = 22.64$. These values provide a measure of the stimulation in the sense that each number indicates the amount of one of the three primary stimuli that would be required for a color match if the CIE observer were to use a colorimeter that incorporated the CIE X, Y, Z primaries.

Table 1.1. Tristimulus values of the spectrum colors (CIE 1931 color-matching data, per watt of indicated wavelength)

Wavelength [nm]	$\bar{x}$	$\bar{y}$	$\bar{z}$
400	0.0143	0.0004	0.0679
410	0.0435	0.0012	0.2074
420	0.1344	0.0040	0.6456
430	0.2839	0.0116	1.3856
440	0.3483	0.0230	1.7471
450	0.3362	0.0380	1.7721
460	0.2908	0.0600	1.6692
470	0.1954	0.0910	1.2876
480	0.0956	0.1390	0.8130
490	0.0320	0.2080	0.4652
500	0.0049	0.3230	0.2720
510	0.0093	0.5030	0.1582
520	0.0633	0.7100	0.0782
530	0.1655	0.8620	0.0422
540	0.2904	0.9540	0.0203
550	0.4334	0.9950	0.0087
560	0.5945	0.9950	0.0039
570	0.7621	0.9520	0.0021
580	0.9163	0.8700	0.0017
590	1.0263	0.7570	0.0011
600	1.0622	0.6310	0.0008
610	1.0026	0.5030	0.0003
620	0.8544	0.3810	0.0002
630	0.6424	0.2650	0.0000
640	0.4479	0.1750	0.0000
650	0.2835	0.1070	0.0000
660	0.1649	0.0610	0.0000
670	0.0874	0.0320	0.0000
680	0.0468	0.0170	0.0000
690	0.0227	0.0082	0.0000
700	0.0114	0.0041	0.0000

The computational procedure just indicated is unnecessarily tedious. Several modifications that simplify manual calculations will be discussed in Chap. 5. Spectrophotometers have been combined with computers that automatically perform the calculations, either simultaneously with spectrophotometry or after storage of the spectrophotometric data with any desired illuminant and observer data.

Photoelectric colorimeters have been designed for determination of tristimulus values without calculation. In these instruments, the response of a photoelectric detector to the light reflected from the sample is recorded when each of three filters is placed in the beam. To yield valid results, the spectral transmission characteristics of the filters must be designed strictly with regard to the spectral energy distribution of the source and the spectral sensitivity of the detector, so that tristimulus values are either indicated directly or can be derived by linear transformation. Even if such an instrument were so constructed, it would give valid colorimetric results only as long as the spectral characteristics of the light source, detector, and filter did not change.

An instrument that consists of a photoelectric detector and a set of filters may be used for some purposes, even though it does not adequately determine tristimulus values. For example, in many problems a sample is to be compared with a standard that has very similar spectral reflection characteristics. The filters should preferably be selected in such a manner as to isolate the region or regions of the spectrum where departures of the sample from the standard are most likely to occur. The resulting instrument would not yield CIE tristimulus values but abridged spectrophotometric data.

1.5 Two Methods of Color Matching

The tristimulus values just given for the green paint represent a stimulus that is equivalent to the paint only when the paint is illuminated by light that has the spectral quality of illuminant C, when the sample is observed by the standard CIE observer, and when the observing conditions are like those used for determination of the basic CIE data. A green appears bluer on a yellow background and yellower on a blue background. Phenomena of this sort are important to artists and designers and also to those who try to understand the nature of the visual process. In the vast majority of instances, however, the chief problem is to know how to indicate that a sample from one lot of material can be used interchangeably with a sample from another lot. If the tristimulus values are the same in the two cases, the two samples will be regarded as a match by a normal observer, in the sense that they may be used interchangeably under light that has the same spectral quality as was used for determination of the tristimulus values[19].

If the additional condition is imposed that the two samples must match for all observers under all conditions of illumination (including such extreme cases as illumination by light of a single wavelength), the two samples must have identical spectral reflection characteristics. Strictly speaking, the two samples must also be alike in all other respects. In particular, they must have identical surface structures and identical gloss characteristics[20].

Occasionally, it is necessary to match the colors of materials that differ widely in some of their other characteristics. For example, it is sometimes desired to match the color of a glossy automobile finish with the color of a pile upholstery fabric. It is impossible to make such materials so that they could be used interchangeably. The best that can be done is to produce a color match for some particular mode of illumination and observation. Experience has shown that samples of glossy and matte materials that have identical tristimulus values for diffuse illumination and normal observation are regarded as a commercial color match. An appropriate method of measurement for such problems is described in Sect. 3.6.

1.6 Need for a Universal Color Language

Students of history agree that human progress was slow until language developed by which experience acquired by one person could be imparted to others. Until the development of spectrophotometry, there was no unambiguous basis upon which to build a universal language of color. Because spectrophotometers have been developed quite recently in the history of the uses of color, the existence of the instrument and the concepts associated with it are still unknown even to many who deal with color as a matter of daily routine. However, the spectrophotometric method is so straightforward that, as soon as people become familiar with the concept, they find it virtually impossible to think in any other terms. In fact, until they have sensed the possibility of a universal and unambiguous language of color, they are not likely to realize the handicap caused by the lack of such a language. It does not strike them as incongruous that, when purchasing almost any article, they can read and understand the specifications of all of its important physical characteristics (such as size and weight) but are unable to get even an approximate idea of its color without seeing a sample. To construct a color language on the basis of samples of colored materials is not a satisfactory solution of the problem, because samples are of questionable permanence and difficult to reproduce and distribute. On the other hand, spectrophotometry depends only on measurements of the wavelength of light and measurements of reflectance or transmittance, both of which can be determined with accuracy. Although tristimulus values do not provide so much information as spectrophotometric data, they are adequate for color matching and can be derived from spectrophotometric data by a straightforward computation procedure. They therefore provide a fundamental basis for a language of color.

1.7 Lightness

If two materials have identical tristimulus values, they constitute a color match under the conditions for which the tristimulus values were determined. However, tristimulus values do not indicate in a readily comprehensible manner the nature of the color difference, when a difference exists. In a simple case, if two colors are represented by $X = 40$, $Y = 50$, $Z = 30$ and $X' = 20$, $Y' = 25$, and $Z' = 15$, respectively, it can be reasoned that the two colors are alike in chromatic quality, but that one is lighter than the other, in the sense that it reflects twice as much light. If the ratios of the tristimulus

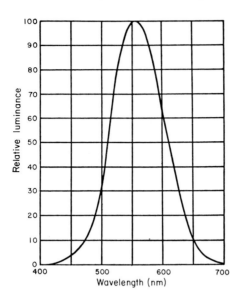

Fig. 1.10 Luminosity of radiant power. One watt of any wavelength produces the indicated multiple of 683 lumens of light. The wavelength of maximum luminous efficiency (1.0) is 555 nm. Luminous efficiency is substantially zero at 400 nm and 700 nm

values are different, the comparison of lightness would be more difficult if it were not for the foresight employed when the basic CIE data were derived. Seven years before its 1931 meeting, the International Commission on Illumination obtained general agreement concerning the relative luminances, called *luminosities,* of equal amounts of energy at various wavelengths. These data are shown in Fig. 1.10. When the data obtained with the actual primaries used in the experiments of Wright and Guild were transformed by linear combinations to a set of primaries that avoided negative tristimulus values, those primaries were also chosen so as to make one of the three functions (the $\bar{y}$ function given in Table 1.1) exactly equal to the luminosities shown in Fig. 1.10. Hence, the relative luminance of a sample is indicated directly by the value of Y, on a scale that represents an absolute black by zero and a perfect white by 100. Thus, the green whose tristimulus values are given in Sect. 1.4 has a luminance relative to the white standard of 24.19%. That ratio is called the luminance factor.

1.8 Chromaticity Coordinates

The evaluation of the quality of a color (chromaticity) is accomplished by defining three new quantities:

$$x = \frac{X}{X + Y + Z} \tag{a}$$

$$y = \frac{Y}{X + Y + Z} \qquad \text{(b)}$$

$$z = \frac{Z}{X + Y + Z}. \qquad \text{(c)}$$

These quantities are called *chromaticity coordinates*. Only two of these quantities are independent, because

$$x + y + z = 1,$$

regardless of the values assigned to X, Y, `and Z. Hence, to specify the chromaticity of a sample, it is only necessary to give the values of two of the coordinates; x and y are generally selected for this purpose. Instead of using the tristimulus values for color specification, more easily understood information is given if the color is specified in terms of Y, x, and y. As a practical example, compare the color considered in Sect. 1.4, specified by $X = 15.50$, $Y = 24.19$, $Z = 22.64$ with another for which $X' = 25.26$, $Y' = 39.42$, $Z' = 36.89$. When these are specified in the new notation, they become, respectively, $Y = 24.19$, $x = 0.2487$, $y = 0.3881$, and $Y' = 39.42$, $x' = 0.2487$, $y' = 0.3881$. It is then apparent that the two colors have the same chromaticity; the difference between them is merely a difference of luminance factor. This relationship is not immediately evident from the tristimulus values.

1.9 Graphical Representation of Chromaticity

For the same reason that it would be very difficult to learn geography without the use of maps, it is impossible to understand the subject of color without some graphical representation of the relationships of various colors one to another. To represent tristimulus values graphically would require a three-dimensional structure; this spatial relationship is not clearly perceived and is mechanically impracticable. Chromaticity can be conveniently represented, however, merely by plotting the trichromatic coefficients, x and y, on a flat "map". This has been done in Fig. 1.11 for certain colors of outstanding interest. The solid curve is the locus of all of spectrum colors. This locus is determined by computing the chromaticity coordinates of each of the spectrum colors from the tristimulus values that were given in Table 1.1. Thus, in the case of radiation that has a wavelength of 600 nm, the tristimulus values are $\bar{x} = 1.0622$, $\bar{y} = 0.6310$, and $\bar{z} = 0.0008$. From these, we can calculate that the chromaticity coordinates are $x = 0.6270$ and $y = 0.3725$. The tristimulus values of illuminant C can be determined, by a numerical integration process (discussed in Chap. 3) to be $X = 98.04$, $Y = 100.00$, and $Z = 118.12$. The corresponding coordinates, $x = 0.3101$ and $y = 0.3163$, locate the chromaticity of illuminant C.

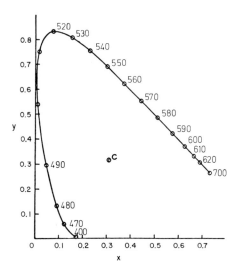

The graphical representation in Fig. 1.11 is called the chromaticity diagram. Earlier graphical representations of colors employed trilinear coordinate systems, rather than the cartesian system that is used in Fig. 1.11. In trilinear coordinate systems, the primary stimuli appeared in the apices of an equilateral triangle, and the diagram was called a color triangle. The term still persists although it is not so appropriate in reference to the CIE x, y chromaticity diagram.

In the CIE chromaticity diagram, Fig. 1.11, the chromaticity coordinates of the primaries are $x = 1$, $y = 0$; $x = 0$, $y = 1$; and $x = 0$, $y = 0$.

1.10 Dominant Wavelength and Purity

A chromaticity diagram has one property that makes it of immense value in connection with the additive mixture of two or more colors. This property of the diagram follows directly from the fact that the tristimulus values of an additive mixture are the sums of the tristimulus values of the components. Various types of additive mixtures are discussed in Sect. 4.2. The tristimulus specification is not adequate for calculation of the results of subtractive mixtures such as mixtures of dyes and pigments; in this case it is necessary to use spectrophotometric data.

In Fig. 1.12, suppose that a certain red is located at **R** and a certain green at **G**. Regardless of the proportions in which these colors are additively mixed, the resultant color will always lie on the line segment that joins **R** and **G**; the exact position of the point can be determined by a procedure that is discussed in Sect. 4.2. Because of this additive property of the diagram, all real colors must lie within the area enclosed by the solid line, because every real color can

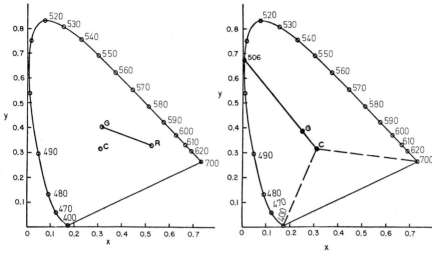

Fig. 1.12 Additive mixtures of colors R and G lie on the line RG in the chromaticity diagram. Extension of this rule to all mixtures of spectrum colors shows that all realizable colors are represented by points within the region enclosed by the solid line. That region is called the gamut of chromaticities of real colors

Fig. 1.13 Green (G) may be produced by mixture of illuminant C with 506 nm spectrum color. Its dominant wavelength is 506 nm

be considered to be an additive mixture of its spectral components. Furthermore, any real color that lies within the solid line but above the dashed line in Fig. 1.13 can be considered to be a mixture of illuminant C and spectrum light of a certain wavelength. For example, the green G whose tristimulus values were previously computed is shown to be a mixture of illuminant C and spectrum light that has a wavelength of 506 nm. This wavelength is known as the dominant wavelength. It was referred to previously without definition in connection with Figs. 1.1 – 6. Because green G lies on a line that terminates at a pure spectrum color at one end and at the illuminant point at the other end, the sample is evidently not so pure a green as the corresponding spectrum color. A numerical specification for the purity of this sample can be obtained by merely determining on the chromaticity diagram the relative distances of the sample point and the corresponding spectrum point from the illuminant point. In this case, the distance of the sample point from the illuminant point is 20% of the distance of the spectrum locus from the illuminant point. The sample is therefore said to have a purity of 20%.

The portions of the diagram that lie within the solid line but below the dashed line in Fig. 1.13 represent the purples or magentas. It is evident that purple cannot be obtained by mixing white light with a single spectrum color. Hence, an artifice is necessary if the concepts of dominant wavelength and purity are to be extended to the specification of purples. The artifice makes use of the principle that the complement of a color always lies on the opposite side of the illuminant point, on the line through the illuminant point. Thus, in Fig. 1.14 the complement of the purple P is green with a dominant wavelength of 550 nm. The wavelength that characterizes the purple P is generally written 550c, which is called the complementary wavelength.

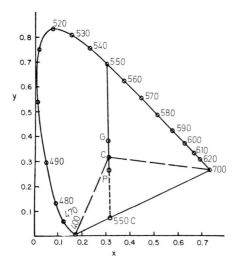

Fig. 1.14 Purple (P) is characterized by the complementary wavelength, which is determined by extending the line PC until it intersects the spectrum locus. In this case, the complementary wavelength is 550 nm, which is written 550c to indicate the complementary

The concept of purity is likewise inapplicable to a purple unless some arbitrary procedure is adopted. The most plausible procedure is to regard the lower boundary of the area of real colors as the locus of purples of highest purity. When a purity of 100% is assigned to each color that lies on this line, the purity of the color represented at P is found to be 21%.

Figure 1.15, which is a reduced-scale reproduction of Chart 23 from the *Handbook of Colorimetry,* is very useful for determination of dominant or complementary wavelength and purity, for the CIE 1931 observer and any preferred illuminant (white point). Figure 1.16, which is a reduced-scale reproduction of Chart 12A from the *Handbook of Colorimetry,* provides highly accurate evaluations of dominant and complementary wavelengths and purities for low-purity colors for the CIE 1931 observer and illuminant C. Figure 1.17, a reduced-scale reproduction of Chart 18, is an example of 22 large-scale charts in the *Handbook of Colorimetry* that facilitate determinations of all dominant and complementary wavelengths and purities for the CIE 1931 observer and illuminant C. For those charts, the *Handbook of Colorimetry* is an indispensable tool for serious colorimetry.

The procedure of regarding every color as a mixture of illuminant C and spectrum light of some wavelength is the basis of the monochromatic-plus-white method of colorimetry. Visual colorimeters have been constructed in which one part of a two-part field of view is filled with the sample color that is

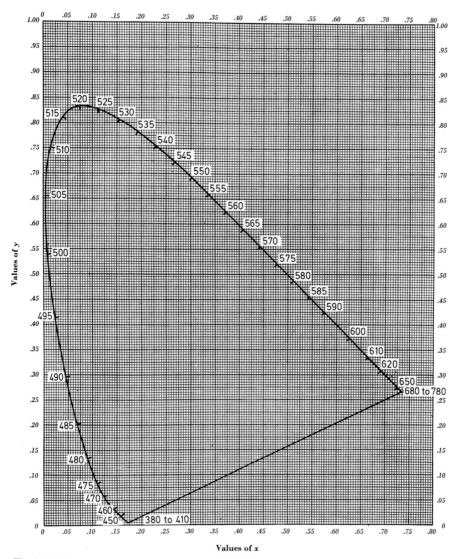

Fig. 1.15 Chromaticity diagram for CIE 1931 observer

to be measured and the other part is filled with a mixture of controlled amounts of white light and light of an adjustable wavelength. By adjustment of the wavelength and the luminances, the colors of the two parts of the field can be made to match. In the case of purple, the match is made by adding the spectral component (usually green) to the sample part of the field. In that sense, purple can be regarded as a mixture of white light and a negative amount of green light of the appropriate wavelength. In every case, the

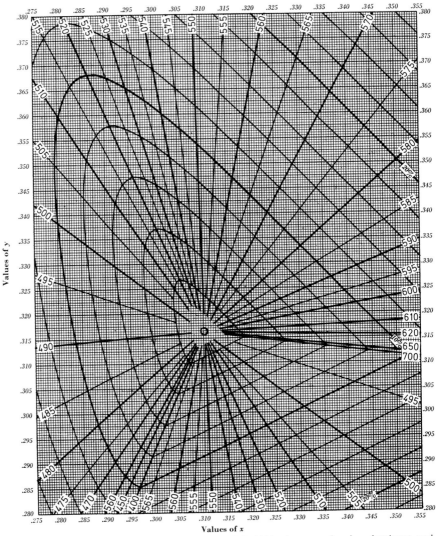

Fig. 1.16 Portion of chromaticity diagram for CIE 1931 observer, showing dominant and complementary wavelengths and low purities, based on illuminant C

dominant or complementary wavelength of the unknown color is determined directly from the wavelength scale of the instrument. The luminance of the sample color is the sum (or, in the case of purple, the difference) of the luminance of the white and the luminance of the spectral component. In such colorimetry, purity is usually taken as the ratio of the luminance of the spectral component to the sum (or difference) of the luminance of the white and the luminance of the spectral component. Purity determined in this manner is called the *colorimetric purity*. Because the values of colorimetric

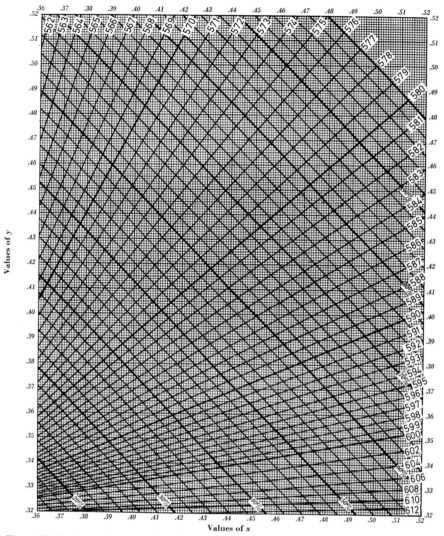

Fig. 1.17 Portion of chromaticity diagram for CIE 1931 observer, showing dominant wavelengths and purities in yellow region, based on illuminant C

purity are negative in the case of purple samples and the lines of constant purity on a chromaticity diagram are discontinuous near dominant wavelengths 400 and 700 nm, the definition of purity given previously is preferred. Purity, thus defined, in terms of ratios of distances on the chromaticity diagram, has been called *excitation purity* to distinguish it from colorimetric purity. Throughout this volume, the term *purity* will mean excitation purity. For reasons similar to those mentioned in connection with visual colorimeters in general, monochromatic-plus-white colorimeters are rarely used.

Table 1.2 may be of interest to those who are accustomed to associate color names with certain colors. In this table are listed the luminance factor, dominant wavelength, and purity of a few colors whose names have been used so widely that some degree of standardization of nomenclature has been achieved. This table is not intended as a dictionary for translation from one color language into another; neither is the table to be interpreted as an attempt to standardize color nomenclature. It is included merely to illustrate the reasonableness of color specification in terms of luminance factor, dominant (or complementary) wavelength, and purity.

The colors whose spectral reflectance curves were shown in Figs. 1.1 – 6 are specified in terms of luminance factor, dominant (or complementary) wavelength, and purity in Table 1.3.

Table 1.2. Typical luminance factors, dominant (or complementary) wavelengths, and purities of a few common colors

	Luminance factors [%]	Dominant Wavelength [nm]	Purity [%]
Cardinal	9	617	55
Baby Pink	50	610	10
Old Rose	23	608	20
Blood Red	17	600	65
Maroon	7	600	35
Henna	8	587	60
Chocolate	5	586	30
Russet	12	585	45
Goldenrod	45	576	70
Ivory	55	575	25
Olive Green	14	572	45
Apple Green	35	568	40
Turquoise	32	500	30
Lupine	32	476	27
Slate	12	476	10
Navy Blue	3	475	20
Royal Purple	4	560c	50
Orchid	33	500c	16

Table 1.3. Luminance factors, dominant (or complementary) wavelengths, and purities of specimens whose spectral reflectances are shown in Figs. 1.1 – 6

Figs.	Luminance Factor [%]	Dominant Wavelength [nm]	Purity [%]
1.1	24	506	20
1.2	33	483	31
1.3	63	576	80
1.4	32	595	87
1.5	13	619	60
1.6	46	550c	21

1.11 Color Tolerances

The value of an explicitly defined color language expressed in numerical terms is immediately obvious, but it is not always appreciated that such a language provides the solution to another important problem – namely, the specification of color tolerances. In every field where a system of measurement has been established, the custom of specifying tolerances has soon been developed. For example, no one conversant with machine-shop practice would submit a drawing that shows a set of dimensions without at the same time indicating the allowable departures from those dimensions. The machinist, in the absence of any information concerning the tolerances, would not know whether the part was intended to be used as a Johansson gauge, which may not deviate more than a micrometer (μm) from its nominal value, or whether the crudest machine work would be satisfactory. In the field of color, use of the expression "color match" without indication of the allowable departure is similarly ambiguous; it is the cause of a great deal of misunderstanding. A method of specifying color tolerances is also useful as a means of indicating the extent to which a color can be allowed to vary with time as a result of exposure to light or to some other deleterious agent.

The physical basis of color specification has been presented in some detail in order that the reader may be assured of the rigor of every step of the procedure. Some may be disappointed to find that it is based upon the use of a spectrophotometer as the fundamental measuring instrument. Such an approach is inevitable, because the eye is not analytical. Specification of color in terms of equivalent stimuli may at times be useful, but many color problems require the wavelength-by-wavelength analysis furnished by a spectrophotometer. Furthermore, the concepts associated with spectrophotometry are of considerable usefulness in themselves. There is enough interest in this subject to justify a belief that spectrophotometers will become more readily available. This will result partly from improvements in the design of the instrument, which will effect economies in its production without sacrifice of precision, and partly from increase of the number of laboratories that provide spectrophotometric service.

2. Sources of Light

Every usual source of light is merely a group of radiating atoms[21]. If one atom could be isolated for study, it would be found to emit radiation of a single frequency, or wavelength, during any interval throughout which it radiates. This type of radiation is often called *homogeneous* or *monochromatic* in optics or radiation physics. However, the terms homogeneous and monochromatic have inappropriate connotations in discussions of appearance and color. For colorimetry, light that consists of a narrow range or "band" of frequency or wavelength is better described by the straightforward name *spectrum light*. This term is employed in this volume. However, the name *monochromator* will be used for any device that provides spectrum light, because there is no recognized alternative. It should not cause confusion.

An atom is capable of radiating energy only when it has previously absorbed energy as a result of thermal, electrical, or some other form of excitation. Extensive experiments have shown that an atom is capable of absorbing only certain amounts of energy, each amount being associated with a definite state of the electrons of which the atom is composed. If, as a result of some form of excitation, an atom is at an energy level higher than the minimum, it is then capable of radiating energy during its transition to a lower level. The frequency or wavelength of this radiation is determined by the difference between the initial and final energy levels. Although an atom can radiate at only a single frequency during a change from one energy level to another, it may later radiate at a different frequency, during a transition between a different pair of energy levels. Hence, a group of atoms isolated from one another, as they are in the gaseous state, is generally observed to emit a group of frequencies or wavelengths. When analyzed by a prism or diffraction grating, the light from such a group of atoms produces a spectrum which consists of certain bright lines with darkness between. The wavelengths of the bright lines are characteristic of the nature of the atoms in the group; in other words, they are characteristic of the chemical element of which each atom is a unit.

Most light sources by which colors are observed do not produce line spectra. Common sources, such as the sun, the filament of an incandescent-tungsten lamp, or the crater of a carbon arc, consist of very hot dense materials. In a dense material, solid, liquid, or gaseous, the atoms are crowded so closely together that they cannot radiate their characteristic lines. For this reason, the radiation from a dense incandescent material is practically independent of the material of which it is composed; the spectral distribution depends only on the temperature of the material. The most efficient thermal radiator is called a *blackbody*. The closest approach to a blackbody that can be realized experimentally is a small opening in a large cavity whose walls are maintained at a uniform temperature. When the radiation from a blackbody is analyzed, it is found that all frequencies, or wavelengths, are present. A spectrum of this type is called a *continuous* spectrum.

2.1 Thermal Radiators

The spectral power distribution of the radiation from a blackbody varies with temperature in accordance with Planck's law. This law can be written in the form

$$E = \frac{c_1 \lambda^{-5}}{\varepsilon^{c_2/\lambda T} - 1},$$

where E is the power radiated in ergs per second per square centimeter of radiating surface, within a spectral band one nanometer in width, c_1 is a constant whose value is 3.7415×10^{23}, ε is the base of the natural system of logarithms, c_2 is a constant whose value is 1.4388×10^7, λ is the wavelength of light in nanometers, and T is the absolute or Kelvin temperature of the body (Celsius degrees plus 273.15). This law holds to the limit of accuracy obtained with the most refined experimental technique.

The relative distribution of power in the radiation from blackbodies at various temperatures is shown in Fig. 2.1. In conformity with the usual convention, each curve has been plotted on such a scale that the power is 100 at 560 nm. Actually, the amount of power radiated within a band one nanometer wide at 560 nm varies in accordance with the values in Table 2.1, which has been computed from Planck's law[22].

The energy radiated by many incandescent solids can be expressed by the equation

$$E = \frac{e\, c_1 \lambda^{-5}}{\exp(c_2/\lambda T) - 1},$$

which is identical with Planck's law except for the insertion of a constant e, which is known as the *emissivity*. A tungsten filament, for example, has an emissivity of approximately 0.3 at the ordinary operating temperature of tungsten lamps. This means that a tungsten filament radiates only about $\frac{1}{3}$ as much power at every wavelength as a blackbody at the same temperature. This proportional reduction of the emission affects only the quantity of radiation and not the quality. Materials whose spectral distributions of power can be represented by the last equation are known as *graybody* radiators.

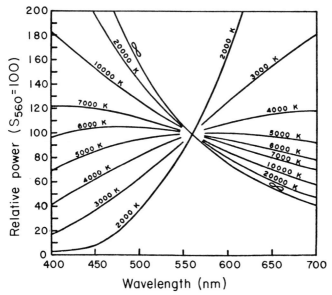

Fig. 2.1 Relative spectral distributions of power in the radiation from blackbodies at the indicated temperatures

Table 2.1. Power radiated by a blackbody in the band from 559.5 to 560.5 nm

Temperature [K]	Radiated [ergs/s · cm^2]
2000	1.86×10^4
2200	5.98×10^4
2400	1.58×10^5
2600	3.58×10^5
2800	7.22×10^5
3000	1.33×10^6
4000	1.12×10^7
5000	4.05×10^7
6000	9.58×10^7
7000	1.78×10^8
8000	2.86×10^8
9000	4.16×10^8
10,000	5.64×10^8
15,000	1.49×10^9
20,000	2.59×10^9
25,000	3.77×10^9

The chromaticity of the radiation from a blackbody at various temperatures is shown in Fig. 2.2. A source may radiate a spectral distribution that does not conform to Planck's law but nevertheless has the same chromaticity as a blackbody at some temperature. That temperature is called the *color temperature* of the radiation. The chromaticities of the CIE illuminants A and C are indicated in Fig. 2.2. The chromaticity of illuminant C is not identical

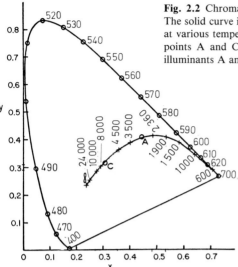

Fig. 2.2 Chromaticities of various important illuminants. The solid curve is the locus of radiations from blackbodies at various temperatures, some of which are indicated. The points A and C represent the chromaticities of the CIE illuminants A and C

with the chromaticity of a blackbody at any temperature. It lies so close to the locus of chromaticities of blackbody radiators, however, that its chromaticity may be indicated with fair precision by stating the temperature of the blackbody to which it most nearly corresponds, 6750 K. The color temperature of a black- or graybody radiator is the same as its true (absolute) temperature. For other radiators, color temperature has no necessary relation to the true temperature. The blue sky, for example, has a color temperature in the neighborhood of 20,000 K.

2.2 Spectroradiometry

The experimental procedure for determining the spectral power distribution of a source of light is known as *spectroradiometry*. In principle, the method consists of dispersing the radiation into its spectral components, allowing the radiation within a narrow wavelength interval to fall on a thermopile or other detector of radiant power, and noting the temperature rise or other indication of the power received. The detector is then exposed to a different portion of the spectrum; the operation is repeated until the entire spectrum has been examined. Although the principles involved in spectroradiometric measurements are thus simple, the power available is ordinarily so small that accurate measurements can be made only with the most meticulous technique, using highly specialized apparatus. Consequently, such measurements are avoided as much as possible. Fortunately, only a few significantly different sources of light are commonly used for definitive examination of colors or need be considered in colorimetry.

The CIE has published the requisite spectroradiometric data for a few sources that are generally accepted for use in colorimetric calculations. They include illuminants A, C, and D_{65}, for which the data at 10 nm intervals from 380 nm to 770 nm are given in Table 2.2. Figure 2.3 shows those spectral

Table 2.2. Relative spectroradiometric data for CIE illuminants A, C, and D_{65}

Wavelength [nm]	S_A	S_C	$S_{D_{65}}$
380	9.80	33.0	50.0
390	12.09	47.4	54.6
400	14.71	63.3	82.8
410	17.68	80.6	91.5
420	20.99	98.1	93.4
430	24.67	112.4	86.7
440	28.70	121.5	104.9
450	33.09	124.0	117.0
460	37.81	123.1	117.8
470	42.87	123.8	114.9
480	48.24	123.9	115.9
490	53.91	120.7	108.8
500	59.86	112.1	109.4
510	66.06	102.3	107.8
520	72.50	96.9	104.8
530	79.13	98.0	107.7
540	85.95	102.1	104.4
550	92.91	105.2	104.0
560	100.00	105.3	100.0
570	107.18	102.3	96.3
580	114.44	97.8	95.8
590	121.73	93.2	88.7
600	129.04	89.7	90.0
610	136.35	88.4	89.6
620	143.62	88.1	87.7
630	150.84	88.0	83.3
640	157.98	87.8	83.7
650	165.03	88.2	80.0
660	171.96	87.9	80.2
670	178.77	86.3	82.2
680	185.43	84.0	78.3
690	191.93	80.2	69.7
700	198.26	76.3	71.6
710	204.41	72.4	74.3
720	210.36	68.3	61.6
730	216.12	64.4	69.9
740	221.67	61.5	75.1
750	227.00	59.2	63.6
760	232.12	58.1	46.4
770	237.01	58.2	66.8
780	241.68	59.1	63.4

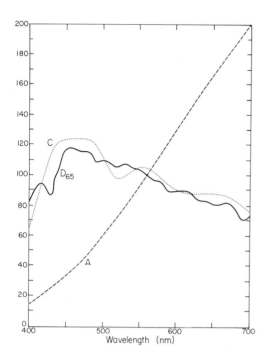

Fig. 2.3 Spectral distributions of power in CIE illuminants A, C and D$_{65}$

distributions. Illuminant A is an incandescent-tungsten lamp at a color temperature of 2856 K. Illuminant C consists of illuminant A combined with a 2-solution filter that converts the light to an approximately daylight quality, with a color temperature of about 6750 K. The actual source is very rarely used, but the tabulated data have been used extensively for colorimetry since their adoption by the CIE in 1931. They have been supplanted, to a large extent, but not formally superseded by D$_{65}$, which consists of only a set of numerical data. Those data are a good representation of the spectral power of average daylight, at 6500 K color temperature. The CIE data for D$_{65}$ extend from 300 nm to 830 nm at 5 nm intervals, although for the purpose of colorimetry only the data for 380 nm to 770 nm are necessary. The data from 300 nm to 375 nm were recommended to facilitate interlaboratory comparison of the colors of fluorescent materials, which are excited by wavelengths in that range, as well as by the visible blue components of daylight. Illuminant C entirely lacks the near uv. The disadvantage of D$_{65}$ is that no source of such light, except daylight itself, is available. Several artificial sources have been proposed, but none gives a very close approximation to the CIE D$_{65}$ data; agreement has not been obtained on any such source. For colorimetric measurement of fluorescent materials, a laboratory realization of D$_{65}$ is needed. For colorimetric calculations from spectrophotometric data of non-fluorescent materials, however, the tabulated data are sufficient, as are also those of illuminant C.

2.3 Sources of Light for Color Matching

Everyone who has had occasion to match colors recognizes that an artificial source of constant intensity and quality is preferable to daylight, which varies considerably in both respects and is not always available. Because of a common misconception, the demand is frequently made that the artificial source be so constructed that, when colors appear to match under its light, they will also match under the light from all other sources. No source can ever be obtained that will satisfy that requirement. If a match must be valid under all types of illumination, the only infallible procedure is to examine the match successively under spectrum light of all wavelengths. This, in effect, is the procedure used in spectrophotometry. The spectrophotometric curves of different specimens must be identical if those specimens are to match in all illuminations.

It is frequently sufficient to require that the match be valid for a certain temperature range of blackbody radiation. In this case, examining the match successively under two properly chosen sources is ordinarily adequate. One source should preferably correspond to a color temperature only slightly higher than that of the yellowest light source that would normally be encountered; the other should correspond to a color temperature only slightly lower than that of the bluest light source that would normally be encountered. If the match is valid under both sources, there is a strong probability that it will be valid under the light from a thermal radiator at any intermediate temperature. To set the limits over which color matches must ordinarily be valid, it is necessary to have information concerning the various aspects of both artificial light and natural light.

2.4 Tungsten Lamps

Small tungsten lamps of the vacuum type, when operated at their rated voltage, have color temperatures about 2400 K. Larger gas-filled lamps have normal operating color temperatures that vary from about 2670 K to slightly more than 3000 K in the largest sizes. These values are for the bare lamp; the spectral distribution of the radiation that illuminates a material under examination may be considerably altered by shades and reflectors or by reflection from the walls of the room. For most practical purposes, however, illuminant A may be considered to be a fair representation of the spectral quality of tungsten lamps.

2.5 Solar Radiation

Above the earth's atmosphere, the radiation from the sun is substantially constant in both quality and quantity. Until a few years ago, measurements of the spectral power distribution of sunlight had to be made under the atmosphere. Corrections for absorption and scattering in the atmosphere were computed from measurements with the sun at several different elevations. Figure 2.4 shows the relative spectral distribution of power in sunlight above the atmosphere, that is, after correction of ground-level data for the effect of the atmosphere. The values from which the curve in this figure was plotted are given in Table 2.3.

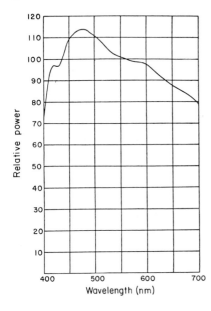

Fig. 2.4 Spectral distribution of power in sunlight outside the earth's atmosphere

On a clear day, solar radiation is scattered selectively in its passage through the earth's atmosphere. This selective scattering causes the sky to be blue and causes the intensities of short wavelengths to be correspondingly reduced in the residual direct beam. At noon on a clear summer day, the illumination on a horizontal surface due to direct sunlight is approximately 80,000 lumens per square meter and that due to the diffuse skylight is about 20,000 lumens per square meter. The spectral distribution of power in average noon light at Washington D.C. is given in Table 2.4 and is represented graphically in Fig. 2.5. Its color temperature is about 5000 K. In the limit, if the scattering particles in the atmosphere are very small, the scattering follows Rayleigh's inverse fourth-power law. This means that radiation with a wavelength of 400 nm has a scattering coefficient nearly ten times as great as radiation with a wavelength of 700 nm. If solar radiation outside the atmosphere

Table 2.3. Spectral distribution of sunlight above the atmosphere

Wavelength [nm]	Relative power	Wavelength [nm]	Relative power
360	60.0	560	100.0
370	63.8	570	99.1
380	62.0	580	98.6
390	63.9	590	98.3
400	73.4	600	97.4
410	91.5	610	95.2
420	97.0	620	93.1
430	96.9	630	91.0
440	102.9	640	89.3
450	109.6	650	87.5
460	112.0	660	86.0
470	113.5	670	84.6
480	113.6	680	83.3
490	112.1	690	81.4
500	110.7	700	79.1
510	108.5	710	76.8
520	105.9	720	74.4
530	103.4	730	72.2
540	101.7	740	70.2
550	100.9	750	68.2

Table 2.4. Spectral distribution of average noon sunlight in Washington, D.C.

Wavelength [nm]	Relative power	Wavelength [nm]	Relative power
360	17.3	560	100.0
370	21.6	570	99.5
380	24.6	580	100.0
390	29.5	590	100.4
400	44.8	600	101.3
410	60.3	610	100.7
420	67.2	620	100.3
430	69.6	630	99.9
440	78.5	640	100.0
450	86.9	650	99.9
460	92.0	660	100.1
470	97.0	670	99.6
480	99.7	680	99.5
490	100.9	690	98.2
500	102.3	700	96.5
510	101.0	710	94.0
520	100.2	720	92.0
530	99.2	730	89.7
540	99.0	740	88.1
550	100.5	750	85.8

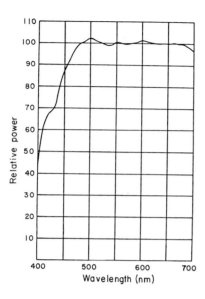

had a strictly uniform distribution of power per nanometer throughout spectrum, the distribution of power per nanometer in skylight, if due to Rayleigh scattering, would be

$$E = \frac{a \; constant}{\lambda^4}.$$

By comparison of this equation with Planck's law, it can be shown that such radiation is identical in quality to the radiation that a blackbody would emit if it could be raised to an infinite temperature.

It rarely happens that the conditions for Rayleigh scattering are fulfilled by the atmosphere. In the extreme case of a completely overcast day, the scattering becomes spectrally almost nonselective. The spectral quality of radiation from any part of the sky is then a close approximation to the spectral quality of solar radiation outside the earth's atmosphere. Light from the north sky, which is frequently used as a source for color matching, is therefore subject to large variations of quality with changing weather conditions; the limits correspond to a blackbody at a very high temperature (20,000 K or higher) on the one hand, and to a blackbody at about 6500 K on the other.

By definition, daylight is the light from the entire sky, including direct sunlight if the sky is clear. The spectral quality of daylight is a close approximation to solar radiation outside the atmosphere, regardless of the state of the weather or the altitude of the sun. For this reason, illuminants C or D_{65}, which rather closely approximate daylight, are the preferred sources on which to base the color language discussed in the preceding chapter.

3. Spectrophotometry

The principles that underlie spectrophotometric measurements were discussed briefly in Chap. 1 on the tacit assumption that the test object was opaque. In general, when light falls on an object, a portion of the incident light is reflected, a portion is absorbed within the material, and the remainder is transmitted. Objects are said to be opaque when the transmitted component is so small as to be negligible. The converse case of a transparent object with a negligible reflectance is never realized. Even a piece of clear white optical glass reflects (from its two surfaces) about 8% of the incident light, absorbs a fraction of 1% in ordinary thicknesses, and transmits nearly 92%. For this reason, an object will be called transparent if the proportion of the incident light that it transmits is too large to be ignored. On this basis, a sheet of paper or cloth must usually be considered transparent.

No attempt is made here to distinguish between *transparency* and *translucency*. Etymologically, translucency is the better word to use for the generic term. Precedent, however, favors the use of "transparency." For example, it has long been customary to speak of the transparency of a photographic deposit, even though the scattering of light within such a deposit makes it impossible to obtain a clear view of objects lying behind it. Such distinction as may be necessary between transparency and translucency will be dealt with in Sect. 3.4 in connection with the method by which the transmittance is determined for inhomogeneous materials.

3.1 Transmittance of Homogeneous Materials

Spectrophotometers were originally devised for determination of transmittance of homogeneous transparent materials. When used for this purpose, the principle that underlies their operation consists of first dispersing the light from a source into its spectral components. A nearly monochromatic beam of a known average wavelength is then isolated and is divided in some manner into two beams of equal intensity. If the test sample is inserted in one of these beams, the intensities will no longer be equal. The balance may be restored, however, by reducing the intensity of the comparison beam by use of an adjustable diaphragm or an equivalent device. When the balance is restored, the ratio of the final intensity of the comparison beam to its original intensity

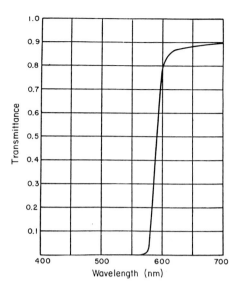

Fig. 3.1 Spectral transmittance of a red signal glass

can then be read directly from the calibrated scale of the diaphragm or other modulator. This ratio is the transmittance of the sample at the wavelength of the original beam. The operation is repeated with monochromatic light of other wavelengths in turn until the entire visible spectrum has been adequately examined. A typical transmittance curve is shown in Fig. 3.1.

In an optical sense, transparent materials may be either homogeneous or inhomogeneous. In the ordinary use of the terms, a homogeneous material would be called transparent and an inhomogeneous material, translucent. In measuring the transmittance of a homogeneous material, such as a piece of colored glass, the usual procedure is to prepare the sample in the form of a flat plate with plane parallel faces. If the material is a liquid, it is placed in a cell with plane parallel walls as illustrated in Fig. 3.2. Because the amount of absorption depends upon the distance that the light travels through the material, it is important that the length of the optical path be known. Ordinarily the length of the optical path is made equal to one dimension of the sample. This is the case in Fig. 3.2, where a collimated (parallel) beam of light is incident normally on the face of the cell.

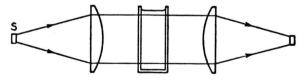

Fig. 3.2 Schematic diagram of a portion of the optical system employed for measurement of transmittance of homogeneous liquids

In the arrangement shown in Fig. 3.2, absorption by the glass of which the cell walls are composed may not be negligible. Also, every air – glass interface reflects approximately 4% of the light incident upon it. Hence, even if the cell walls were constructed of glass that has no absorption and if the cell were filled with a clear, nonabsorbing liquid, the measured value of the transmittance would be in the neighborhood of 92%. It is desirable in many applications of spectrophotometry to determine the absorption of a dye in a solution that has a definite thickness and consists of a known concentration of the dye in some solvent. To isolate the absorption due to the dye alone, the transmittance of the cell filled with pure solvent may first be determined. Dividing the measured transmittance of the cell when it contains the dye solution by the transmittance of this "dummy" cell corrects the transmittance of the dye for reflection and absorption losses due to the cell and solvent. An alternative procedure is to use two identical cells, one of which is filled with the dye solution and the other with pure solvent. The cell that contains the dye solution is placed in the sample beam and the cell that contains the solvent is placed in the comparison beam of the spectrophotometer. The presence of the dummy cell in the comparison beam automatically corrects the values of transmittance for the absorption and reflection losses in the cell and solvent.

Similar considerations apply to measurements of transmittance of solid materials, such as colored glasses. The transmittances that are determined in the manner first described include the reflection losses of the air – glass interfaces. Before the values thus measured can be used to calculate the transmittances for some other thickness of the material by application of Bouguer's law (to be discussed in the next section), they must be corrected for the reflection losses. They may be determined by measuring two samples of the same material that have different thicknesses. From these data, the reflection losses can be eliminated by computation. If the index of refraction of the material is known, the surface reflection losses can be computed by application of Fresnel's equations. In the case of normal (perpendicular) incidence, Fresnel's equations reduce to the form

$$R = \left(\frac{n' - n}{n' + n} \right)^2,$$

where R is the reflectance of a boundary surface, n is the index of refraction of the medium on one side of the boundary and n' that of the medium on the other side. For the boundary surface between air and a glass with an index of 1.5, the value of R is 0.04. However, because of intersurface reflections, the transmittance of two or more surfaces in series is not exactly the product of their several transmittances.

3.2 Bouguer's Law

The transmittance of a homogeneous material, after correction for surface losses, varies with the thickness of the sample in accordance with Bouguer's law. Bouguer set forth this law in 1729. Because it was rediscovered some years later by Lambert, it is frequently called Lambert's law of absorption. If unit thickness of the material has transmittance t, Bouguer's law is that the thickness x of the material has the transmittance

$$T = t^x.$$

This law is frequently written in the form

$$T = \varepsilon^{-ax}$$

where ε is the base of the natural system of logarithms (2.71828 ...) and a is the absorption coefficient. Spectral transmittance curves for different thicknesses of a certain glass are illustrated in Fig. 3.3.

It is often convenient to express the results of spectrophotometric measurements in terms of a quantity called *optical density*. By definition, optical density

$$D = \log_{10} \tfrac{1}{T}.$$

From Bouguer's law $T = t^x$, it follows that

$$D = xD_0,$$

where D is the density of a material of thickness x, and D_0 is the density of a unit thickness of the same material. In other words, the density of a material is directly proportional to its thickness. The curves in Fig. 3.3 have been replotted on a density scale in Fig. 3.4.

The curves in both Figs. 3.3 and 3.4 change their shape as the thickness of the sample varies. One of the useful applications of spectrophotometry is for identification of an unknown coloring material. Identification is often facilitated by plotting the spectrophotometric data in such a manner that the shape of the curve does not vary with the thickness of the sample or concentration of a dye. From $T = \varepsilon^{-ax}$, it follows that

$$D = \log_{10} \tfrac{1}{T} = 0.4343\,ax,$$

whence

$$\log_{10} D = \log_{10}(\log_{10} \tfrac{1}{T}) = \log_{10} 0.434\,a + \log_{10} x.$$

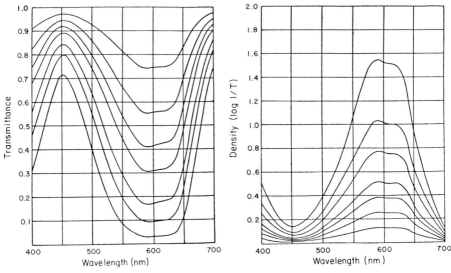

Fig. 3.3 Spectral transmittance curves (corrected for surface reflection) of various thicknesses of a pink glass. The thicknesses were 1, 2, 3, 4, 6, 8, and 12 mm, respectively, from top to bottom

Fig. 3.4 Density curves of the glasses whose spectral transmittance curves are shown in Fig. 3.3

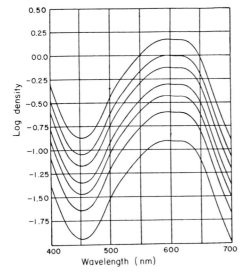

Fig. 3.5 Curves of the logarithms of the densities of the glasses whose spectral transmittances are shown in Fig. 3.3

The *absorption coefficient, a,* varies with the wavelength, whereas x (the thickness of the sample) is independent of the wavelength. Hence, the first term on the right side of the last equation determines the shape of the curve; variations of the thickness merely shift the curve vertically, without altering its shape. The advantage of this plotting procedure is exemplified in Fig. 3.5 for the material whose spectral transmittance curves for various thicknesses were plotted in Fig. 3.3. It is useful for identifying the constituents of mixtures of two or three dyes, for which purpose an atlas of log density curves of pure solutions of possible constituents is prepared. If the details in the high parts of the curve for any pure dye are found at the same wavelengths in the curve for the mixture, then that dye is almost certainly a constituent of the mixture.

3.3 Beer's Law

Many of the applications of spectrophotometry are concerned with determination of the transmittances of dye solutions. If c is the concentration of a dye, Beer's law states that the transmittance of a sample of constant thickness is

$$T = t^c,$$

where t is the transmittance of a solution of unit concentration. Combining Beer's law with Bouguer's law for samples of thickness and concentration c, we obtain

$$T = t^{cx},$$

where t is the transmittance of a sample of unit thickness and unit concentration. Corresponding to the exponential form of Bouguer's law, this expression may be written

$$T = \varepsilon^{-acx}.$$

This and Bouguer's law involve different values of the constant a unless unit concentration is employed in connection with Bouguer's law.

The density of a definite thickness of dye solution is directly proportional to the concentration of the dye. The device of plotting the spectrophotometric curve of a dye solution in terms of log density again leads to a shape that is often invariant with changes of either thickness or concentration. Bouguer's law is rigorously true in the case of homogeneous materials, but Beer's law is sometimes merely an approximation, especially at high concentrations, because of molecular aggregation or other chemical or physicochemical effects.

3.4 Transmittance of Inhomogeneous Materials

If an optically inhomogeneous material is inserted in the collimated beam shown in Fig. 3.2, the scattering of light that takes place within the material

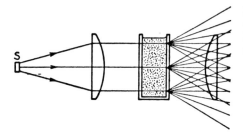

Fig. 3.6 Schematic diagram showing the unsuitability of the optical system shown in Fig. 3.2 for the measurement of nonhomogeneous materials

produces the effect illustrated diagrammatically in Fig. 3.6. Much of this scattered light is not admitted to the photometer. A value for the transmittance at each wavelength can still be determined, but it is significant only if the material is inserted in an optical system that is geometrically equivalent to that of the measuring instrument. It will be recalled in this connection that the transmittance of homogeneous materials depends upon the length of the optical path and that, by convention, the light is made to travel parallel to the shortest dimension of the sample, thereby obtaining the maximum transmittance. The maximum value of the transmittance of an inhomogeneous material is obtained if the optical system is so arranged as to collect all of the light that emerges from the material, regardless of its direction. One method by which this is accomplished is illustrated in Fig. 3.7, where the sample is placed over the window of an integrating sphere. If the inside of the sphere is painted white, the same amount of power will be measured by a probe inserted in the

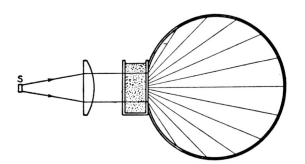

Fig. 3.7 Schematic diagram of an optical system (integrating sphere) designed for the measurement of the transmittance of inhomogeneous materials

sphere regardless of the direction in which the light enters the sphere. An arrangement like that of Fig. 3.7 is said to measure the *diffuse* transmittance, whereas an arrangement like Fig. 3.2 is said to measure the *specular* transmittance. Unless a material is almost perfectly homogeneous, it is usually more significant to determine its diffuse transmittance. If a homogeneous material is illuminated by a collimated beam, the specular and diffuse transmittances are equal. Hence, spectrophotometers are of more general usefulness if designed to measured diffuse transmittance.

3.5 Specular and Diffuse Reflectances

An opaque material whose surface is perfectly smooth behaves like a mirror. If, as shown in Fig. 3.8, a collimated beam of light is incident on a smooth surface at an angle *a,* the beam is still collimated after reflection and makes an angle $-a$ with the normal to the surface. The reflectance of the surface at any wavelength is the ratio of the intensity of a monochromatic beam after reflection to its intensity before reflection. This type of reflectance is called *specular,* from the Latin word *speculum,* meaning a mirror. The specular reflectance varies somewhat with the angle of incidence; a specification of this angle should be part of the report of the measurement. Measurements of specular reflectance are not of much importance in the field of colorimetry, because materials that exhibit purely specular reflection are not often encountered.

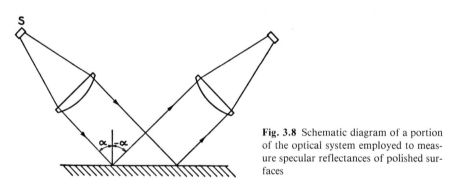

Fig. 3.8 Schematic diagram of a portion of the optical system employed to measure specular reflectances of polished surfaces

In general, materials encountered in colorimetry have surfaces that are rough in comparison with the wavelength of light, or because of optical inhomogeneities within them, scatter reflected light in all directions; such materials are said to be *diffusing.* The procedure used to measure *diffuse* reflectance is illustrated diagrammatically in Fig. 3.9. A collimated beam passes through a sphere and illuminates the test sample; the reflected light is collected by the white interior walls of the sphere. Owing to the geometry of a sphere, a window in the sphere wall occupied by the measuring detector is illuminated to the same extent by a given amount of light reflected from the test sample, regardless of the direction in which the light is reflected. Such an arrangement is called an *integrating sphere.* When the test sample is replaced by a white standard of known reflectance, the reflectance of the former can be computed from the ratio of the powers detected through the window in the two cases.

Although this method requires a relatively simple optical system, it is subject to an error, because replacing the test sample by a white standard changes the average reflectance of the walls of the sphere, even if the test sample occupies what might be thought to be a negligible portion of the sphere wall. A direct-comparison method is better than the substitution method. In direct-comparison methods, the sample and the white standard occupy positions in the sphere wall simultaneously, but are illuminated alternately.

It will be recalled that an instrument that measures diffuse transmittances of inhomogeneous materials can be used also to measure specular transmittances of homogeneous materials. In the same way, an arrangement like that shown in Fig. 3.9 can be used to obtain the specular reflectance of a smooth surface, provided that the sample is oriented in such a manner that the reflected beam strikes the sphere wall rather than the aperture through which the light enters the sphere. In this case, it is necessary that the reflectance of the white lining of the sphere be high, especially where the reflected beam first strikes it.

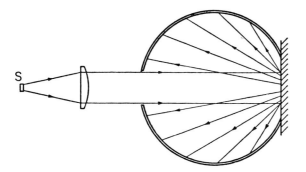

Fig. 3.9 Schematic diagram of an optical system (integrating sphere) designed for measurement of diffuse reflectances of rough surfaces

It is evident that the methods outlined for determination of reflectances of opaque materials are applicable to materials that are not opaque under the definition given in the first paragraph of this chapter. In the case of non-opaque materials, the reflectance often depends to a considerable extent on the reflectance of the material with which the sample is backed. Thus, if the test sample is backed with a perfectly white material, higher values are obtained than with a black backing. Because it is impossible to obtain a black material that has a reflectance of zero, the test sample may be supported in such a manner as to have no backing whatsoever. The light transmitted by the sample can then be absorbed by the walls of a darkened room. Many materials that are ordinarily assumed to be opaque have measurable transmittances. This is usually true of textile fabrics, paper samples, and films of paint, ink, lacquer, or enamel. For such samples, much valuable information concerning the *opacity* is acquired by measuring diffuse reflectances with both a white and a black backing. Tests of this sort will almost invariably demonstrate that the opacity is a function of wavelength, even in the case of nearly white materials.

3.6 Gloss

A reflecting surface that is perfectly diffusing is equally bright for all directions of viewing. This is true regardless of the mode of illumination. On the other hand, a perfect mirror illuminated by a single source of light appears bright for only a single direction of viewing, and black for all other directions. Neither type of surface can be fully realized in practice; all actual surfaces have diffusing characteristics that are intermediate between these two extremes. A surface that approaches closely the conditions of specular reflection is ordinarily said to be *glossy*; one that approaches more closely the conditions of diffuse reflection is said to be *matte*. Every color specification should be accompanied by a statement of the geometry of the illuminating beam and the geometry of that portion of the reflected (or transmitted) beam that is evaluated in the measurement.

There is no conclusive reason for mandating any particular mode of illumination and observation. Colored materials are ordinarily examined under a wide diversity of modes of illumination and viewing.

Correspondingly, many modes of illumination and observation have been incorporated into the design of color-measuring instruments. One design that has been used rather extensively employs diffuse illumination of the sample and observation of the sample by a nearly unidirectional beam normal to the surface. The color specification obtained with such an instrument corresponds to placing the sample horizontally where it is illuminated by the completely overcast sky and viewing the sample from above, avoiding obstruction of the illumination. In the design of an instrument that employs this mode of illumination and observation, it is frequently simpler to illuminate the sample normally by a unidirectional beam of light and then to collect all of the reflected light by means of an integrating sphere. A fundamental law of optics ensures that this reversal of the direction of the light yields identical results.

For example, in the description of the principles that underlie the operation of a spectrophotometer, the light was said to be dispersed into its spectral components before it was incident on the sample. For nonfluorescent samples, an equivalent procedure is to illuminate the sample by undispersed white light and subsequently to disperse the reflected light into its spectral components. Fluorescent samples, however, should be illuminated with undispersed white light that has the spectral composition, including any ultraviolet wavelengths that excite fluorescence, of the illuminant relevant for final use – e.g., daylight.

4. Color Mixture

Anyone who works continually with colors acquires, in time, the ability to anticipate the result of mixing familiar colors. Knowledge acquired in this manner cannot be imparted to others and cannot be applied to new colors without an extended series of experiments with them. It is often possible to calculate the result of mixing colors from the characteristics of the components. When valid, this procedure yields quantitative results of high precision and does not require familiarity with the component colors. The principles upon which such calculations are based are discussed in this chapter.

4.1 Absorptive Color Mixture

If two homogeneous materials, such as two pieces of glass or two cells that contain clear liquids, are placed in series in the same beam of light, the transmittance of the combination at any wavelength is the product of their individual transmittances, provided that corrections are made for interreflections between surfaces. Hence, if the spectral transmittances of two samples are known, the spectral transmittances of the combination can be determined by computation. This has been done in Fig. 4.1 for a combination of a yellow and a blue glass. The resulting curve corresponds to a green glass, as would be expected. This principle may be generalized. Thus, if several materials are placed in series in the same beam of light, the transmittance of the combination at any wavelength is the product of their individual transmittances. It is frequently simpler in dealing with combinations like this to plot the results on a density scale. The density of the combination at any wavelength is the sum of the individual densities. Hence, the density curve of the combination can be readily obtained by graphical construction from density curves of the components. In the case of mixtures of two or more colored solutions in the same cell, the spectral transmittance curve of the mixture is obtained by taking the product at each wavelength of the individual transmittances of the components, provided there is no chemical or other interaction between the components. It is necessary, of course, to correct the measured values of the transmittances for reflectance and transmittance losses due to the cell. It is also necessary to take into account mutual dilution, when solutions are mixed.

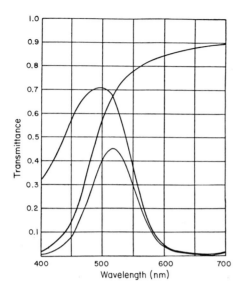

Fig. 4.1 Transmittance curves of a blue glass, a yellow glass, and their combination

The simple law of subtractive mixtures is not applicable for computation of the spectral reflectances of mixtures of opaque or semi-opaque materials, paints, and other pigmented materials. These materials usually consist of a nearly transparent vehicle in which one or more insoluble pigments are suspended in finely divided states. In some printing inks, the pigment particles have nearly the same refractive index as the vehicle in which they are suspended. Such inks are therefore optically nearly homogeneous, and the simple law of subtractive mixtures may be applicable. When this law is used, allowance must be made for reflection at the air – vehicle boundary, for the reflectances of the vehicle-wetted support to which the ink is applied, for the thickness of the film (the optical thickness is twice the actual thickness because incident light must pass through the film, be reflected from the underlying paper, and pass again through the film before it can be seen), and for mutual dilution of the components when they are mixed.

A pigmented film in which the vehicle has the same refractive index as the pigmented particles would be worthless as a paint, because it would be transparent. Such a film would have no hiding power. The hiding power, or opacity, of a pigmented film results from the innumerable reflections that take place at the pigment – vehicle interfaces. The magnitude of each individual reflection depends on the difference between the two indices of refraction. The optical behavior of such materials is complex; it is not to be expected that these materials will obey the simple law just explained for homogeneous materials. Formulae for computation of the spectral reflectances of such mixtures will be given and discussed in Sect. 7.3. It is often safer and simpler to determine the mixture curves experimentally.

Absorptive color mixture is sometimes called *subtractive* color mixture, although there is no sense in which arithmetic subtraction is pertinent.

4.2 Additive Color Mixture

In so-called *additive* color mixture, the light from each component reaches the eye in an unmodified state. The simplest type of additive mixture is the simultaneous projection of two or more beams of colored light on the same area of a white screen. An equivalent procedure is to project the several beams, one at a time, in such rapid succession that they are combined by persistence of vision into a single color perception. The result of that would be averaging, rather than addition of colors. Colors of opaque materials, such as colored papers, may be added or, again, more precisely, averaged by cutting the materials so that they can be mounted as segments of a circular disk. By spinning the disk the colors may be made to appear to fuse. Such an arrangement is often called a color wheel or Maxwell disk. Another method of obtaining an additive mixture takes advantage of the limited resolving power of the eye. Thus, a roofing material composed of red and green particles may appear a dark yellow (brown) when viewed from such a distance that the individual particles cannot be resolved. In the same way, a gray cloth is often made from a combination of black and white threads. In all such cases, the colors of the constituents are averaged rather than added.

   In the case where two or more beams of light are added together, such as by projection together on a screen, the energy distribution curve of the mixture can be computed by adding the energies of the components at each wavelength. In the other cases, in which one of the components replaces another, either in time or in space, allowance must be made for the proportion that each bears to the total time or total space. Thus, in the case of a Maxwell disk that contains two colors that occupy fractional areas a and b, the reflectance of the rotating disk at each wavelength is obtained by multiplying the reflectance of one component by a, the other component by b, and summing the results. This principle can be extended to include the addition of any number of colors.

   It is not necessary to have spectrophotometric data in order to compute the result of an additive mixture. Thus, if two beams of light whose tristimulus values are X_1, Y_1, Z_1 and X_2, Y_2, Z_2 are projected on the same white screen, the tristimulus values of the mixture are

$$X = X_1 + X_2$$
$$Y = Y_1 + Y_2$$
$$Z = Z_1 + Z_2.$$

If the colors of the two beams are specified in terms of Y_1, x_1, y_1 and Y_2, x_2, y_2, the luminance and chromaticity of the mixture can be computed by use of the formulae

$$Y = Y_1 + Y_2$$

$$x = \frac{m_1 x_1 + m_2 x_2}{m_2 + m_2}$$

$$y = \frac{m_1 y_1 + m_2 y_2}{m_1 + m_2},$$

$$Y_2 \left(\frac{x_2 + Y_2 + Z_2}{Y_2} \right) = x_2 + Y_2 + Z_2$$

where $m_1 = Y_1/y_1$ and $m_2 = Y_2/y_2$. The equations for x and y are those familiar for the center of gravity of two masses m_1 and m_2 located at x_1, y_1, and x_2, y_2, respectively. This is the precise statement of the *center-of-gravity law* of color mixture enunciated over 300 years ago by Sir Isaac Newton. Note that the *masses* are Y/y. They are also the sums of the tristimulus values $m = X + Y + Z$.

If two colors that have fractional areas a and b are mixed on a Maxwell disk, the tristimulus values of the mixture are

$$X = aX_1 + bX_2$$

$$Y = aY_1 + bY_2$$

$$Z = aZ_1 + bZ_2.$$

If the two colors on the Maxwell disk are expressed in terms of Y_1, x_1, y_1 and Y_2, x_2, y_2, the result of their mixture would be

$$Y = aY_1 + bY_2$$

$$x = \frac{am_1 x_1 + bm_2 x_2}{am_1 + bm_2}$$

$$y = \frac{am_1 y_1 + bm_2 y_2}{am_1 + bm_2},$$

where again $m_1 = Y_1/y_1$ and $m_2 = Y_2/y_2$. The equations for x and y may be extended to mixtures of three or more colors by adding corresponding terms to both the numerator and denominator.

Examination of the equations for x and y show that, like the center of gravity, regardless of the ratio in which two colors are mixed, the point thus determined on a chromaticity diagram lies on the straight line that joins the points x_1, y_1 and x_2, y_2. This property of a chromaticity diagram was used extensively in Chap. 1.

4.3 Complementary Colors

When the line that joins the points that represent the two components passes through the white point, the components and their dominant wavelengths are said to be complementary. Table 4.1 gives a list of pairs of complementary dominant wavelengths, when the CIE illuminant C is taken as white. If two materials have dominant wavelengths that are complementary, as indicated in this table, and are mixed additively in the proper proportions, they will

Table 4.1. Complementary wavelengths [nm] for illuminant C (white)

Wavelength [nm]	Complementary [nm]	Wavelength [nm]	Complementary [nm]
380	567.0	576	475.4
400	567.1	577	476.7
420	567.3	578	478.0
430	567.5	579	479.0
440	568.0	580	480.0
450	568.9	581	480.8
455	569.6	582	481.6
460	570.4	583	482.3
470	573.1	584	482.9
471	573.6	585	483.5
472	574.0	586	484.1
473	574.5	587	484.6
474	575.1	588	485.1
475	575.7	589	485.5
476	576.4	590	485.9
477	577.2	591	486.3
478	578.0	592	486.7
479	579.0	593	487.0
480	580.0	594	487.3
481	581.2	595	487.6
482	582.6	596	487.9
483	584.1	597	488.1
484	585.8	598	488.4
485	587.8	599	488.6
486	590.2	600	488.8
487	593.0	605	489.7
488	596.5	610	490.4
489	600.9	615	490.9
490	607.0	620	491.2
491	616.8	625	491.5
492	640.2	630	491.7
568	439.3	640	492.0
569	450.7	650	492.2
570	457.9	660	492.3
571	463.1	670	492.3
572	466.8	680	492.4
573	469.7	690	492.4
574	471.9	700	492.4
575	473.8	780	492.4

produce a mixture whose chromaticity coordinates are the same as those of illuminant C.

4.4 Photometric Relations Between Complementary Colors[23]

The concepts of Y/y as a mass and of additive mixture as defining a center of gravity lead to some far-reaching conclusions. For example, the ratio of the number of lumens, Y_2/Y_1, of two complementary colors whose additive mixture is white or neutral gray, is the inverse ratio of the moments of the masses per lumen ($Y = 1$) of those chromaticities with respect to the chromaticity of the illuminant (i.e., the white point). Recall that the white point lies on the straight line that connects the points that represent any pair of complementary colors in the chromaticity diagram. If we designate the distances of these points from the illuminant point as s_1 and s_2, then the *moments* per lumen of the colors, with respect to the white point, are s_1/y_1 and s_2/y_2. The ratio of the numbers of lumens of those colors required for a white mixture is $Y_2/Y_1 = (s_1/y_1)/(s_2/y_2)$. Because the moment per lumen of any chromaticity with respect to the illuminant point is simply the ratio s/y of the distances of that chromaticity point from the illuminant point and from

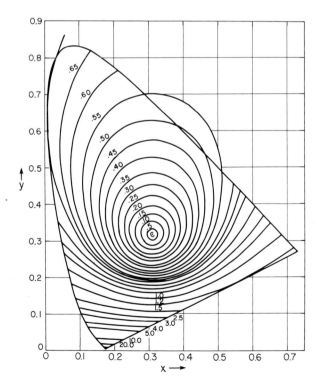

Fig. 4.2
Moment per lumen with respect to illuminant C

the $y = 0$ base line, the locus of all chromaticities that have any one value of moment per lumen is a conic section with a focus at the illuminant point and the base line for its directrix, Fig. 4.2. In particular, all chromaticities for which the moment per lumen is unity (1) are on the parabola whose focus is the illuminant point. It passes through the point that has the same x coordinate as the illuminant and a y coordinate exactly half that of the illuminant. The locus of chromaticities for which the moment per lumen is any value less than 1 is an ellipse that lies above that parabola. One of its foci is the illuminant point.

The locus of chromaticities for which the moment per lumen is any value greater than 1 is an hyperbola below the parabola.

4.5 Color Moment

The mass per watt of any spectrum color is simply $\bar{x} + \bar{y} + \bar{z}$. The mass per watt is shown as a function of wavelength in Fig. 4.3. When those values are multiplied by the distance of the corresponding point on the spectrum locus from the illuminant point, the moment per watt shown in Fig. 4.4 is obtained.

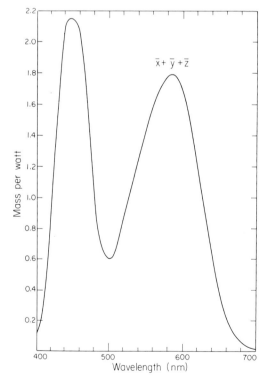

Fig. 4.3 Mass per watt of spectrum colors

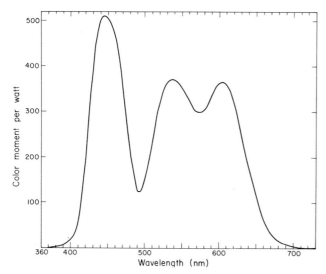

Fig. 4.4 Moment per watt of spectrum colors with respect to illuminant C

When the values in Fig. 4.4 are divided by $\bar{y}$, the moments per lumen shown in Fig. 4.5 are obtained. These are exactly the values of the moments indicated in Fig. 4.2 for the intersections of the conics and the spectrum locus. Although the significance of the data in Figs. 4.4, 5 is specialized in that they show effectiveness of spectrum colors in complementary mixtures, they are indicative of the effectiveness of wavelengths in color mixtures in general[24]. For this reason, they are called color moments. The very great values of moment per lumen (Fig. 4.5) in the short wavelengths is especially notable. In consequence, although the luminosities of short wavelengths are quite low, their effectiveness in additive mixtures is very great. Therefore, provided that they have high purity, i.e., are near the spectrum locus, blue primaries for color television or additive color photography need not have as much luminance as the green or red primaries. Similarly, the blue phosphor component in the white coating on the interiors of fluorescent lamps need not be very luminous, compared to the other components.

The blue maximum of the curve in Fig. 4.4 has the consequence that the maximum possible *luminous efficiency* (lumens/watt) with which any chromaticity can be produced is obtained by use of a spectrum component in the wavelength range from 438 – 448 nm. To produce any particular chromaticity, a single other wavelength is coupled with the blue. It must be "complementary" in the sense that the desired chromaticity plays the role of the "illuminant" or "white" point. The necessary lumen ratio of the blue to the other wavelength is the inverse ratio of their moments per lumen (s/y) with respect to the desired chromaticity. The particular blue wavelength that gives the maximum luminous efficiency must be determined by an iterative procedure. It varies appreciably from 448 nm only for the production of

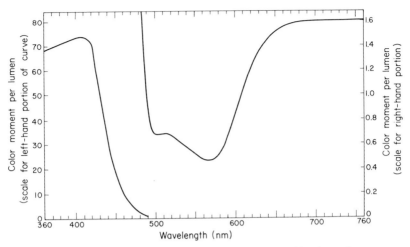

Fig. 4.5 Moment per lumen of spectrum colors with respect to illuminant C

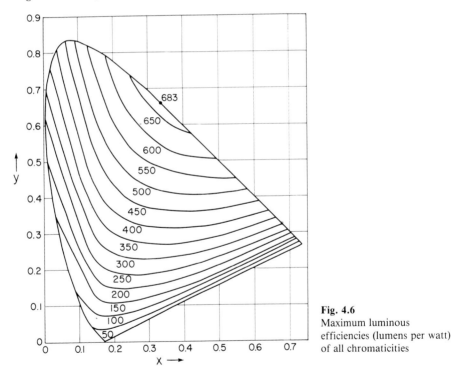

Fig. 4.6
Maximum luminous
efficiencies (lumens per watt)
of all chromaticities

chromaticities with y less than 0.03. For all other cases, the second wavelength is longer than 448 nm. The maximum luminous efficiencies for typical chromaticities are shown in Fig. 4.6. Values can be interpolated for intermediate chromaticities.

The tristimulus value X is simply the moment of a color around the y axis. Likewise, in addition to being the luminance (or luminance factor in the case of a reflecting or transparent material) the tristimulus value Y is the moment of the color around the x axis. The former (X) can be appropriately called the x moment of the color and Y the y moment. In these terms, the x moment of the additive mixture of any number of colors is the sum of the x moments of the constituent colors and the y moment of the combination is the sum of the y moments of the constituents. The color mass of the combination is the sum of the masses Y/y of the constituents.

In strict analogy with the mechanical center of gravity, the chromaticity coordinates of a color mixture are the sums of the x moments and the y moments divided by the sum of the color masses. Of course, this is merely a restatement of the definitions of x and y; the sum of the x moments is the tristimulus value X of the mixture — the sum of the X tristimulus values of its constituents; the sum of the y moments is the tristimulus value Y — the sum of the Y tristimulus values of the constituents; the sum of the color masses is the sum of the tristimulus values $X + Y + Z$ of the mixture. As mentioned previously, $m = X + Y + Z$ for each of the constituents and for any combination of them because, by definition, tristimulus values of each kind are additive, $y = Y/(X + Y + Z)$, and $m = Y/y$.

5. Determination of Tristimulus Values

As explained in Chap. 1, the objective method of evaluating the appearance of a color consists of determining a stimulus that is equivalent under the viewing conditions. The stimulus ordinarily employed is an additive mixture of three basic or primary stimuli. In the calculation of the equivalent stimulus from spectrophotometric data, it is necessary to use the tristimulus values for the spectrum colors. Table 1.1 lists the values of $\bar{x}$, $\bar{y}$, $\bar{z}$ that were adopted by the CIE in 1931. Those values indicate the amounts of each of the chosen primaries that are required by a normal observer to match the colors of equal amounts of power at the indicated wavelengths.

5.1 Tristimulus Values of the Spectrum Colors

As an example of the use of the tristimulus values of the spectrum, consider the problem of determining the chromaticity coordinates for illuminant C. The relative distribution of power E_C from this source is known from Table 2.2. These values are listed in column two of Table 5.1 against the corresponding wavelength entries in column one. The wavelength interval used is 10 nm. In general, the wavelength interval should be so small that the use of smaller intervals would not produce significant changes of the final results. Column three in Table 5.1 gives the corresponding values of $\bar{x}$ from Table 1.1; column four gives the product of columns two and three. The sum of the entries in the fourth column is a measure of X, one of the tristimulus values for illuminant C. Repetition of this procedure, with $\bar{y}$ and $\bar{z}$ substituted in turn for $\bar{x}$, gives

$X = 1043.8$

$Y = 1064.7$

$Z = 1257.4$.

Recall that the values in column two are only the relative amounts of energy at each wavelength, not the absolute amounts. Furthermore, the computed values of X, Y, and Z are the sums of entries at intervals of 10 nm; different sums would have been obtained if a different wavelength interval had been selected. Fortunately, the vast majority of problems in colorimetry

Table 5.1. Sample calculation of a tristimulus value of a source by the weighted-ordinate method

Wavelength [nm]	E_c	$\bar{x}$	$E_c\bar{x}$	Wavelength [nm]	E_c	$\bar{x}$	$E_c\bar{x}$
380	33.0	0.0014	0.05	600	89.7	1.0622	95.28
390	47.4	0.0042	0.20	610	88.4	1.0026	88.63
400	63.3	0.0148	0.91	620	88.1	0.8544	75.27
410	80.6	0.0435	3.51	630	88.0	0.6424	56.53
420	98.1	0.1344	13.18	640	87.8	0.4479	39.33
430	112.4	0.2839	31.91	650	88.2	0.2835	25.00
440	121.5	0.3483	42.32	660	87.9	0.1649	14.49
450	124.0	0.3362	41.69	670	86.3	0.0874	7.54
460	123.1	0.2908	35.80	680	84.0	0.0468	3.93
470	123.8	0.1954	24.19	690	80.2	0.0227	1.82
480	123.9	0.0956	11.84	700	76.3	0.0114	0.87
490	120.7	0.0320	3.86	710	72.4	0.0058	0.42
500	112.1	0.0049	0.55	720	68.3	0.0029	0.20
510	102.3	0.0093	0.95	730	64.4	0.0014	0.09
520	96.9	0.0633	6.13	740	61.5	0.0007	0.04
530	98.0	0.1655	16.22	750	59.2	0.0003	0.02
540	102.1	0.2904	29.65	760	58.1	0.0002	0.01
550	105.2	0.4334	45.59	770	58.2	0.0001	0.01
560	105.3	0.5945	62.60				
570	102.3	0.7621	77.96				
580	97.8	0.9163	89.61				
590	93.2	1.0263	95.65				

Sum = 1043.8

are concerned with the quality of the light source, not with the quantity of light that it emits. Multiplying X, Y, and Z by a common factor does not alter the specification of quality, which is evaluated by the chromaticity coordinates,

$$x = X/(X + Y + Z)$$
$$y = Y/(X + Y + Z).$$

Substitution in these equations in the case of illuminant C gives $x = 0.3101$, $y = 0.3163$. These are the chromaticity coordinates of illuminant C.

5.2 Tristimulus Values of the Spectrum Colors Weighted by the CIE Illuminants

Most of the problems of importance in colorimetry require determination of tristimulus values of either transparent or opaque materials. Such problems

Table 5.2. Color-matching functions (CIE 1931 tristimulus values of the spectrum) multiplied by relative spectral power distribution of CIE illuminant A

Wavelength [nm]	$\bar{x}S_A$	$\bar{y}S_A$	$\bar{z}S_A$	Wavelength [nm]	$\bar{x}S_A$	$\bar{y}S_A$	$\bar{z}S_A$
380	0.01	0.00	0.06	600	137.07	81.42	0.10
390	0.05	0.00	0.24	610	136.70	68.58	0.04
				620	122.71	54.72	0.03
400	0.21	0.01	1.00	630	96.90	39.97	0.00
410	0.77	0.02	3.67	640	70.76	27.65	0.00
420	2.82	0.08	13.56				
430	7.00	0.29	34.18	650	46.79	17.66	0.00
440	10.00	0.66	50.14	660	28.36	10.49	0.00
				670	15.62	5.72	0.00
450	11.12	1.26	58.64	680	8.68	3.15	0.00
460	11.00	2.27	63.11	690	4.36	1.57	0.00
470	8.38	3.90	55.20				
480	4.61	6.71	39.22	700	2.26	0.81	0.00
490	1.73	11.21	25.08	710	1.19	0.43	0.00
				720	0.61	0.21	0.00
500	0.29	19.33	16.28	730	0.30	0.11	0.00
510	0.61	33.23	10.45	740	0.16	0.04	0.00
520	4.59	51.48	5.67				
530	13.10	68.21	3.34	750	0.07	0.02	0.00
540	24.96	82.00	1.74	760	0.05	0.02	0.00
				770	0.02	0.00	0.00
550	40.27	92.45	0.81				
560	59.45	99.50	0.39				
570	81.68	102.04	0.23				
580	104.86	99.56	0.19				
590	124.93	92.15	0.13				
				Sum =	1185.05	1078.93	383.89

far outnumber evaluations of the chromaticities of light sources. The tristimulus values for either a transparent or an opaque material may be computed by multiplying at each wavelength the relative amount of power of the source by the reflectance or transmittance of the sample. The product gives the relative amount of power at that wavelength that enters the eye of the observer. This product must then be multiplied by $\bar{x}$, $\bar{y}$, and $\bar{z}$, in turn. An equivalent procedure, which greatly economizes on the amount of arithmetic needed for any light source that is to be the illuminant for many samples, is to multiply first the relative amount of power from the source by the corresponding values of $\bar{x}$, $\bar{y}$, $\bar{z}$. It is then only necessary to multiply tabulated values of those products by the spectral reflectances or transmittances of the sample. Tables 5.2 – 4 list values of $E\bar{x}$, $E\bar{y}$, and $E\bar{z}$ for the CIE illuminants A, C, and D_{65}, respectively. Those values were obtained by multiplying, at each wavelength, values taken from the appropriate columns of Table 2.2 by the corresponding values of $\bar{x}$, $\bar{y}$, and $\bar{z}$ for the CIE 1931 observer, given in Table 1.1.

Table 5.3. Color-matching functions (CIE 1931) multiplied by relative spectral power distribution of CIE illuminant C

Wavelength [nm]	$\bar{x}S_c$	$\bar{y}S_c$	$\bar{z}S_c$	Wavelength [nm]	$\bar{x}S_c$	$\bar{y}S_c$	$\bar{z}S_c$
380	0.05	0.00	0.21	600	95.28	56.60	0.07
390	0.20	0.00	0.95	610	88.63	44.47	0.03
400	0.91	0.03	4.30	620	75.27	33.57	0.02
410	3.51	0.10	16.72	630	56.53	23.32	0.00
420	13.18	0.39	63.33	640	39.33	15.37	0.00
430	31.91	1.30	155.74	650	25.00	9.44	0.00
440	42.32	2.79	212.27	660	14.49	5.36	0.00
450	41.69	4.71	219.74	670	7.54	2.76	0.00
460	35.80	7.39	205.48	680	3.93	1.43	0.00
470	24.19	11.27	159.40	690	1.82	0.66	0.00
480	11.84	17.22	100.73	700	0.87	0.31	0.00
490	3.86	25.11	56.15	710	0.42	0.15	0.00
500	0.55	36.21	30.49	720	0.20	0.07	0.00
510	0.95	51.46	16.18	730	0.09	0.03	0.00
520	6.13	68.80	7.58	740	0.04	0.01	0.00
530	16.22	84.48	4.14	750	0.02	0.01	0.00
540	29.65	97.40	2.07	760	0.01	0.01	0.00
550	45.59	104.67	0.92	770	0.01	0.00	0.00
560	62.60	104.77	0.41				
570	77.96	97.39	0.21				
580	89.61	85.09	0.17				
590	95.65	70.55	0.10				
				Sum =	1044.15	1064.68	1258.75

5.3 Weighted-Ordinate Method

As an example of the use of these tables, consider the problem of determining the chromaticity coordinates and luminance factor of a red signal glass that is to be placed in front of a lamp that has the quality of illuminant A. The computational procedure by which these results are obtained is shown in Table 5.5. Column one gives the wavelength of the light at intervals of 10 nm; column two gives the spectral transmittances of the red glass as determined by a spectrophotometer and shown in Fig. 3.1; column three gives the values of $E\bar{x}$ for illuminant A from Table 5.2; column four is the product of columns two and three. The sum of the entries in the fourth column is a measure of X. Repeating this operation with $E\bar{y}$ and $E\bar{z}$ substituted for $E\bar{x}$ gives $X = 640.2$, $Y = 321.3$, and $Z = 0.0$. From these values, the chromaticity coordinates are $x = 0.6658$ and $y = 0.3342$.[25]

The luminance factor can be found by determining the ratio of the sum for Y to the total for Y of a few centimeters of air, whose transmittance is 1.000 at

Table 5.4. Color-matching functions (CIE 1931) multiplied by relative spectral power distribution of CIE illuminant D_{65}

Wavelength [nm]	$\bar{x}S_{65}$	$\bar{y}S_{65}$	$\bar{z}S_{65}$	Wavelength [nm]	$\bar{x}S_{65}$	$\bar{y}S_{65}$	$\bar{z}S_{65}$
380	0.07	0.00	0.33	600	95.60	56.79	0.07
390	0.23	0.01	1.10	610	89.83	45.07	0.03
				620	74.93	33.41	0.02
400	1.33	0.04	6.30	630	53.51	22.07	0.00
410	3.98	0.11	18.98	640	37.49	14.65	0.00
420	12.55	0.37	60.30				
430	24.61	1.01	120.13	650	22.68	8.56	0.00
440	36.54	2.41	183.27	660	13.22	4.89	0.00
				670	7.19	2.63	0.00
450	39.34	4.45	207.34	680	3.66	1.33	0.00
460	34.26	7.07	196.63	690	1.58	0.57	0.00
470	22.45	10.46	147.95				
480	11.08	16.11	94.23	700	0.82	0.29	0.00
490	3.48	22.63	50.61	710	0.43	0.16	0.00
				720	0.18	0.06	0.00
500	0.54	35.34	29.76	730	0.10	0.04	0.00
510	1.00	54.22	17.05	740	0.05	0.02	0.00
520	6.63	74.41	8.20				
530	17.82	92.84	4.54	750	0.02	0.01	0.00
540	30.32	99.60	2.12	760	0.01	0.00	0.00
				770	0.01	0.00	0.00
550	45.07	103.48	0.90				
560	59.45	99.50	0.39				
570	73.39	91.68	0.20				
580	87.78	83.35	0.16				
590	91.03	67.15	0.10				
				Sum =	1004.35	1056.65	1150.93

Table 5.5. Sample calculation of a tristimulus value of a filter by the weighted-ordinate method (see text for explanation)

Wavelength [nm]	T	$E_a\bar{x}$	$TE_A\bar{x}$	Wavelength [nm]	T	$E_A\bar{x}$	$TE_A\bar{x}$
380	...	...	...	650	0.883	44.66	39.4
				660	0.887	26.81	23.8
...	...	...	...	670	0.890	15.63	13.9
...	...	...	...	680	0.894	8.67	7.8
...	...	...	...	690	0.895	4.35	3.9
570	0.002	81.69	0.2	700	0.897	2.25	2.0
580	0.100	104.85	10.5	710	0.897	1.19	1.1
590	0.500	124.97	62.5	720	0.897	0.61	0.5
				730	0.897	0.31	0.3
600	0.775	137.04	106.2	740	0.897	0.15	0.1
610	0.850	136.73	116.2				
620	0.870	122.72	106.8	750	0.897	0.08	0.1
630	0.876	96.90	84.9	760	0.897	0.04	0.0
640	0.880	68.20	60.0	770	0.897	0.02	0.0
						Sum =	640.2

every wavelength. The sum for Y obtained for the air is 1079.0, as shown at the bottom of Table 5.2, whereas the value obtained for the red glass is 321.3. The ratio is

$$\frac{321.3}{1079.0} = 0.2978 = 29.78\% .$$

This procedure is valid because the $\bar{y}$ function was, by appropriate selection of the primaries, made to correspond to the luminosity function of the eye. The above ratio is, therefore, the ratio of the number of lumens emitted by the lamp and signal-glass combination to the number of lumens that would be emitted by the lamp alone. It is also the ratio of the luminance of a white surface illuminated with illuminant A and viewed through the filter to the luminance of the white surface viewed directly. For this reason, the ratio is called the luminance factor. The luminance factor of a filter depends on the spectral quality of the source with which it is used.

When they are reported, the tristimulus values X, Y, and Z are normalized by dividing the totals of the products by the total for Y in air, as in the calculation of luminance factor. Similarly, they are often expressed as percentages, rather than as decimals. The same divisor is used for all three tristimulus values. The totals for X and Z for air are not used, except for determining the tristimulus values and chromaticity of the illuminant alone. The divisor should be the sum of the products $\bar{y}S$ for only the wavelengths for which spectral transmittances (or reflectances) are available and used. Thus the common divisor is, in general, different when transmittances from 400 to 700 nm are used than when values from 380 to 770 nm are used. The common divisor should also be different (about twice as great) if products at 5 nm intervals are used than when 10 nm intervals are used.

As a second example of the use of Tables 5.2 – 4, consider the problem of evaluating the color of a nearly white paper whose reflectances at the various wavelengths are listed in column two of Table 5.6 and shown in Fig. 5.1. In this table, column one gives the wavelength at intervals of 10 nm. The third column gives the values of $E\bar{x}$ for illuminant C from Table 5.3. The fourth column gives the products of the entries in columns two and three. The sum of the entries in the fourth column is a measure of X. Repeating this operation with $E\bar{y}$ and $E\bar{z}$ substituted in turn for $E\bar{x}$ gives $X = 880$, $Y = 902$, and $Z = 960$. From these, the chromaticity coordinates are $x = 0.3209$, $y = 0.3290$.

As in the previous example, the luminance factor is computed by determining the value of Y for a surface that has a reflectance of 1.000 at all wavelengths. The resulting value of Y for such a surface is 1065, as shown at the bottom of the third column in Table 5.3. Hence the ratio

$$\frac{902}{1065} = 0.847 = 84.7\%$$

is the luminance factor of the white paper. In other words, it is the luminance

Table 5.6. Sample calculation of a tristimulus value for a sheet of "white" paper by the weighted-ordinate method

Wavelength [nm]	R	$E_c\bar{x}$	$RE_c\bar{x}$	Wavelength [nm]	R	$E_c\bar{x}$	$RE_c\bar{x}$
380	0.620	0.05	0.0	570	0.855	77.96	66.7
390	0.640	0.20	0.1	580	0.860	89.61	77.1
				590	0.865	95.65	82.8
400	0.660	0.91	0.6				
410	0.681	3.51	2.4	600	0.870	95.28	82.9
420	0.703	13.18	9.3	610	0.873	88.63	77.4
430	0.727	31.91	23.2	620	0.875	75.27	65.9
440	0.745	42.32	31.4	630	0.878	56.53	49.6
				640	0.880	39.33	34.6
450	0.760	41.69	31.7				
460	0.775	35.80	27.8	650	0.882	25.00	22.1
470	0.787	24.19	19.0	660	0.884	14.49	12.8
480	0.800	11.84	9.5	670	0.884	7.54	6.7
490	0.805	3.86	3.1	680	0.885	3.93	3.5
				690	0.885	1.82	1.6
500	0.815	0.55	0.4				
510	0.822	0.95	0.8	700	0.885	0.87	0.8
520	0.830	6.13	5.1	710	0.885	0.42	0.4
530	0.835	16.22	13.5	720	0.885	0.20	0.2
540	0.840	29.65	24.9	730	0.885	0.09	0.1
				740	0.885	0.04	0.0
550	0.845	45.59	38.5				
560	0.850	62.60	53.2				

Sum $= 880.0$

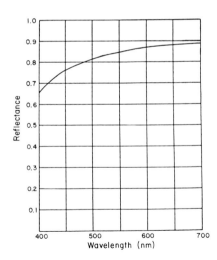

Fig. 5.1 Spectral reflectance curve of a sample of white paper

of the white paper relative to the luminance of a perfect reflector under the same illumination, in this case under illuminant C. As before, this luminance factor depends on the spectral quality of the illumination.

5.4 Truncated Weighted Ordinates

The most commonly used method for evaluation of tristimulus values is the weighted-ordinate method described in Sect. 5.3. It is the well-known trapezoidal-rule method of numerical integration. In effect, it approximates every set of spectrophotometric data with a graph like Fig. 5.2 where, for λ intervals from wavelength $\lambda - \Delta\lambda/2$ to $\lambda + \Delta\lambda/2$, the spectrophotometric curve is assumed to be a straight line through the value R_λ measured at λ, with the slope $(R_{\lambda+\Delta\lambda} - R_{\lambda-\Delta\lambda})/2\Delta\lambda$.[26] Modifications have been proposed and occasionally used: a) to improve the approximation indicated in Fig. 5.2; b) to compensate for limitations of spectrophotometric data; and c) to simplify the calculations.

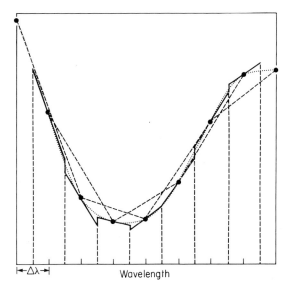

Wavelength

Fig. 5.2 Approximation of spectrophotometric curve implied by trapezoidal rule

Because the CIE values of the color-matching functions were recommended at 5 nm intervals from 380 to 775 nm, for utmost accuracy the integrations should consist of summations of products computed at every 5 nm between and at those limits. In the great majority of actual cases, however, the summations are abridged to $\Delta\lambda = 10$ nm intervals, as in the examples in Tables 5.1,5. Recently, they have often been further abridged to 20 nm intervals, from 400 to 700 nm.

Simpson's rule is sometimes suggested and even used instead of the trapezoidal rule. In effect, it replaces the straight-line segments in Fig. 5.2 with portions of vertical-axis parabolas that pass through $R_{\lambda-\Delta\lambda}$, R_λ, and $R_{\lambda+\Delta\lambda}$. Use of the parabolic approximation in place of straight lines is usually of negligible effect. Furthermore, if the summations are carried from 375 to 775 nm, where the color-matching data are zero, the trapezoidal rule gives exactly the same results as Simpson's rule. Simpson's rule is therefore a useless refinement in colorimetry. It gives different results only when the summations are truncated at wavelength limits at which color-matching data are greater than zero, e.g., at 400 nm and 700 nm. Such truncations, in effect, assume zero values of spectrophotometric data outside the limits of summation. In such cases, Simpson's rule gives different results than the trapezoidal rule because Simpson's rule, in effect, sets $R \equiv 0$ exactly at the limits, whereas the trapezoidal rule sets R equal to the value measured at each limit λ over the entire band $\lambda - \Delta\lambda/2$ to $\lambda + \Delta\lambda/2$. Thus, for $\Delta\lambda = 10$ nm and $\lambda = 400$ nm, Simpson's rule makes $R = 0$ for all λ less than 400 nm, whereas the trapezoidal rule makes $R = R_{400}$ for λ from 395 to 405 nm.

Spectrophotometric data for colorimetry are commonly obtained only for wavelengths from 400 to 700 nm. In most cases, when weighted ordinates are summed at 10-nm intervals, the contributions of 380, 390, 710, 720, 730, 740, 750, 760, and 770 nm to the tristimulus values are simply omitted, ignored. As mentioned in the preceding paragraph, this is equivalent to assuming that spectrophotometric data are zero as far as 395 nm and beyond 705 nm for the trapezoidal rule, or at all wavelengths less than 400 nm and greater than 700 nm for Simpson's rule. Figure 5.3 illustrates the fallacy in the case of the trapezoidal rule, i.e., the usual weighted-ordinate method. Figure 5.4 illustrates the fallacy when Simpson's rule is used from 400 to 700 nm.

The error represented in Fig. 5.3 is sometimes recognized and an effort is made to avoid it by adding the products of the color-matching data by the light-source power at 380 nm and 390 nm to the value of the product at 400 nm and using the sum of those three products as the weight for the spectral reflectance at 400 nm of every sample. The weights $\bar{x}S$ and $\bar{y}S$ at 700 nm are similarly increased by the sums of the corresponding products at 710, 720, 730, 740, 750, 760, and 770. Use of such revised weights at 400 nm and 700 nm

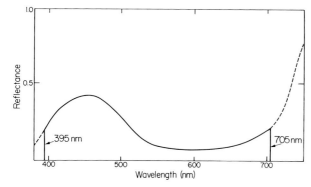

Fig. 5.3 Spectrophotometric data implied by truncation of trapezoidal rule at 400 and 700 nm. Actual spectrophotometric curve is shown dotted

is equivalent to assuming that, for every sample, the spectrophotometric data at 380 nm and 390 nm are exactly the same as the value at 400 nm and that the spectrophotometric data for all wavelengths longer than 700 nm are equal to the value at 700 nm. The fallacy of this is illustrated in Fig. 5.5. This usually

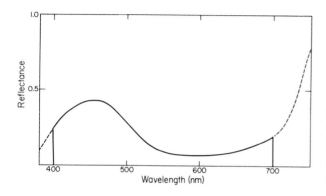

Fig. 5.4 Spectrophotometric data implied by truncation of Simpson's rule at 400 and 700 nm. Actual spectrophotometric curve is shown dotted

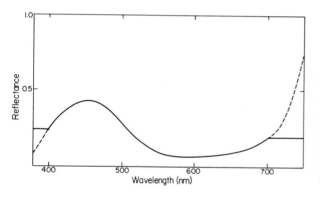

Fig. 5.5 Spectrophotometric data implied by addition of color-matching data at 380 and 390 nm to those for 400 nm and addition of color-matching data at 710 to 770 nm to those for 700 nm. Actual spectrophotometric curve is shown dotted

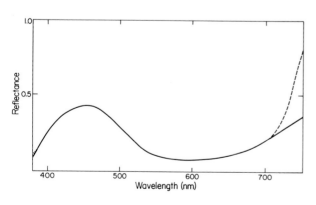

Fig. 5.6 Linear extensions of spectrophotometric curve beyond 400 and 700 nm

gives results closer than the approximations represented by Figs. 5.3,4 to those that would be obtained from measured data complete to 380 nm and 770 nm and integration between those limits. More-probably, better results can be obtained, however, with no more data or work.

Tristimulus values equal to those obtained with the assumption that the spectrophotometric data beyond 400 and 700 nm are linear continuations with the same slopes as between 410 and 400 nm and between 690 and 700 nm, respectively, as indicated in Fig. 5.6, can be obtained by using revised color-matching data for 400 and 410 nm and for 690 and 700 nm. Let f_λ represent $\bar{x}S$, $\bar{y}S$, or $\bar{z}S$. Then, to obtain the effects of linear continuations of spectrophotometric data beyond 400 and 700 nm, use the revised color-matching data f'

$$f'_{400} = f_{400} + 2f_{390} + 3f_{380},$$

$$f'_{410} = f_{410} - f_{390} - 2f_{380},$$

$$f'_{690} = f_{690} - f_{710} - 2f_{720} - 3f_{730} - 4f_{740} - 5f_{750} - 6f_{760} - 7f_{770},$$

$$f'_{700} = f_{700} + 2f_{710} + 3f_{720} + 4f_{730} + 5f_{740} + 6f_{750} + 7f_{760} + 8f_{770}.$$

The revised color-matching data f' for the data for 400 to 680 nm in Tables 5.2 – 4 for the CIE 1931 observer and illuminants A, C and D_{65} are given in Table 5.7. Similarly revised data for use with the data in Tables 5.8 – 10 for the CIE supplementary observer (1964) and sources A, C, and D_{65} are given in Table 5.11.

Table 5.7. Revised color-matching data for linear truncations beyond 400 and 700 nm, for CIE 1931 observer and illuminants A, C, and D_{65}

Illuminant	Wavelength [nm]	$\bar{x}S$	$\bar{y}S$	$\bar{z}S$
A	400	0.34	no change	1.90
	410	0.70	no change	3.13
	690	−0.38	0.01	
	700	9.40	3.20	
C	400	1.46	no change	6.83
	410	3.21	no change	15.35
	690	0.34	0.13	
	700	3.14	1.12	
D_{65}	400	2.00	0.06	9.49
	410	3.61	0.10	17.22
	690	0.13	0.04	
	700	3.06	1.11	

Table 5.8. Color-matching functions (CIE 1964) multiplied by relative spectral power distribution of illuminant A

Wavelength [nm]	$\bar{x}S_A$	$\bar{y}S_A$	$\bar{z}S_A$
380	0.00	0.00	0.01
390	0.03	0.00	0.13
400	0.28	0.03	1.27
410	1.50	0.16	6.88
420	4.29	0.45	20.41
430	7.76	0.95	38.32
440	11.01	1.78	56.46
450	12.27	2.96	66.01
460	11.43	4.85	65.99
470	8.39	7.94	56.49
480	3.88	12.23	37.25
490	0.87	18.28	22.39
500	0.23	27.58	13.08
510	2.48	40.08	7.40
520	8.53	55.23	4.40
530	18.71	69.25	2.41
540	32.39	82.68	1.18
550	49.22	92.15	0.37
560	70.52	99.73	0.00
570	94.18	102.41	0.00
580	116.06	99.44	0.00
590	136.16	94.63	0.00
600	145.04	84.95	0.00
610	140.51	71.99	0.00
620	122.98	57.18	0.00
630	97.67	42.76	0.00
640	68.18	28.40	0.00
650	44.28	17.76	0.00
660	26.24	10.37	0.00
670	14.53	5.68	0.00
680	7.58	2.95	0.00
690	3.82	1.48	0.00
700	1.90	0.73	0.00
710	0.94	0.37	0.00
720	0.46	0.17	0.00
730	0.22	0.09	0.00
740	0.11	0.04	0.00
750	0.07	0.02	0.00
760	0.02	0.02	0.00
770	0.02	0.00	0.00
Sum =	1264.73	1187.88	400.49

Table 5.9. Color-matching functions (CIE 1964) multiplied by relative spectral power distribution of illuminant C

Wavelength [nm]	$\bar{x}S_A$	$\bar{y}S_A$	$\bar{z}S_A$
380	0.01	0.00	0.02
390	0.11	0.01	0.50
400	1.21	0.13	5.44
410	6.83	0.71	31.39
420	20.06	2.10	95.40
430	35.37	4.35	174.61
440	46.62	7.55	239.03
450	45.97	11.10	247.36
460	37.21	15.78	214.86
470	24.22	22.93	163.12
480	9.97	31.42	95.66
490	1.96	40.93	50.13
500	0.43	51.66	24.49
510	3.84	62.07	11.46
520	11.41	73.82	5.88
530	23.18	85.77	2.99
540	38.47	98.22	1.40
550	55.73	104.34	0.42
560	74.26	105.02	0.00
570	89.89	97.75	0.00
580	99.19	84.98	0.00
590	104.24	72.45	0.00
600	100.82	59.05	0.00
610	91.10	46.68	0.00
620	75.44	35.07	0.00
630	56.98	24.95	0.00
640	37.89	15.79	0.00
650	23.66	9.49	0.00
660	13.41	5.30	0.00
670	7.02	2.74	0.00
680	3.44	1.34	0.00
690	1.60	0.62	0.00
700	0.73	0.28	0.00
710	0.33	0.13	0.00
720	0.15	0.05	0.00
730	0.06	0.03	0.00
740	0.03	0.01	0.00
750	0.02	0.01	0.00
760	0.01	0.01	0.00
770	0.01	0.00	0.00
Sum =	1142.92	1174.83	1364.49

Table 5.10. Color-matching functions (CIE 1964) multiplied by relative spectral power distribution of illuminant D_{65}

Wavelength [nm]	$\bar{x}S_{65}$	$\bar{y}S_{65}$	$\bar{z}S_{65}$	Wavelength [nm]	$\bar{x}S_{65}$	$\bar{y}S_{65}$	$\bar{z}S_{65}$
380	0.01	0.00	0.04	580	97.16	83.24	0.00
390	0.13	0.02	0.57	590	99.21	68.96	0.00
400	1.77	0.19	7.98	600	101.16	59.25	0.00
410	7.75	0.81	35.63	610	92.33	47.31	0.00
420	19.10	2.00	90.83	620	75.10	34.91	0.00
430	27.28	3.36	134.69	630	53.94	23.62	0.00
440	40.25	6.51	206.37	640	36.12	15.05	0.00
450	43.37	10.47	233.39	650	21.46	8.61	0.00
460	35.61	15.10	205.61	660	12.24	4.84	0.00
470	22.47	21.28	151.39	670	6.69	2.62	0.00
480	9.33	29.39	89.49	680	3.20	1.24	0.00
490	1.76	36.89	45.18	690	1.39	0.54	0.00
500	0.42	50.41	23.90	700	0.69	0.26	0.00
510	4.04	65.40	12.07	710	0.34	0.13	0.00
520	12.33	79.84	6.36	720	0.14	0.05	0.00
530	25.47	94.26	3.28	730	0.07	0.03	0.00
540	39.34	100.43	1.43	740	0.04	0.02	0.00
550	55.10	103.15	0.42	750	0.02	0.01	0.00
560	70.52	99.73	0.00	760	0.00	0.00	0.00
570	84.62	92.01	0.00	770	0.01	0.00	0.00
				Sum =	1101.78	1161.99	1247.63

Table 5.11. Revised color-matching data for linear truncations beyond 400 and 700 nm, for CIE 1964 observer and illuminants A, C, and D_{65}

Illuminant	Wavelength [nm]	$\bar{x}S$	$\bar{y}S$	$\bar{z}S$
A	400	0.34	no change	1.56
	410	1.47	no change	6.73
	690	0.25	0.12	
	700	7.31	2.80	
C	400	1.46	0.15	6.50
	410	6.70	0.70	30.85
	690	0.44	0.15	
	700	2.50	0.99	
D_{65}	400	0.34	0.09	9.24
	410	1.47	0.95	34.98
	690	0.25	0.12	
	700	7.31	2.80	

Results obtained with those weights from spectrophotometric data confined to the 400 to 700 nm range are more-probably accurate than results obtained with any of the previously described methods.

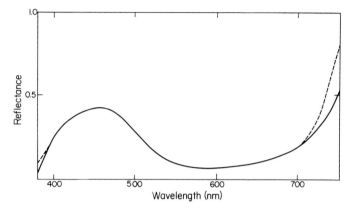

Fig. 5.7 Parabolic extensions of spectrophotometric curve beyond 400 and 700 nm

Even more-probably accurate results from spectrophotometric data confined to the 400 to 700 nm range can be obtained with no longer calculation by assuming that the continuations to shorter and longer wavelengths are given by the parabolas that pass through the spectrophotometric data at 420, 410, 400 nm and 680, 690, 700 nm, respectively, as in Fig. 5.7. That assumption is implemented by using the revised weights

$$f''_{400} = f_{400} + 3f_{390} + 6f_{380}$$

$$f''_{410} = f_{410} - 3f_{390} - 8f_{380}$$

$$f''_{420} = f_{420} + f_{390} + 3f_{380}$$

$$f''_{680} = f_{680} + f_{710} + 3f_{720} + 6f_{730} + 10f_{740} + 15f_{750} + 21f_{760} + 28f_{770}$$

$$f''_{690} = f_{690} - 3f_{710} - 8f_{720} - 15f_{730} - 24f_{740} - 35f_{750} - 48f_{760} - 63f_{770}$$

$$f''_{700} = f_{700} + 3f_{710} + 6f_{720} + 10f_{730} + 15f_{740} + 21f_{750} + 28f_{760} + 36f_{770}.$$

The revised color-matching data f'' for use with the data for other wavelengths in Tables 5.2 – 4, 7 – 9 are given in Table 5.12.[27]

Table 5.12. Revised color-matching data for parabolic truncations beyond 400 and 700 nm for CIE 1931 and 1964 observers and illuminants A, C, and D_{65}

Observer	Illuminant	Wavelength [nm]	$\bar{x}S$	$\bar{y}S$	$\bar{z}S$
1931	A	400	0.42	no change	2.08
		410	0.54	no change	2.47
		420	2.90	no change	13.98
		680	17.76	5.99	
		690	− 18.54	− 5.67	
		700	18.48	6.04	
	C	400	1.81	no change	8.41
		410	2.51	no change	12.19
		420	13.53	no change	64.91
		680	6.68	2.43	
		690	− 5.16	− 1.87	
		700	5.89	2.12	
	D_{65}	400	2.44	0.07	11.58
		410	2.73	0.08	13.04
		420	12.99	0.38	62.39
		680	6.52	2.26	
		690	− 5.66	− 1.82	
		700	6.00	2.04	
1964	A	400	0.37	no change	1.72
		410	1.41	no change	6.41
		420	4.32	no change	20.57
		680	14.35	5.49	
		690	− 13.29	− 4.96	
		700	14.08	5.34	
	C	400	1.60	0.16	7.06
		410	6.42	0.68	29.73
		420	20.20	2.11	95.96
		680	5.67	2.26	
		690	− 4.02	− 1.69	
		700	4.73	1.91	
	D_{65}	400	2.22	0.25	9.93
		410	7.28	0.75	33.60
		420	19.26	2.02	91.52
		680	5.36	2.05	
		690	− 4.09	− 1.53	
		700	4.63	1.76	

5.5 Selected-Ordinate Method

In Sect. 5.3, the tristimulus values were computed by a weighted-ordinate method. This method involves many multiplications and subsequent addition. The selected-ordinate method reduces the process of determining the tristimulus values to mere addition. When computers are used, the reduction of number and complexity of arithmetic operations is not important. That reduction is desirable when the work must be done by hand, even with the aid of an adding machine. The selected-ordinate method has been used to advantage when a high-speed computer was used to calculate the colorimetric results of absorptive ("subtractive") mixtures of different dyes. The selected-ordinate method will be shown to be less seriously affected by random spectrophotometric errors than the weighted-ordinate method. Gaussian quadrature, which is a combination of the weighted- and selected-ordinate methods, is subject to errors peculiar to it, which make it unsuitable for colorimetry.

The process involved in the determination of the tristimulus values of a colored material is, in the language of calculus, expressed by three integrals of the form

$$X = \int_0^\infty SR\bar{x}\,d\lambda$$

$$Y = \int_0^\infty SR\bar{y}\,d\lambda$$

$$Z = \int_0^\infty SR\bar{z}\,d\lambda,$$

where S, a function of wavelength, represents the power distribution of the illuminant, R represents the spectral reflectance (or transmittance) of the test sample, and $\bar{x}$, $\bar{y}$, and $\bar{z}$ are the tristimulus values for the spectrum colors. These functions are too complex to be formulated analytically. Hence, the indicated integrations must be approximated by the determination of the finite sums[28]

$$X = \sum_{380}^{780} SR\bar{x}\Delta\lambda$$

$$Y = \sum_{380}^{780} SR\bar{y}\Delta\lambda$$

$$Z = \sum_{380}^{780} SR\bar{z}\Delta\lambda \ .$$

In the weighted-ordinate method described in Sect. 5.3, the values of $SR\bar{x}$, $SR\bar{y}$, and $SR\bar{z}$ are summed at wavelengths equally spaced throughout the visible region. In other words, $\Delta\lambda$ has a constant value, and the three products

$S\bar{x}$, $S\bar{y}$, and $S\bar{z}$ may be considered to be weights applied to the values of R. In the selected-ordinate method, the wavelength intervals are unequal; they are chosen so as to give constant values to $S\bar{x}\Delta\lambda$, $S\bar{y}\Delta\lambda$, and $S\bar{z}\Delta\lambda$. Each integral in this case is merely the sum of the values of R at the median wavelengths of each of those wavelength intervals. The three sums are multiplied by factors that are proportional to the constants $S\bar{x}\Delta\lambda$, $S\bar{y}\Delta\lambda$, and $S\bar{z}\Delta\lambda$, respectively. The factors are adjusted so that the factor for Y equals the reciprocal of the number of ordinates.[29] The appropriate multiplying factor is given at the foot of each list of selected ordinates in Tables 5.13 – 18. Although from 99 to 117 wavelengths are listed in each table, it is rarely necessary to use that many ordinates. For manual integration, it is usually sufficient to use the 33, 36, or 39 that are marked with asterisks. Then, in wavelength regions where the differences between successive selected ordinates change rapidly, the two ordinates at the closest unmarked wavelengths can be averaged with the ordinate at any marked wavelength to increase the accuracy. Automatic integrators that use the selected-ordinate method might best use all of the tabulated ordinates. These sets of selected ordinates can be further abridged to 11, 12, or 13 ordinates for manual integration of such curves as in Fig. 5.1, by using only the double-starred wavelengths in Tables 5.13 – 18.

For determination of the wavelengths for the selected-ordinate method, a table was prepared that listed the running sum of the values of $S\bar{x}$. This was done by adding the entry at 385 nm to the entry at 380 nm. That sum was recorded in the running-sum table with the wavelength designation 387.5 nm. The value of $S\bar{x}$ for 390 nm was then added to that sum and the new total was recorded with the wavelength designation 392.5 nm. This process was continued for each wavelength up to 772.5 nm. Let the final entry in this table of running sums be represented by T. Then, for 99 selected ordinates, T was multiplied successively by 1/198, 3/198, 5/198 ... 197/198. By means of cubic interpolation in the table of running sums, the 99 wavelengths that correspond to those values were determined. Those are the wavelengths required for the selected-ordinate method when 99 ordinates are desired. A similar procedure was used to determine the selected ordinates for $S\bar{y}$ and $S\bar{z}$. The selected ordinates for each illuminant and the supplementary observer data were determined in the same manner.

The values for T for the three illuminants and for the 1931 and 1964 color-mixture data are

	Values of T					
	1931 data			1964 data		
Illuminant	$S\bar{x}$	$S\bar{y}$	$S\bar{z}$	$S\bar{x}$	$S\bar{y}$	$S\bar{z}$
A	2370.40	2157.86	767.78	2529.45	2275.76	800.98
C	2088.31	2129.37	2517.44	2285.83	2349.66	2728.98
D_{65}	2008.71	2113.29	2301.87	2203.57	2323.98	2495.27

Table 5.13. Selected ordinates for CIE 1931 observer and illuminant A. (For explanation of asterisks, see text)

	(X)	(Y)	(Z)		(X)	(Y)	(Z)
1	427.68	467.58	407.24	48	595.63	569.42	456.14
2*	440.76	486.17	415.23	49	596.45	570.49	456.71
3	450.94	495.41	419.01	50**	597.26	571.56	457.28
4	460.73	501.53	421.56	51	598.07	572.63	457.84
5**	472.25	506.07	423.50	52	598.88	573.70	458.41
6	519.98	509.72	425.10	53*	599.68	574.77	458.97
7	531.80	512.81	426.51	54	600.48	575.84	459.53
8*	537.77	515.50	427.77	55	601.28	576.92	460.10
9	542.17	517.90	428.92	56*	602.08	578.00	460.66
10	545.76	520.10	429.99	57	602.87	579.09	461.22
11*	548.83	522.14	431.00	58	603.66	580.18	461.78
12	551.54	524.05	431.96	59**	604.45	581.28	462.35
13	553.97	525.86	432.87	60	605.24	582.38	462.91
14**	556.19	527.59	433.75	61	606.03	583.50	463.48
15	558.23	529.25	434.60	62	606.82	584.62	464.05
16	560.13	530.85	435.42	63	607.61	585.75	464.62
17*	561.91	532.39	435.22	64	608.41	586.89	465.19
18	563.59	533.88	436.99	65*	609.21	588.05	465.77
19	565.19	535.34	437.75	66	610.01	589.22	466.36
20*	566.70	536.75	438.49	67	610.81	590.40	466.94
21	568.15	538.14	439.22	68**	611.62	591.59	467.54
22	569.54	539.49	439.94	69	612.43	592.80	468.15
23**	570.88	540.81	440.64	70	613.25	594.03	468.77
24	572.17	542.12	441.33	71*	614.07	595.27	469.40
25	573.41	543.39	442.01	72	614.90	596.54	470.04
26*	574.61	544.65	442.69	73	615.74	597.82	470.69
27	575.78	545.89	443.35	74*	616.59	599.13	471.35
28	576.92	547.11	444.01	75	617.44	600.47	472.02
29*	578.03	548.32	444.67	76	618.30	601.83	472.71
30	579.11	549.51	445.31	77**	619.18	603.22	473.41
31	580.16	550.69	445.95	78	620.07	604.64	474.13
32**	581.19	551.85	446.59	79	620.97	606.10	474.87
33	582.20	553.00	447.21	80*	621.89	607.59	475.63
34	583.19	554.15	447.84	81	622.82	609.13	476.40
35*	584.17	555.28	448.46	82	623.77	610.72	477.20
36	585.12	556.40	449.07	83*	624.75	612.36	478.02
37	586.06	557.52	449.68	84	625.74	614.06	478.88
38*	586.99	558.62	450.29	85	626.77	615.82	479.76
39	587.90	559.72	450.89	86**	627.82	617.65	480.67
40	588.80	560.81	451.49	87	628.90	619.57	481.62
41**	589.68	561.90	452.08	88	630.01	621.60	482.62
42	590.56	562.99	452.67	89*	631.17	623.74	483.66
43	591.43	564.07	453.26	90	632.36	626.04	484.75
44*	592.28	565.14	453.84	91	633.59	628.53	485.90
45	593.13	566.21	454.42	92*	634.87	631.24	487.11
46	593.97	567.28	455.00	93	636.21	634.24	488.39
47*	594.80	568.35	455.57	94	637.60	637.61	489.75

Table 5.13. (continued)

	(X)	(Y)	(Z)		(X)	(Y)	(Z)
95**	639.06	641.48	491.20	104**	658.83		511.35
96	640.60	646.11	492.76	105	662.90		515.52
97	642.24	652.01	494.42	106	668.24		521.17
98*	643.98	660.42	496.22	107*	676.22		529.47
99	645.86	677.55	498.17	108	692.59		546.50
100	647.90		500.29				
101*	650.15		502.61				
102	652.66		505.15	Factors	0.010171	0.010101	0.003294
103	655.50		508.01	*	0.030514	0.030303	0.009884
				**	0.091541	0.090909	0.029651

Table 5.14. Selected ordinates for CIE 1931 observer and illuminant C. (For explanation of asterisks, see text)

	(X)	(Y)	(Z)		(X)	(Y)	(Z)
1	415.58	446.83	404.77	33	560.68	539.03	440.22
2*	423.72	464.23	412.45	34	562.30	540.14	440.72
3	428.04	474.07	416.06	35*	563.86	541.23	441.22
4	431.39	480.97	418.48	36	565.37	542.31	441.71
5**	434.31	486.40	420.32	37	566.83	543.39	442.21
6	436.98	490.90	421.83	38*	568.24	544.45	442.70
7	439.52	494.76	423.10	39	569.62	545.51	443.19
8*	441.99	498.14	424.21	40	570.97	546.55	443.69
9	444.44	501.15	425.21	41**	572.28	547.59	444.18
10	446.90	503.86	426.13	42	573.57	548.63	444.67
11*	449.39	506.32	427.00	43	574.83	549.66	445.15
12	451.93	508.59	427.81	44*	576.07	550.69	445.64
13	454.54	510.70	428.58	45	577.30	551.71	446.13
14**	457.25	512.69	429.31	46	578.50	552.73	446.62
15	460.11	514.55	430.01	47*	579.69	553.75	447.10
16	463.18	516.32	430.69	48	580.86	554.76	447.59
17*	466.56	518.00	431.34	49	582.02	555.78	448.07
18	470.59	519.61	431.98	50**	583.17	556.80	448.56
19	475.89	521.16	432.59	51	584.31	557.82	449.05
20*	485.13	522.65	433.20	52	585.44	558.84	449.54
21	523.58	524.10	433.79	53*	586.56	559.86	450.03
22	531.46	525.51	434.37	54	587.67	560.89	450.52
23**	536.44	526.88	434.93	55	588.78	561.92	451.01
24	540.31	528.21	435.49	56*	589.89	562.96	451.50
25	543.55	529.51	436.04	57	590.99	564.00	451.99
26*	546.38	530.78	436.58	58	592.08	565.05	452.48
27	548.91	532.02	437.12	59**	593.18	566.11	452.98
28	551.22	533.24	437.64	60	594.27	567.18	453.47
29*	553.35	534.43	438.17	61	595.37	568.26	453.96
30	555.34	535.61	438.69	62*	596.46	569.35	454.46
31	557.21	536.77	439.20	63	597.56	570.45	454.96
32**	558.99	537.90	439.71	64	598.66	571.57	455.46

Table 5.14. (continued)

	(X)	(Y)	(Z)		(X)	(Y)	(Z)
65*	599.76	572.70	455.96	93	641.05	621.47	471.93
66	600.87	573.85	456.46	94	644.04	625.04	472.67
67	601.98	575.01	456.97	95**	647.48	629.16	473.44
68**	603.10	576.19	457.47	96	651.60	634.08	474.23
69	604.22	577.39	457.98	97	656.85	640.25	475.05
				98*	664.37	648.89	475.90
70	605.36	578.62	458.50	99	679.74	665.36	476.78
71*	606.50	579.87	459.01				
72	607.65	581.14	459.53	100			477.71
73	608.82	582.44	460.05	101*			478.68
74*	610.00	583.78	460.58	102			479.71
75	611.20	585.14	461.10	103			480.79
76	612.41	586.55	461.64	104**			481.94
77**	613.65	587.99	462.17	105			483.18
78	614.91	589.47	462.72	106			484.51
79	616.19	591.00	463.26	107*			485.95
				108			487.53
80*	617.51	592.59	463.81	109			489.28
81	618.86	594.23	464.37				
82	620.24	595.93	464.94	110*			491.23
83*	621.67	597.69	465.51	111			493.45
84	623.16	599.53	466.09	112			496.01
85	624.71	601.46	466.68	113**			499.07
86**	626.32	603.47	467.28	114			502.81
87	628.02	605.58	467.90	115			507.61
88	629.82	607.81	468.53	116*			514.85
89*	631.74	610.16	469.18	117			531.10
90	633.79	612.68	469.84	Factors	0.009906	0.010101	0.010105
91	636.00	615.37	470.52	*	0.029719	0.030303	0.030319
92*	638.40	618.28	471.22	**	0.089156	0.090909	0.090942

Table 5.15. Selected ordinates for CIE 1931 observer and illuminant D_{65}. (For explanation of asterisks, see text)

	(X)	(Y)	(Z)		(X)	(Y)	(Z)
1	414.12	448.61	402.44	14**	460.14	513.28	430.16
2*	423.23	465.57	410.91	15	463.23	514.98	431.02
3	428.26	475.47	414.89	16	466.70	516.59	431.85
4	432.33	482.39	417.60	17*	470.91	518.13	432.64
5**	435.68	487.97	419.64	18	476.59	519.61	433.39
6	438.67	492.63	421.33	19	487.64	521.03	434.11
7	441.43	496.49	422.79				
8*	444.10	499.78	424.06	20*	524.41	522.40	434.81
9	446.72	502.64	425.22	21	531.16	523.73	435.49
				22	535.77	525.01	436.15
10	449.30	505.17	426.30	23**	539.49	526.26	436.80
11*	451.88	507.46	427.32	24	542.69	527.48	437.43
12	454.52	509.55	428.31	25	545.49	528.66	438.05
13	457.27	511.48	429.26	26*	548.02	529.82	438.65

Table 5.15. (continued)

	(X)	(Y)	(Z)		(X)	(Y)	(Z)
27	550.34	530.96	439.25	70	605.70	578.04	462.19
28	552.49	532.09	439.84	71*	606.79	579.29	462.76
29*	554.51	533.21	440.42	72	607.88	580.57	463.33
				73	608.99	581.87	463.91
30	556.43	534.32	440.99	74*	610.12	583.22	464.49
31	558.25	535.42	441.55	75	611.25	584.60	465.09
32**	560.00	536.51	442.11	76	612.41	586.03	465.69
33	561.67	537.60	442.66	77**	613.59	587.50	466.31
34	563.28	538.68	443.22	78	614.79	589.04	466.94
35*	564.83	539.75	443.77	79	616.02	590.62	467.58
36	566.34	540.82	444.31				
37	567.80	541.89	444.85	80*	617.27	592.26	468.24
38*	569.22	542.95	445.39	81	618.56	593.93	468.93
39	570.61	544.00	445.92	82	619.89	595.64	469.63
				83*	621.26	597.41	470.35
40	571.96	545.04	446.46	84	622.69	599.23	471.09
41**	573.27	546.09	446.98	85	624.19	601.12	471.85
42	574.55	547.12	447.51	86**	625.77	603.08	472.64
43	575.79	548.16	448.03	87	627.44	605.13	473.46
44*	577.02	549.19	448.55	88	629.22	607.29	474.30
45	578.21	550.22	449.06	89*	631.14	609.56	475.18
46	579.38	551.25	449.58				
47*	580.54	552.28	450.09	90	633.18	611.98	476.09
48	581.68	553.32	450.60	91	635.37	614.58	477.04
49	582.81	554.36	451.11	92*	637.74	617.39	478.04
				93	640.34	620.47	479.09
50**	583.94	555.41	451.63	94	643.27	623.94	480.20
51	585.07	556.46	452.14	95**	646.70	627.99	481.38
52	586.19	557.51	452.65	96	650.90	632.91	482.65
53*	587.31	558.57	453.16	97	656.28	639.04	484.04
54	588.43	559.64	453.68	98*	663.98	647.63	485.56
55	589.55	560.71	454.20	99	679.19	664.53	487.25
56*	590.66	561.79	454.72				
57	591.71	562.88	455.24	100			489.14
58	592.87	563.98	455.76	101*			491.29
59**	593.95	565.09	456.28	102			493.72
				103			496.51
60	595.03	566.20	456.81	104**			499.77
61	596.10	567.33	457.33	105			503.69
62*	597.17	568.47	457.86	106			508.62
63	598.23	569.62	458.39	107*			515.91
64	599.29	570.79	458.92	108			531.49
65*	600.35	571.97	459.46				
66	601.41	573.16	460.00				
67	602.47	574.36	460.54	Factors	0.009601	0.010101	0.010086
68**	603.54	575.57	461.09	*	0.028803	0.030303	0.030257
69	604.62	576.80	461.64	**	0.086410	0.090909	0.090770

Table 5.16. Selected ordinates for CIE 1964 observer and illuminant A. (For explanation of asterisks, see text)

	(X)	(Y)	(Z)		(X)	(Y)	(Z)
1	424.41	453.25	405.88	48	592.58	567.88	453.01
2*	438.55	472.94	412.06	49	593.41	569.00	453.56
3	448.60	483.05	415.43	50**	594.24	570.13	454.11
4	458.21	490.17	417.91	51	595.06	571.25	454.66
5**	469.40	495.74	419.90	52	595.88	572.37	455.21
6	514.50	500.26	421.61	53*	596.70	573.50	455.76
7	527.00	504.09	423.13	54	597.51	574.63	456.31
8*	533.21	507.43	424.50	55	598.33	575.76	456.86
9	537.76	510.41	425.76	56*	599.13	576.90	457.41
10	541.44	513.11	426.93	57	599.94	578.04	457.97
11*	544.60	515.58	428.03	58	600.75	579.19	458.52
12	547.39	517.87	429.07	59**	601.55	580.35	459.08
13	549.90	520.02	430.06	60	602.36	581.51	459.64
14**	552.18	522.04	431.00	61	603.16	582.67	460.20
15	554.29	523.97	431.91	62*	603.97	583.84	460.76
16	556.24	525.82	432.77	63	604.78	585.02	461.33
17*	558.07	527.59	433.61	64	605.59	586.20	461.90
18	559.79	529.30	434.41	65*	606.40	587.39	462.47
19	561.42	530.96	435.19	66	607.22	588.59	463.04
20*	562.97	532.56	435.95	67	608.04	589.79	463.62
21	564.45	534.12	436.68	68**	608.86	591.01	464.20
22	565.87	535.63	437.40	69	609.69	592.24	464.79
23**	567.23	537.10	438.10	70	610.52	593.49	465.38
24	568.54	538.53	438.79	71*	611.36	594.75	465.98
25	569.81	539.94	439.46	72	612.21	596.02	466.50
26*	571.04	541.32	440.12	73	613.06	597.32	467.19
27	572.24	542.67	440.77	74*	613.92	598.64	467.81
28	573.40	544.00	441.41	75	614.80	599.98	468.43
29*	574.54	545.32	442.03	76	615.68	601.34	469.07
30	575.64	546.61	442.65	77**	616.57	602.73	469.71
31	576.73	547.89	443.27	78	617.47	604.16	470.37
32**	577.79	549.15	443.87	79	618.39	605.61	471.03
33	578.83	550.40	444.47	80*	619.33	607.10	471.72
34	579.85	551.64	445.07	81	620.28	608.63	472.41
35*	580.86	552.86	445.66	82	621.24	610.21	473.14
36	581.84	554.07	446.24	83*	622.22	611.84	473.88
37	582.81	555.26	446.82	84	623.23	613.53	474.65
38*	583.76	556.45	447.39	85	624.25	615.28	475.44
39	584.69	557.62	447.97	86**	625.30	617.11	476.26
40	585.61	558.79	448.54	87	626.37	619.03	477.11
41**	586.52	559.94	449.10	88	627.47	621.04	478.00
42	587.41	561.09	449.67	89*	628.61	623.16	478.92
43	588.30	562.23	450.23	90	629.78	625.41	479.89
44*	589.17	563.37	450.79	91	630.99	627.83	480.91
45	590.03	564.50	451.35	92*	632.25	630.43	481.98
46	590.89	565.63	451.90	93	633.57	633.31	483.11
47*	591.74	566.76	452.45	94	634.95	636.56	484.30

Table 5.16. (continued)

	(X)	(Y)	(Z)		(X)	(Y)	(Z)
95**	636.40	640.34	485.57	104**	656.13		504.22
96	637.94	644.89	486.94	105	660.16		508.20
97	639.57	650.69	488.41	106	665.38		513.44
98*	641.32	658.99	490.00	107*	673.02		520.65
99	643.20	675.46	491.74	108	688.83		533.12
100	645.25		493.65				
101*	647.49		495.78	Factors	0.010275	0.010101	0.003259
102	649.98		498.19	*	0.030825	0.030303	0.009777
103	652.82		500.96	**	0.092476	0.090909	0.029330

Table 5.17. Selected ordinates for CIE 1964 observer and illuminant C. (For explanation of asterisks, see text)

	(X)	(Y)	(Z)		(X)	(Y)	(Z)
1	412.42	432.27	404.34	34	558.44	533.53	438.62
2*	420.31	447.94	410.00	35*	560.02	534.83	439.12
3	425.06	457.64	413.04	36	561.55	536.11	439.61
4	428.79	464.83	415.23	37	563.02	537.37	440.10
5**	432.00	470.50	417.01	38*	564.45	538.60	440.58
6	434.87	475.17	418.50	39	565.84	539.82	441.06
7	437.53	479.25	419.81	40	567.20	541.02	441.54
8*	440.04	482.91	421.00	41**	568.53	542.21	442.01
9	442.48	486.19	422.09	42	569.83	543.39	442.49
10	444.90	489.24	423.09	43	571.10	544.56	442.96
11*	447.31	492.09	424.03	44*	572.36	545.72	443.43
12	449.79	494.76	424.92	45	573.59	546.87	443.90
13	452.33	497.27	425.76	46	574.81	548.02	444.36
14**	454.98	499.64	426.56	47*	576.02	549.16	444.83
15	457.78	501.90	427.34	48	577.21	550.30	445.29
16	460.82	504.07	428.08	49	578.40	551.43	445.76
17*	464.17	506.15	428.80	50**	579.57	552.56	446.22
18	468.04	508.16	429.49	51	580.73	553.69	446.68
19	472.96	510.10	430.16	52	581.88	554.81	447.15
20*	481.54	511.98	430.82	53*	583.03	555.94	447.61
21	518.06	513.80	431.45	54	584.16	557.06	448.08
22	526.45	515.56	432.07	55	585.29	558.18	448.55
23**	531.71	517.27	432.68	56*	586.41	559.31	449.01
24	535.77	518.93	433.27	57	587.52	560.44	449.48
25	539.14	520.54	433.84	58	588.64	561.57	449.95
26*	542.06	522.12	434.41	59**	589.74	562.71	450.42
27	544.68	523.65	434.96	60	590.85	563.86	450.90
28	547.06	525.16	435.51	61	591.96	565.01	451.37
29*	549.26	526.63	436.05	62*	593.06	566.18	451.85
30	551.32	528.07	436.57	63	594.17	567.35	452.32
31	553.24	529.47	437.10	64	595.29	568.54	452.81
32**	555.06	530.85	437.61	65*	596.41	569.74	453.29
33	556.79	532.21	438.12	66	597.53	570.96	453.78

Table 5.17. (continued)

	(X)	(Y)	(Z)		(X)	(Y)	(Z)
67	598.66	572.19	454.27	94	641.18	623.62	469.62
68**	599.80	573.45	454.76	95**	644.65	627.67	470.33
69	600.95	574.73	455.25	96	648.79	632.44	471.07
70	602.10	576.03	455.75	97	654.05	638.48	471.83
71*	603.27	577.36	456.26	98*	661.57	647.05	472.61
72	604.45	578.71	456.76	99	676.50	663.42	473.44
73	605.64	580.10	457.27	100			474.30
74*	606.85	581.51	457.79	101*			475.20
75	608.08	582.95	458.31	102			476.14
76	609.32	584.43	458.84	103			477.14
77**	610.59	585.94	459.38	104**			478.20
78	611.88	587.49	459.91	105			479.34
79	613.19	589.08	460.46	106			480.56
80*	614.54	590.71	461.01	107*			481.87
81	615.93	592.40	461.57	108			483.31
82	617.35	594.14	462.13	109			484.88
83*	618.81	595.95	462.70	110*			486.64
84	620.33	597.83	463.28	111			488.62
85	621.90	599.79	463.86	112			490.92
86**	623.53	601.83	464.46	113**			493.65
87	625.24	603.98	465.06	114			497.05
88	627.03	606.23	465.68	115			501.58
89*	628.93	608.61	466.30	116*			508.41
90	630.95	611.15	466.94	117			522.82
91	633.13	613.87	467.59				
92*	635.52	616.81	468.25	Factors	0.009827	0.010101	0.009927
93	638.17	620.03	468.93	*	0.029480	0.030303	0.029780
				**	0.088439	0.090909	0.089341

Table 5.18. Selected ordinates for CIE 1964 observer and illuminant D_{65}. (For explanation of asterisks, see text)

	(X)	(Y)	(Z)		(X)	(Y)	(Z)
1	410.98	433.62	402.76	14**	457.79	501.64	426.74
2*	419.35	449.94	408.68	15	460.86	503.80	427.67
3	424.61	459.38	411.84	16	464.26	505.84	428.59
4	429.05	466.44	414.15	17*	468.25	507.78	429.49
5**	432.97	472.10	416.04	18	473.51	509.63	430.35
6	436.27	476.81	417.67	19	483.53	511.41	431.19
7	439.20	480.93	419.08	20*	518.88	513.11	431.99
8*	441.93	484.64	420.37	21	526.16	514.76	432.76
9	444.56	488.05	421.57	22	530.92	516.35	433.49
10	447.14	491.26	422.70	23**	534.72	517.89	434.19
11*	449.69	494.20	423.77	24	537.98	519.40	434.88
12	452.26	496.87	424.80	25	540.88	520.87	435.54
13	454.95	499.34	425.79	26*	543.49	522.30	436.19

Table 5.18. (continued)

	(X)	(Y)	(Z)		(X)	(Y)	(Z)
27	545.88	523.69	436.82	70	602.53	575.53	459.39
28	548.09	525.04	437.43	71*	603.65	576.88	459.95
29*	550.17	526.37	438.03	72	604.78	578.25	460.51
30	552.12	527.67	438.62	73	605.92	579.64	461.08
31	553.98	528.94	439.19	74*	607.08	581.06	461.66
32**	555.76	530.19	439.76	75	608.24	582.50	462.25
33	557.46	531.42	440.32	76	609.43	583.99	462.84
34	559.10	532.64	440.87	77**	610.63	585.53	463.45
35*	560.68	533.85	441.41	78	611.86	587.11	464.06
36	562.21	535.06	441.95	79	613.12	588.75	464.69
37	563.70	536.25	442.48	80*	614.41	590.44	465.33
38*	565.14	537.44	443.01	81	615.73	592.18	465.98
39	566.54	538.61	443.53	82	617.09	593.96	466.64
40	567.92	539.79	444.06	83*	618.49	595.78	467.32
41**	569.26	540.95	444.57	84	619.94	597.65	468.02
42	570.58	542.11	445.09	85	621.45	599.58	468.74
43	571.87	543.27	445.60	86**	623.03	601.59	469.47
44*	573.13	544.42	446.11	87	624.69	603.67	470.23
45	574.37	545.57	446.61	88	626.45	605.86	471.01
46	575.59	546.71	447.11	89*	628.32	608.17	471.82
47*	576.79	547.85	447.61	90	630.34	610.61	472.66
48	577.97	548.99	448.11	91	632.51	613.23	473.55
49	579.13	550.12	448.61	92*	634.88	616.06	474.47
50**	580.27	551.26	449.10	93	637.50	619.17	475.44
51	581.41	552.40	449.60	94	640.44	622.64	476.46
52	582.54	553.54	450.09	95**	643.86	626.63	477.55
53*	583.67	554.69	450.58	96	648.01	631.40	478.71
54	584.79	555.85	451.08	97	653.39	637.39	479.95
55	585.91	557.00	451.57	98*	661.10	645.85	481.29
56*	587.03	558.17	452.07	99	675.94	662.62	482.76
57	588.16	559.33	452.56	100			484.40
58	589.28	560.51	453.07	101*			486.25
59**	590.40	561.69	453.58	102			488.38
60	591.52	562.89	454.09	103			490.88
61	592.64	564.09	454.60	104**			493.88
62*	593.74	565.30	455.12	105			497.56
63	594.84	566.53	455.64	106			502.38
64	595.94	567.77	456.16	107*			509.49
65*	597.03	569.02	456.69	108			523.73
66	598.13	570.29	457.22				
67	599.22	571.58	457.75	Factors	0.009578	0.010101	0.00942
68**	600.32	572.88	458.29	*	0.028733	0.030303	0.029825
69	601.43	574.20	458.84	**	0.086199	0.090909	0.089475

In the selected-ordinate method, most of the labor is concentrated in the determination of the appropriate wavelengths, a task that, when once accomplished, need not be repeated. Integration by this method is then

Table 5.19. Example of selected-ordinate integration of Fig. 5.1 for CIE 1931 observer and illuminant C

Ordinate Number	(X)	(Y)	(Z)
1	0.734	0.801	0.707
2	0.772	0.822	0.721
3	0.841	0.833	0.729
4	0.851	0.841	0.746
5	0.856	0.845	0.751
6	0.864	0.851	0.757
7	0.867	0.855	0.765
8	0.871	0.859	0.773
9	0.875	0.865	0.781
10	0.876	0.871	0.783
11	0.881	0.876	0.791
12			0.789
13			0.811
	Sum = 9.288	Sum = 9.319	Sum = 9.913
	X = 0.828	Y = 0.847	Z = 0.901

exceedingly simple. Consider, for example, the nearly white material selected for illustration in Sect. 5.4. In this case, 11 selected ordinates are sufficient for X and Y and 13 for Z; the double-starred entries in Table 5.15 are the appropriately selected wavelengths. The values of R that correspond to these wavelengths are the desired selected ordinates. The values are listed in Table 5.19. Multiplying the sum of each set of selected ordinates by the indicated factors gives the tristimulus values X = 0.828, Y = 0.847, and Z = 0.901. The chromaticity coordinates are the same as before,

$$x = 0.3209$$

and

$$y = 0.3290.$$

The luminance factor is given directly by the value of Y, 84.7%.

5.6 Sensitivity of Tristimulus Values to Random Spectrophotometric Errors

The best-designed, best-constructed, and best-calibrated spectrophotometers, even when used most carefully, yield data that differ from one instrument to another. The results also differ from one measurement to the next, even on the same instrument. The differences should be quite small and randomly different. The differences among readings are net results of combinations of a great many small fluctuations due to mutually unrelated variations of different components of the instrument, different factors in the environment (e.g., temperature, humidity, vibration), and manipulation (e.g., sample centering, rotation, pressure).

Random variations are customarily assessed by their root-mean-square (rms) deviations from the average (mean) of a very large number of readings. Usually, the rms deviations (which are also called uncertainties or errors) are unknown; in most cases they are estimated from only a few measurements.

With well-designed and carefully used spectrophotometers, such estimates (σ) are about 0.1% reflectance. That means that differences as great as 0.2% from the average of many readings occur in about 5% of the measurements. Significant variations of σ with wavelength are not usually found.

A typical application of spectrophotometry to color measurement uses only a single value of reflectance at each of a limited number (n) of wavelengths. In some instruments, each value is the average of several or even many separate measurements. However, when the whole process is repeated, small differences inevitably occur. The latter differences are the ones with which this discussion is concerned. The values of spectral reflectance used for any particular calculation of tristimulus values inevitably differ from the averages that would be obtained by a large number of remeasurements. Those averages are, in general, unknown. The differences of the actual results from those unknown averages are estimated by the rms deviations.

Because the tristimulus value Y given by the selected-ordinate method is simply the average of the selected spectral reflectances, the estimated uncertainty of Y is the rms value of the estimated uncertainties of those reflectances divided by the square root of the number (n) of selected reflectances. If the estimated rms uncertainties (σ) of the spectral reflectances are all equal, then the estimated uncertainty of Y is $\sigma/\sqrt{n}$. The estimated uncertainties of the tristimulus values X and Z are greater or smaller in proportion to the tristimulus values X_w, Y_w, Z_w of white for the same observer and illuminant. For $n = 33$, the uncertainty of Y is 0.174 times the uncertainty of each spectral reflectance. Differences as great as twice this, or slightly more than one third the uncertainty σ of the spectral reflectances, can be expected in about 5% of redeterminations of tristimulus values with the selected-ordinate method.

If the estimated uncertainties of the spectral reflectances are not all equal, the uncertainties of the tristimulus values obtained with the selected-ordinate method are greater by the factor

$$G = \sqrt{1 + \sum_{\lambda_1}^{\lambda_n} (\sigma_\lambda - \bar{\sigma})^2/\bar{\sigma}^2},$$

where $\bar{\sigma}$ is the average value of the estimated uncertainties σ_λ for the selected wavelengths.

The uncertainties of tristimulus values obtained by the weighted-ordinate method are greater than those that result by use of the same number of selected ordinates by factors (F) that depend on the variations of the weights. As in Sect. 5.5, let f_λ represent $\bar{x}S$, $\bar{y}S$, or $\bar{z}S$, and assume the same uncertainties of spectral reflectances as for the selected ordinates. Then the average value of the weights is

$$\bar{f} = \sum_{\lambda_1}^{\lambda_n} f_\lambda/n \quad \text{and}$$

$$F = \sqrt{1 + \sum_{\lambda_1}^{\lambda_n} (f_\lambda - \bar{f})^2/\bar{f}^2} \ .$$

For equal weights, such as are used in the selected-ordinate method, all of the differences $f_\lambda - \bar{f}$ are zero and $F = 1$. For unequal weights, as used in the weighted-ordinate method, F is greater than 1. Therefore, the uncertainties of tristimulus values computed with the weighted-ordinate method are always greater than those obtained by summing an equal number of equally accurate selected-ordinate spectral reflectances. This is true whether or not the estimated uncertainties of spectral reflectances depend on wavelength.

When the uncertainties of spectral reflectances do not vary with wavelength, the values of F for six combinations of CIE observers and illuminants are

Illuminant	1931 observer			1964 observer		
	$\bar{x}$	$\bar{y}$	$\bar{z}$	$\bar{x}$	$\bar{y}$	$\bar{z}$
A	1.77	1.66	2.15	1.73	1.59	2.16
C	1.55	1.65	2.27	1.54	1.56	2.29
D$_{65}$	1.56	1.66	2.26	1.53	1.56	2.24

In effect, because of the variations of the weights, the results yielded by the weighted-ordinate method are subject to uncertainties as great as those of averages of only n/F^2 values of spectral reflectance. The weighted-ordinate method from 400 to 700 nm at 10 nm intervals $(n = 31)$ is only as accurate as the selected-ordinate method with the following numbers of ordinates.

Illuminant	1931 observer			1964 observer		
	$\bar{x}$	$\bar{y}$	$\bar{z}$	$\bar{x}$	$\bar{y}$	$\bar{z}$
A	10	11	7	10	12	6
C	13	11	6	13	13	6
D$_{65}$	13	11	6	13	13	6

The effective numbers of spectral reflectances for the Z tristimulus values are especially low because appreciable weights are applied to only half of the 31 available reflectances. Six of those together have only 10% of the total of all of the weights, whereas more than half of the total weight is applied to only three. In the wavelength range of those three, 16 or more of the 33 selected ordinates are used. Selected ordinates are used where, and only where, they are needed. The number of selected ordinates within any constant interval, such as 10 nm, is proportional to the weights used in the weighted-ordinate method.

The selected-ordinate method was devised when spectral reflectance values were customarily read visually from recorded curves, which was as easy for the selected wavelengths as for wavelengths at equal intervals. Selected ordinates were also digitized and entered automatically into adding machines in 1936 and 1950 [30], many years prior to the first use of automatic equipment for tristimulus integration with the weighted-ordinate method. Although those early machines are obsolete and abandoned long ago, modern spectrophotometers that employ computer-controlled stepping-motor wavelength drives could be programmed to supply selected ordinates. They would have the merit of reduced uncertainties of tristimulus values, as indicated in the foregoing.

When σ is independent of wavelength, the uncertainties of the chromaticity coordinates are related to the uncertainties of the tristimulus values by

$$
\sigma_x^2 = \left(\frac{\partial x}{\partial X} \right)^2 \sigma_x^2 + \left(\frac{\partial x}{\partial Y} \right)^2 \sigma_Y^2 + \left(\frac{\partial x}{\partial Z} \right)^2 \sigma_Z^2
$$

$$
+ 2\sigma^2 \left(\frac{\partial x}{\partial X} \frac{\partial x}{\partial Y} r_{XY} + \frac{\partial x}{\partial Y} \frac{\partial x}{\partial Z} r_{YZ} + \frac{\partial x}{\partial Z} \frac{\partial x}{\partial X} r_{XZ} \right)
$$

$$
\sigma_y^2 = \left(\frac{\partial y}{\partial X} \right)^2 \sigma_X^2 + \left(\frac{\partial y}{\partial Y} \right)^2 \sigma_Y^2 + \left(\frac{\partial y}{\partial Z} \right)^2 \sigma_Z^2
$$

$$
+ 2\sigma^2 \left(\frac{\partial y}{\partial X} \frac{\partial y}{\partial Y} r_{XY} + \frac{\partial y}{\partial Y} \frac{\partial y}{\partial Z} r_{YZ} + \frac{\partial y}{\partial Z} \frac{\partial y}{\partial X} r_{XZ} \right),
$$

where σ_X, σ_Y, σ_Z, and σ are the previously discussed uncertainties of the tristimulus values and of the spectral reflectances, respectively, and r_{XY}, r_{YZ}, r_{XZ} are related to the correlations of the pairs of weights used in the weighted-ordinate method of determining the indicated pairs of tristimulus values [31].

When the selected-ordinate method is used, the factors r_{XY}, r_{YZ}, r_{XZ} are zero, so the uncertainties of the chromaticity coordinates are given by the first three terms.

When the weighted-ordinate method is used,

$$r_{XY} = \sum_1^n \bar{x}\bar{y}S^2, \quad r_{YZ} = \sum_1^n \bar{y}\bar{z}S^2, \quad r_{XZ} = \sum_1^n \bar{x}\bar{z}S^2,$$

where S is the spectral distribution of power in the illumination, expressed in such units that

$$\sum_1^n \bar{y}S = 1.$$

The values of the r's are all positive, but the effects of the last three terms in σ_x^2 and σ_y^2 may be either to increase or decrease those uncertainties, according to the signs of the partial derivatives,

$$\frac{\partial x}{\partial X} = (1 - x)y/Y, \quad \frac{\partial x}{\partial Y} = \frac{\partial x}{\partial Z} = -xy/Y$$

$$\frac{\partial y}{\partial X} = \frac{\partial y}{\partial Z} = -y^2/Y, \quad \frac{\partial y}{\partial Y} = (1 - y)y/Y.$$

The values of r_{XY}, r_{YZ}, and r_{XZ} for six combinations of observer data and illuminants are

Illuminant	1931 observer			1964 observer		
	r_{XY}	r_{YZ}	r_{XZ}	r_{XY}	r_{YZ}	r_{XZ}
A	2.38	0.09	0.11	2.38	0.13	0.06
C	1.49	0.31	0.85	1.48	0.43	0.94
D_{65}	1.43	0.39	1.08	1.38	0.27	1.04

5.7 Gaussian Quadrature

Gaussian quadrature has been suggested for determination of tristimulus values. In practice, it is a combination of the selected- and weighted-ordinate methods. It uses significantly fewer wavelengths (ordinates) than either of those methods. It yields the most accurate numerical integration of a function (e.g., a spectral reflectance curve) that can be fitted exactly with a polynomial (e.g., a sum of powers of wavelength multiplied by numerical coefficients) of order $2n - 1$, where n is the number of ordinates used. The wavelengths at which the ordinates are selected and the weights by which they are multiplied can be calculated from the weighting function ($f = \bar{x}S$, $\bar{y}S$, or $\bar{z}S$).[32] The wavelengths and weights for the 7th to 10th orders for all combinations of the CIE 1931 and 1964 observer data and illuminants A, C and D_{65} are given in Tables 5.20 – 25. Although some of those wavelengths are outside of the range from 400 to 700 nm, their weights are extremely small compared to the totals of the weights. They can be omitted with negligible effect on accuracy.

An n-point gaussian method is equivalent to a $2n$-point conventional method, i.e., selected or weighted ordinates. This is true, however, only for integration of spectral reflectance data that are exactly fitted by a $(2n - 1)$-

Table 5.20. Wavelengths and weights for gaussian quadrature with CIE 1931 observer data and illuminant A for orders 7 to 10

Order	$\lambda(\bar{x})$ [nm]	$\omega(\lambda)$	$\lambda(\bar{y})$ [nm]	$\omega(\lambda)$	$\lambda(\bar{z})$ [nm]	$\omega(\lambda)$
7	416.3	0.0079	424.3	0.0024	398.2	0.0017
	449.9	0.0383	472.9	0.0410	419.7	0.0322
	529.5	0.0887	523.8	0.2539	442.6	0.1209
	580.4	0.4810	572.3	0.4365	467.5	0.1281
	625.0	0.4278	620.3	0.2408	496.1	0.0467
	671.9	0.0545	670.0	0.0253	519.0	0.0255
	731.7	0.0001	733.5	0.0001	546.0	0.0004
8	411.5	0.0041	417.2	0.0009	393.6	0.0006
	441.8	0.0338	458.1	0.0186	413.7	0.0175
	485.8	0.0254	505.3	0.1383	433.8	0.0777
	556.4	0.2561	550.0	0.3751	455.9	0.1392
	600.4	0.5235	595.0	0.3420	479.7	0.0774
	641.6	0.2388	638.9	0.1186	509.8	0.0353
	687.5	0.0162	687.1	0.0064	527.3	0.0076
	740.8	0.0002	743.7	0.0001	548.4	0.0001
9	406.3	0.0018	411.4	0.0004	390.0	0.0002
	432.6	0.0218	446.1	0.0088	408.2	0.0074
	463.4	0.0301	488.8	0.0670	426.1	0.0511
	539.1	0.1110	531.0	0.2610	445.8	0.1133
	580.5	0.4196	572.6	0.3766	466.9	0.1079
	619.0	0.4029	614.0	0.2330	489.3	0.0422
	657.7	0.1072	655.2	0.0520	514.5	0.0311
	701.8	0.0038	701.4	0.0013	535.0	0.0024
	746.7	0.0001	749.7	0.0000	550.6	0.0000
10	402.4	0.0009	406.5	0.0002	386.7	0.0001
	426.9	0.0156	436.5	0.0045	403.9	0.0033
	455.5	0.0338	474.5	0.0328	420.2	0.0326
	513.4	0.0288	514.5	0.1536	438.2	0.0821
	558.7	0.2342	553.1	0.3262	457.4	0.1122
	597.1	0.4614	592.1	0.3189	477.5	0.0741
	633.0	0.2748	630.2	0.1432	500.0	0.0235
	670.6	0.0481	669.5	0.0205	517.1	0.0263
	712.5	0.0006	713.0	0.0001	538.5	0.0014
	750.2	0.0000	753.2	0.0000	551.6	0.0000

order polynomial. The most serious shortcoming of the gaussian method is that spectral-reflectance data are rarely, if ever, exactly fitted by such a polynomial, even of order 19. An example is shown in Fig. 5.8. As shown most clearly by the curve of the differences between the values of the best-fitting polynomial of order 19 and actual reflectances, the former is exactly equal to the latter at only 19 wavelengths, two less than 400 nm and four longer than 700 nm; between them, differences as great as 2.6% occur, with a rms difference of 1.2%. Therefore, in this case the rms error of fit with order 19 is more than ten times the rms error expected in spectrophotometry[33].

Table 5.21. Wavelengths and weights for gaussian quadrature with CIE 1931 observer data and illuminant C, for orders 7 to 10

Order	$\lambda(\bar{x})$ [nm]	$\omega(\lambda)$	$\lambda(\bar{y})$ [nm]	$\omega(\lambda)$	$\lambda(\bar{z})$ [nm]	$\omega(\lambda)$
7	412.6	0.0176	426.6	0.0032	395.3	0.0058
	443.8	0.1377	469.7	0.0517	423.7	0.2081
	493.1	0.0647	518.6	0.2901	448.1	0.5633
	568.2	0.3512	564.5	0.4399	476.8	0.3534
	615.9	0.3535	613.0	0.1935	513.1	0.0498
	663.3	0.0557	663.0	0.0216	560.7	0.0005
	724.1	0.0001	725.9	0.0000	606.3	0.0000
8	404.4	0.0059	417.8	0.0010	390.6	0.0025
	434.1	0.0946	455.4	0.0248	417.2	0.1063
	465.6	0.0974	500.6	0.1595	439.2	0.4523
	549.3	0.1861	543.8	0.3998	464.6	0.4617
	593.3	0.3883	587.1	0.3175	494.0	0.1454
	635.5	0.1930	632.6	0.0917	531.2	0.0127
	681.1	0.0150	680.3	0.0056	577.7	0.0002
	736.5	0.0001	738.1	0.0000	611.1	0.0000
9	398.8	0.0024	409.7	0.0004	387.0	0.0011
	428.6	0.0678	444.3	0.0116	411.1	0.0467
	457.2	0.1171	484.5	0.0778	432.2	0.3557
	520.7	0.0565	525,5	0.2935	454.6	0.4667
	569.1	0.3018	565.5	0.3875	479.8	0.2562
	610.3	0.3339	607.2	0.1892	510.5	0.0520
	650.3	0.0967	649.4	0.0389	546.5	0.0024
	695.1	0.0041	695.5	0.0013	588.0	0.0001
	743.9	0.0001	745.8	0.0000	614.3	0.0000
10	393.8	0.0009	402.6	0.0001	385.0	0.0006
	422.8	0.0418	435.9	0.0062	405.7	0.0194
	448.0	0.1151	470.9	0.0440	426.3	0.2230
	480.8	0.0477	509.2	0.1781	446.2	0.4739
	550.4	0.1766	547.2	0.3709	469.1	0.3425
	589.5	0.3363	585.0	0.2789	495.0	0.1057
	626.8	0.2207	624.4	0.1056	525.9	0.0158
	664.8	0.0404	664.1	0.0160	560.5	0.0000
	707.8	0.0008	708.1	0.0002	594.4	0.0000
	749.0	0.0000	750.6	0.0000	616.2	0.0000

Table 5.22. Wavelengths and weights for gaussian quadrature with CIE 1931 observer data and illuminant D_{65}, for orders 7 to 10

Order	$\lambda(\bar{x})$ [nm]	$\omega(\lambda)$	$\lambda(\bar{y})$ [nm]	$\omega(\lambda)$	$\lambda(\bar{z})$ [nm]	$\omega(\lambda)$
7	410.2	0.0140	424.3	0.0025	394.1	0.0069
	443.5	0.1249	468.8	0.0478	422.1	0.1734
	492.6	0.0641	518.4	0.3002	447.9	0.5201
	567.5	0.3397	563.8	0.4337	476.4	0.3365
	615.2	0.3540	612.2	0.1949	513.3	0.0507
	662.9	0.0534	662.4	0.0208	560.0	0.0006
	724.5	0.0001	726.1	0.0000	606.3	0.0000
8	402.4	0.0048	415.1	0.0007	389.6	0.0035
	433.3	0.0827	455.0	0.0218	415.3	0.0886
	465.0	0.0946	500.8	0.1590	438.9	0.4012
	548.2	0.1815	542.8	0.4082	464.2	0.4433
	592.8	0.3852	586.7	0.3128	494.2	0.1374
	634.6	0.1867	631.9	0.0919	530.6	0.0139
	680.6	0.0146	679.9	0.0055	577.5	0.0002
	736.1	0.0001	737.4	0.0000	611.0	0.0000
9	397.2	0.0021	407.3	0.0002	386.3	0.0012
	427.2	0.0580	444.2	0.0107	409.4	0.0389
	456.6	0.1143	484.4	0.0755	431.4	0.2980
	519.9	0.0554	525.3	0.3139	454.3	0.4504
	568.4	0.2981	564.9	0.3648	479.6	0.2437
	609.8	0.3246	606.7	0.1951	510.6	0.0531
	649.7	0.0935	648.9	0.0386	545.8	0.0027
	694.9	0.0041	695.4	0.0012	588.0	0.0001
	742.9	0.0001	744.7	0.0000	614.2	0.0000
10	392.6	0.0009	401.1	0.0001	383.1	0.0000
	420.9	0.0343	435.3	0.0052	404.5	0.0551
	447.6	0.1075	570.4	0.0402	425.2	0.2521
	480.3	0.0470	510.0	0.1937	446.1	0.4526
	549.4	0.1658	546.3	0.3698	468.8	0.2472
	589.1	0.3332	584.7	0.2710	495.2	0.0723
	626.0	0.2218	623.8	0.1050	525.6	0.0078
	664.4	0.0389	663.8	0.0150	560.1	0.0010
	707.9	0.0007	708.4	0.0002	594.5	0.0000
	747.8	0.0000	749.5	0.0000	616.2	0.0000

Table 5.23. Wavelengths and weights for gaussian quadrature with CIE 1964 observer data and illuminant A, for orders 7 to 10

Order	$\lambda(\bar{x})$ [nm]	$\omega(\lambda)$	$\lambda(\bar{y})$ [nm]	$\omega(\lambda)$	$\lambda(\bar{z})$ [nm]	$\omega(\lambda)$
7	416.3	0.0080	424.3	0.0024	398.2	0.0017
	449.9	0.0388	472.9	0.0410	419.7	0.0319
	529.5	0.0898	523.8	0.2539	442.6	0.1198
	580.4	0.4868	572.3	0.4365	467.5	0.1268
	625.0	0.4330	620.3	0.2408	496.1	0.0462
	671.9	0.0552	670.1	0.0253	519.0	0.0253
	731.7	0.0001	733.5	0.0001	546.0	0.0004

Table 5.23. (continued)

Order	$\lambda(\bar{x})$ [nm]	$\omega(\lambda)$	$\lambda(\bar{y})$ [nm]	$\omega(\lambda)$	$\lambda(\bar{z})$ [nm]	$\omega(\lambda)$
8	411.5	0.0042	417.2	0.0009	393.6	0.0006
	441.8	0.0342	458.1	0.0186	413.7	0.0173
	485.8	0.0257	505.3	0.1383	433.8	0.0769
	556.4	0.2592	550.0	0.3751	455.9	0.1378
	600.4	0.5299	594.9	0.3420	479.7	0.0767
	641.6	0.2417	638.9	0.1186	509.8	0.0350
	687.5	0.0164	687.1	0.0064	527.3	0.0075
	740.8	0.0002	743.7	0.0001	548.4	0.0001
9	406.3	0.0019	411.4	0.0004	390.0	0.0002
	432.6	0.0220	446.1	0.0088	408.2	0.0074
	463.4	0.0305	488.8	0.0670	426.1	0.0506
	539.1	0.1123	531.0	0.2610	445.8	0.1122
	580.5	0.4247	572.6	0.3766	466.9	0.1068
	619.0	0.4078	614.0	0.2330	489.3	0.0418
	657.7	0.1085	655.2	0.0520	514.5	0.0308
	701.8	0.0038	701.4	0.0013	535.0	0.0024
	746.7	0.0001	749.7	0.0000	550.6	0.0000
10	402.4	0.0009	406.4	0.0002	386.7	0.0001
	426.9	0.0158	436.5	0.0045	403.9	0.0033
	455.5	0.0342	474.5	0.0328	420.2	0.0322
	513.4	0.0291	514.5	0.1536	438.2	0.0813
	558.7	0.2370	553.1	0.3262	457.4	0.1111
	597.1	0.4670	592.1	0.3189	477.5	0.0733
	633.1	0.2782	630.2	0.1432	500.0	0.0233
	670.6	0.0487	669.5	0.0205	517.1	0.0260
	712.5	0.0006	713.0	0.0001	538.5	0.0014
	750.2	0.0000	753.2	0.0000	551.6	0.0000

Table 5.24. Wavelengths and weights for gaussian quadrature with CIE 1964 observer data and illuminant C, for orders 7 to 10

Order	$\lambda(\bar{x})$ [nm]	$\omega(\lambda)$	$\lambda(\bar{y})$ [nm]	$\omega(\lambda)$	$\lambda(\bar{z})$ [nm]	$\omega(\lambda)$
7	414.1	0.0279	420.0	0.0065	397.8	0.0067
	444.3	0.1349	461.3	0.0699	418.5	0.1453
	498.0	0.0649	510.4	0.2767	439.7	0.4139
	566.5	0.3614	559.3	0.4204	463.5	0.4257
	614.2	0.3311	609.3	0.2020	489.9	0.1228
	661.3	0.0527	659.4	0.0246	517.1	0.0464
	722.1	0.0001	723.3	0.0000	545.2	0.0006
8	408.8	0.0127	414.0	0.0029	393.5	0.0023
	435.1	0.1051	448.9	0.0375	413.0	0.0714
	466.7	0.0848	492.8	0.1705	432.0	0.3298
	547.5	0.1981	538.9	0.3705	453.1	0.4305
	591.5	0.3816	583.7	0.3142	476.3	0.2440

Table 5.24. (continued)

Order	$\lambda(\bar{x})$ [nm]	$\omega(\lambda)$	$\lambda(\bar{y})$ [nm]	$\omega(\lambda)$	$\lambda(\bar{z})$ [nm]	$\omega(\lambda)$
8 (cont.)	633.8	0.1764	629.5	0.0979	505.5	0.0659
	678.9	0.0143	677.3	0.0064	523.4	0.0177
	735.4	0.0001	737.5	0.0000	547.5	0.0002
9	404.9	0.0078	409.0	0.0013	390.1	0.0007
	429.0	0.0733	439.2	0.0206	407.8	0.0340
	457.3	0.1104	478.1	0.1020	424.9	0.1722
	524.6	0.0720	520.1	0.2755	443.7	0.4103
	568.9	0.3130	562.0	0.3672	464.2	0.3425
	609.6	0.3047	604.4	0.1896	486.2	0.1417
	649.1	0.0878	646.6	0.0422	513.2	0.0555
	693.1	0.0039	692.7	0.0014	532.8	0.0045
	743.1	0.0000	746.0	0.0000	550.0	0.0000
10	401.1	0.0028	404.7	0.0006	386.7	0.0002
	423.8	0.0510	431.5	0.0126	403.6	0.0148
	449.6	0.1071	465.4	0.0628	419.3	0.1035
	486.1	0.0385	503.6	0.1845	436.2	0.3641
	548.9	0.1843	543.4	0.3297	454.5	0.3450
	587.9	0.3402	582.2	0.2822	474.1	0.2177
	625.2	0.2103	622.0	0.1106	495.5	0.0694
	663.0	0.0380	661.6	0.0168	516.0	0.0446
	705.3	0.0008	705.7	0.0002	537.5	0.0021
	747.9	0.0000	751.1	0.0000	551.2	0.0000

Table 5.25. Wavelengths and weights for gaussian quadrature with CIE 1964 observer data and illuminant D_{65}, for orders 7 to 10

Order	$\lambda(\bar{x})$ [nm]	$\omega(\lambda)$	$\lambda(\bar{y})$ [nm]	$\omega(\lambda)$	$\lambda(\bar{z})$ [nm]	$\omega(\lambda)$
7	412.2	0.0233	417.8	0.0048	397.2	0.0068
	444.2	0.1237	460.8	0.0649	417.2	0.1334
	498.1	0.0649	510.7	0.2842	439.6	0.3614
	565.9	0.3518	559.0	0.4188	463.3	0.4004
	613.7	0.3340	608.7	0.2036	490.1	0.1223
	661.0	0.0504	658.8	0.0238	517.1	0.0486
	722.9	0.0001	723.4	0.0000	545.0	0.0008
8	407.3	0.0113	412.1	0.0022	392.9	0.0023
	434.5	0.0851	448.8	0.0345	411.6	0.0681
	466.3	0.0831	493.0	0.1656	431.3	0.2784
	546.4	0.1962	538.0	0.3833	452.9	0.4096
	591.2	0.3808	583.3	0.3095	476.0	0.2306
	633.0	0.1779	628.6	0.0987	505.9	0.0657
	678.6	0.0138	676.8	0.0062	523.4	0.0188
	735.3	0.0001	736.7	0.0000	547.3	0.0003
9	403.6	0.0065	407.5	0.0011	389.0	0.0010
	427.9	0.0647	438.8	0.0187	406.5	0.0354

Table 5.25. (continued)

Order	$\lambda(\bar{x})$ [nm]	$\omega(\lambda)$	$\lambda(\bar{y})$ [nm]	$\omega(\lambda)$	$\lambda(\bar{z})$ [nm]	$\omega(\lambda)$
9 (cont.)	457.0	0.1055	477.7	0.0978	423.8	0.1634
	524.2	0.0735	520.0	0.2762	443.5	0.3609
	568.4	0.3033	561.4	0.3682	463.9	0.3227
	609.1	0.3063	604.0	0.1947	486.1	0.1290
	648.6	0.0846	646.1	0.0419	513.3	0.0567
	693.0	0.0037	692.6	0.0014	532.6	0.0046
	742.4	0.0000	744.9	0.0000	549.9	0.0001
10	400.2	0.0029	403.5	0.0005	386.1	0.0002
	422.4	0.0456	430.5	0.0107	402.6	0.0169
	449.4	0.1010	465.0	0.0546	418.3	0.1051
	486.1	0.0380	504.0	0.1863	435.8	0.3037
	547.8	0.1834	542.6	0.3410	454.3	0.3289
	587.6	0.3376	581.9	0.2785	474.0	0.2044
	624.5	0.2024	621.3	0.1121	495.7	0.0650
	662.6	0.0366	661.3	0.0161	516.0	0.0472
	705.5	0.0008	706.0	0.0002	537.3	0.0023
	747.0	0.0000	749.9	0.0000	551.2	0.0000

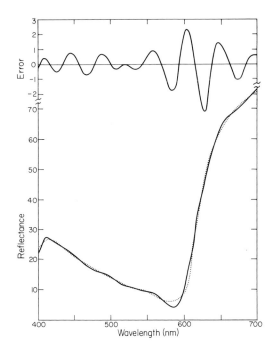

Fig. 5.8 Approximation of spectro-photometric curve by 19th-order polynomial. Error curve is shown at top. It is zero at 19 wavelengths; in general, they are not at the wavelengths of measurement or at the gaussian-selection wavelengths

Other spectrophotometric curves have been fitted more successfully, but the least rms error of fit obtained with a 19th-order polynomial was 0.1%. Because the errors of fit are in addition to, and unrelated to the errors of spectrophotometry, even in that most successful case they multiply the rms error by $\sqrt{2}$, an increase of 40%. The rms error of fit of a 6th-order polynomial to the spectrophotometric curve that was most successfully fitted was 8 times as great as for the 10th-order fit.

Finally, the uncertainty of the results of gaussian quadrature follows the same rules as those of weighted-ordinate integration in general. If only 10 ordinates are used, even though equal weights were used, the uncertainty would be $\sqrt{3.3}$ times as great as with 33 equally weighted ordinates selected from the polynomial approximation, or from $\sqrt{6.6}$ to 10 times as great as with 33 ordinates selected from the spectral-reflectance data measured at the wavelengths of the selected-ordinate method. Because the weights in the gaussian-quadrature method are not equal to each other as in Sect. 5.6, the uncertainty is multiplied by yet another factor

Table 5.26. Multiplying factors for rms errors of gaussian quadrature with CIE 1931 and 1964 observer data and illuminants A, C, and D_{65} for orders 7 to 10 (omitting ordinates at wavelengths less than 400 and more than 700 nm, and those with weights less than 0.0002)

Observer	Illuminant	Order	(X)	(Y)	(Z)
1931	A	7	1.46	1.38	1.29
		8	1.52	1.43	1.26
		9	1.46	1.38	1.29
		10	1.52	1.42	1.31
	C	7	1.31	1.38	1.33
		8	1.33	1.44	1.39
		9	1.31	1.52	1.34
		10	1.24	1.35	1.32
	D_{65}	7	1.32	1.38	1.33
		8	1.34	1.45	1.40
		9	1.32	1.49	1.34
		10	1.26	1.35	1.41
1964	A	7	1.46	1.38	1.29
		8	1.52	1.44	1.25
		9	1.46	1.38	1.29
		10	1.52	1.42	1.31
	C	7	1.30	1.34	1.33
		8	1.32	1.39	1.38
		9	1.37	1.44	1.33
		10	1.34	1.38	1.37
	D_{65}	7	1.31	1.35	1.31
		8	1.34	1.40	1.37
		9	1.38	1.45	1.40
		10	1.35	1.40	1.42

$$F = \sqrt{1 + \sum_1^n (w_i - \bar{w})^2 / \bar{w}^2}\,,$$

where

$$\bar{w} = \sum_1^n w_i / n\,.$$

Those factors, for the same combinations of observer data and illuminants as in Tables 5.20 – 25 are given in Table 5.26. The uncertainty of tristimulus values obtained by use of 10th-order gaussian quadrature is therefore at least 3 times and possibly 20 times as great as the uncertainty of 33 selected-ordinate results.

Consequently, although gaussian quadrature may be useful for iterative investigations that require large numbers of calculations of tristimulus values, such as for color matching with dye or pigment mixtures, accuracy is sacrificed.

If accuracy limited only by the uncertainties of spectrophotometry is wanted, the selected-ordinate method had best be used rather than either the weighted-ordinate or the gaussian-quadrature methods.

6. Color of Light

Color can be seen only if there is light. Unlike the absolute sense of musical pitch, possessed by some persons, there is no absolute sense of color. All color perception is relative. For wide ranges of variation of spectral distributions and of location in the chromaticity diagram of the point that represents it, any light source looks white, as do all objects illuminated by it that have reflectances that are both high and independent of wavelength. Such objects are called white, almost regardless of the quality of their illumination. Chromatic objects are those that in these same illuminations, appear qualitatively different from white. The points that represent chromatic objects in the chromaticity diagram have locations different from the point that represents both the illumination and white objects. Chromatic qualities of common sources or illuminations can be sensed only by comparison with some reference illumination. For the colorimetry of reflecting or transmitting objects, illuminants A, C, or D_{65} are commonly used for reference. They can also be used for assessing the color of light and often are so used to specify the colors of highly chromatic sources. However, to designate commonly encountered qualities of illumination, a continuous series of sources that span the expected range and that are determined by a single parameter is useful. Such a series is provided by the ideal thermal radiators commonly called blackbodies. Their parameter is temperature, expressed on the Kelvin scale.

6.1 Color Temperature

The unique feature of blackbody radiators is that, for any temperature, the spectral distribution of power is specified by Planck's formula,

$$S_\lambda = c_1/\lambda^5 \, [\exp(c_2/\lambda T) - 1],$$

where S_λ is given in units of microwatt per square millimeter of the source per nanometer wavelength interval, $c_1 = 3.7415 \times 10^{20}$ microwatt per square millimeter, $c_2 = 1.4388 \times 10^7$ nanometer Kelvin, λ is expressed in nanometers (nm), and T is expressed on the Kelvin scale (K).

For so-called graybodies, S_λ given by Planck's formula is multiplied by a constant, called emissivity, less than 1. For example, tungsten, the most usual practical thermal radiator – used in ordinary incandescent lamps – has emissivity about 0.3.

The emissivity of tungsten is not quite constant. Strictly speaking, therefore, tungsten is not a graybody. However, as usually occurs in incandescent lamps in which the tungsten is in the form of coiled or even coiled-coil filaments, the light, after much interreflection within adjacent turns of the coils, nearly follows Planck's formula, with emissivity close to 0.5.

Despite the variation of emissivity with wavelength, the spectral distribution of light from a tungsten lamp is almost exactly the same as that of a graybody of a slightly different temperature. That temperature is called the color temperature of the lamp. Because the emissivity of tungsten is higher in the blue than in the red, the color temperature is higher than the actual temperature of the tungsten.

Many other sources, notably the sun, moon, and stars, as well as carbon arcs, produce light with spectral distributions similar to those of graybodies. Because their spectral distributions are not exactly the same as the spectral distributions of a graybody at some temperature, color temperatures cannot be determined for them by matching spectral-distribution curves, as can be done for tungsten lamps. By visual color matching or, more conveniently and objectively, by colorimetry, a graybody can be found that has almost exactly the same color as the sun, moon, stars, arcs, or any source that appears white when seen alone. The color qualities of such sources commonly are reported in terms of their color temperatures, the temperatures of graybodies that in direct comparisons, most-nearly match their colors. The color temperature of a source is usually different than its actual temperature. In some cases it is very different. For example, a "daylight" fluorescent lamp may have 5000 K color temperature, whereas the lamp itself is barely warm, or a clear blue sky may have 12,000 K color temperature whereas the air itself is cold.

When a source is compared to one that has a lower color temperature, the former appears bluer than the latter. This is in conflict with common terminology: A bluer color is commonly called colder than one that is less blue, but a bluer white light has the higher color temperature! Similarly, a source that has a lower color temperature than another appears yellower or, for color temperatures less than 2000 K, even orange compared to a source that has a higher color temperature. However, because it is yellower or even orange, the light with the lower color temperature is said to be warmer, in common terminology! Things at still lower temperatures, such as 1500 K, appear red. They are called red hot to express the idea of extremely hot. Our ancestors had no experience with hotter things – except the sun whose higher temperature was (and still is, to most persons) inconceivable. That the yellowness of the sun (or its whiteness in clear atmosphere) indicated a temperature four times as great as the hottest things on earth never occurred to them – or even to Aristotle or Leonardo da Vinci. Anaxagoras was accused of impiety because he maintained that the sun was a hot object.

It would be futile to advocate change of common terminology. The paradox should simply be kept in mind.

The essential tool for colorimetric determination of color temperature is the chromaticity diagram. On it, by calculation with the CIE 1931 observer data as illustrated in Sect. 5.3, the chromaticities of blackbodies at various temperatures can be represented, as in Fig. 2.2. Graybodies at the same temperatures are represented by exactly the same points. The curve drawn through the calculated points is called the blackbody locus, or sometimes the planckian locus, or locus of complete radiators.

By spectroradiometry, or calculations based on spectroradiometry and spectrophotometric data for any filters or reflectors used in composite sources, the spectral distribution of power can be obtained for any source. Only relative data are necessary for determination of color temperature, so spectroradiometry or calculation of power in absolute units is not needed.

The tristimulus values of the source can be calculated from the relative spectral-distribution data, by use of the method presented in Sect. 5.3. From the tristimulus values, the chromaticity coordinates are computed and plotted as explained in Sect. 1.9. The value of Y is not otherwise significant for determination of color temperature. It has no significance at all if the spectroradiometric data used are only relative, i.e., expressed in arbitrary units.

On the other hand, if the spectroradiometric data are expressed in watts, then Y multiplied by 683 (called the maximum luminous efficiency of radiant energy, K_m) gives the equivalent number of lumens (i.e., for the same geometrical parameters as were used to express the spectroradiometric data, e.g., per square millimeter). This is the fundamental basis of physical photometry.

To determine color temperature of any source (such as a tungsten lamp) whose chromaticity is represented by a point on the blackbody locus, interpolate the temperature that corresponds to the location of that point on the locus. For sources such as the sun, sky, arcs, or fluorescent lamps, whose chromaticities are represented by points that are not exactly on the blackbody locus, it is necessary to determine the point on the blackbody locus that represents the most nearly similar blackbody chromaticity. That point is not the geometrically nearest point, which would be at the foot of the perpendicular from the point that represents the source to the blackbody locus. Rather, the line from the source point to the point on the locus that represents the most nearly similar blackbody is one of the line segments drawn transverse to the blackbody locus in Fig. 6.1, or as nearly as possible parallel to the nearest two of those line segments. The basis for those transverse lines will be explained in Sect. 8.1. They are called *isotemperature* lines. The temperature that corresponds to the blackbody whose chromaticity is represented by the point where the isotemperature line from the source point intersects the blackbody locus is called the *correlated color temperature* of the source. It is commonly used to designate the colors of light, including daylight, skylight,

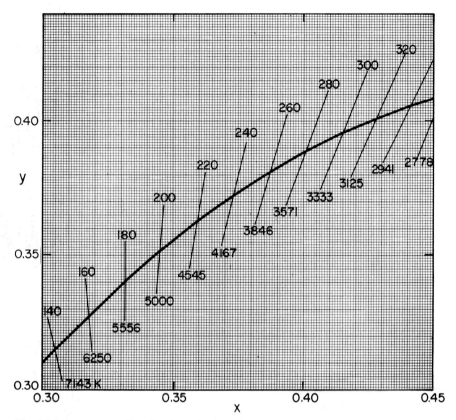

Fig. 6.1 Isotemperature lines for determination of correlated color temperature

fluorescent light, and other illuminations that, seen by themselves, are usually called white.

The extent to which the point that represents the chromaticity of any source of light departs from the blackbody locus along its isotemperature line indicates how much the color of the light differs from that of the most nearly similar blackbody. Points above the blackbody locus appear greenish, compared to the most nearly similar blackbodies. Points below the locus appear pinkish compared to blackbodies that have the same color temperatures. Points at the ends of the line segments in Fig. 6.1 represent colors that differ from blackbodies at the same color temperatures by about twice the just-noticeable difference. Incidentally, the separations between adjacent line segments in Fig. 6.1 also represent differences of color temperature about twice the just-noticeable difference. Just-noticeable differences of chromaticity will be discussed in Sect. 8.1.

Just-noticeable differences of color temperature amount to about ten reciprocal megakelvins (RMK). The reciprocal temperature (in RMK) of any color temperature is 1,000,000/T, where T is expressed is absolute Kelvin units. Thus, the reciprocal temperature that corresponds to 5000 K is 200 RMK. The color temperature that is just noticeably higher than 5000 K has a reciprocal temperature 10 RMK lower, or 190 RMK. That just-noticeably higher color temperature is therefore 1,000,000/190 = 5250 K. The RMK values at which the isotemperature lines in Fig. 6.1 intersect the blackbody locus are 140, 160, ... , 200, 220, ... , 340, 360 RMK, which correspond to 7143, 6250, 5556, 5000, 4545, 4167, 3846, 3571, 3333, 3125, 2941, and 2778 K.

6.2 Colors of Daylight and Sky

Spectral distributions of sunlight and daylight in all kinds of weather have been measured many times in many parts of the world – Canada, the United States of America, England, Germany, Egypt, South Africa, and Australia. Most of the chromaticities computed from such data are above (on the greenish side of) the blackbody locus, as shown in Fig. 6.2. Reported correlated color temperatures have ranged from 4000 K, for light from a low sun shining through a reddish haze, to 100,000 K for light from a very clear north sky at a high-altitude observatory.

In order to promote uniformity of practice in colorimetry – to make results obtained in different laboratories comparable – the CIE recommend-

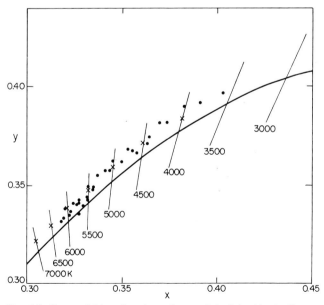

Fig. 6.2 Chromaticities of various phases of daylight (dots). Chromaticities of CIE sources D (crosses)

ed a procedure for calculating the spectral distribution of daylight for any correlated color temperature. That method was based on over 600 measurements of natural daylight made in Rochester, New York; Ottawa, Canada; and Enfield, England[34]. The chromaticities of the phases of daylight measured in Rochester are shown in Fig. 6.2.

For correlated color temperatures from approximately 4000 K to 7000 K, the CIE defined the x chromaticity coordinate of daylight in terms of the correlated Kelvin temperature T_c by

$$x_D = -4.607 \times 10^9/T_c^3 + 2967800/T_c^2 + 99.11/T_c + 0.244063.$$

For correlated color temperatures from 7000 K to approximately 25,000 K,

$$x_D = -2.0064 \times 10^9/T_c^3 + 1901800/T_c^2 + 247.48/T_c + 0.23704.$$

Then,

$$y_D = -3x_D^2 + 2.87x_D - 0.275.$$

A few of the chromaticities thus defined are indicated by $\times$'s in Fig. 6.2. The spectral distribution of daylight of correlated color temperature T_c is

$$S_\lambda = S_0(\lambda) + M_1 S_1(\lambda) + M_2 S_2(\lambda),$$

where $S_0(\lambda)$, $S_1(\lambda)$, $S_2(\lambda)$ are the functions of wavelength λ listed in Table 6.1, and

$$M_1 = \frac{-1.3515 - 1.7703x_D + 5.9114y_D}{0.0241 + 0.2562x_D - 0.7341y_D},$$

$$M_2 = \frac{0.03 - 31.4424x_D + 30.0717y_D}{0.0241 + 0.2562x_D - 0.7341y_D}.$$

Although these formulas apply to all correlated color temperatures between 4000 K and 25,000 K, the CIE recommended that, when possible, colorimetry should be based on the distribution for 5500 K, 6500 K, or 7500 K. Those illuminants are designated D_{55}, D_{65}, D_{75}. Practice has concentrated on D_{65}, for which the spectral distribution is given in Table 2.2.

The formulas for x_D were based on correlated color temperatures determined from the chromaticities of blackbodies calculated by use of $c_2 = 1.4380$ cm K. The most recent value of c_2 is 1.4388 cm K, on which basis the correlated color temperature of D_{65} is 6504 K. For the sake of continuity and uniformity of practice, however, the spectral distribution labelled D_{65} in Table 2.2 remains the illuminant most frequently assumed for colorimetric

Table 6.1. Characteristic components $S_0(\lambda)$, $S_1(\lambda)$, and $S_2(\lambda)$ for CIE daylight

λ [nm]	$S_0(\lambda)$	$S_1(\lambda)$	$S_2(\lambda)$	λ [nm]	$S_0(\lambda)$	$S_1(\lambda)$	$S_2(\lambda)$
300	0.04	0.02	0.0	580	95.1	−3.5	0.5
310	6.0	4.5	2.0	590	89.1	−3.5	2.1
320	29.6	22.4	4.0	600	90.5	−5.8	3.2
330	55.3	42.0	8.5	610	90.3	−7.2	4.1
340	57.3	40.6	7.8	620	88.4	−8.6	4.7
350	61.8	41.6	6.7	630	84.0	−9.5	5.1
360	61.5	38.0	5.3	640	85.1	−10.9	6.7
370	68.8	42.4	6.1	650	81.9	−10.7	7.3
380	63.4	38.5	3.0	660	82.6	−12.0	8.6
390	65.8	35.0	1.2	670	84.9	−14.0	9.8
400	94.8	43.4	−1.1	680	81.3	−13.6	10.2
410	104.8	46.3	−0.5	690	71.9	−12.0	8.3
420	105.9	43.9	−0.7	700	74.3	−13.3	9.6
430	96.8	37.1	−1.2	710	76.4	−12.9	8.5
440	113.9	36.7	−2.6	720	63.3	−10.6	7.0
450	125.6	35.9	−2.9	730	71.7	−11.6	7.6
460	125.5	32.6	−2.8	740	77.0	−12.2	8.0
470	121.3	27.9	−2.6	750	65.2	−10.2	6.7
480	121.3	24.3	−2.6	760	47.7	−7.8	5.2
490	113.5	20.1	−1.8	770	68.6	−11.2	7.4
500	113.1	16.2	−1.5	780	65.0	−10.4	6.8
510	110.8	13.2	−1.3	790	66.0	−10.6	7.0
520	106.5	8.6	−1.2	800	61.0	−9.7	6.4
530	108.8	6.1	−1.0	810	53.3	−8.3	5.5
540	105.3	4.2	−0.5	820	58.9	−9.3	6.1
550	104.4	1.9	−0.3	830	61.9	−9.8	6.5
560	100.0	0.0	0.0				
570	96.0	−1.6	0.2				

calculations. No actual light source that has that distribution is available except, rarely and quite unnoticed, when actual daylight briefly attains that correlated color temperature.

Many practical light sources, including many other phases of daylight, have spectral distributions sufficiently similar to D_{65} that they can be used in place of it for visual inspection. The visual results obtained with them are consistent with the calculated results of colorimetry. However, because, in the long term, all practical light sources are as ephemeral as any particular phase of daylight, and because their availability is vulnerable to all the fluctuations of technology, economics, and style, it would be futile to standardize any one or to use its spectral distribution. For example, illuminant "C" was obsolete as a practical light source less than ten years after it was recommended by the CIE in 1931. Its spectral distribution, which is still used for colorimetry and will probably continue to be so used for decades more, is a poor approximation to the spectral distribution of any phase of daylight. The details of its spectral distribution, which are crucial to whether or not color matches are correctly indicated by colorimetry, are seriously different from natural daylight and from D_{65}. Although the correlated color temperature of illuminant C is 6750 K, well within the normal range of daylight, and although it is about as greenish as D_{65} or daylight of its correlated color temperature, its spectral distribution is much inferior to that of D_{65} for colorimetry. Therefore, D_{65} is to be preferred as the illuminant of choice for colorimetry, even though it consists of only a table of numerical data. It should not be abandoned in favor of the spectral distribution of any practical light source, because the latter can only be a poorer representation of daylight and will probably become as obsolete as illuminant C within a decade or so.

6.3 Colorimetry with Fluorescent Light

The spectral distributions of power from thermal sources, such as incandescent tungsten-filament lamps, are smooth and continuous over the entire visible range. Such a distribution in the spectrum is called a *continuum*. Thermal sources usually have much greater power at the long-wavelength (700 nm) red end of the visible spectrum than at the short-wavelength (400 nm) blue end, but there are not extreme maxima or minima (bumps or dips) between. Filtered sources, such as illuminant C, have bumps and dips, but they are not extreme (not as much as 2:1 in a short-wavelength range, e.g., from 400 to 430 nm). Daylight is similar.

The spectral distributions from fluorescent lamps are quite different. They are characterized by a few very narrow, intense concentrations of power superimposed on a continuum. Those concentrations are called lines, because they appear as bright lines in a spectroscope. Although they are very narrow, less than 0.1 nm, they have a lot of power. If the spectral concentration of power in one of them were expressed in the same terms as that of the continuum with which they are combined, for example, microwatts per nanometer, the values in the lines would be tens or hundreds of times the values in the neighboring continuum. It is practically impossible to show such composite spectra on a graph; the continuum would be crowded down so as to be almost indistinguishable from the zero base line if a scale sufficiently small to show the brightest lines were used. Some of the less bright but yet significant lines would also be almost invisibly graphed. For this reason, the power in each line is customarily shown as an area, as if it were spread out over a much wider spectrum band, centered on the wavelength at which all of the power of the line is actually radiated. The width of that band is equal to the interval normally used for weighted-ordinate calculation of tristimulus values. The spectral distribution from a daylight fluorescent lamp is shown in that manner in Fig. 6.3.

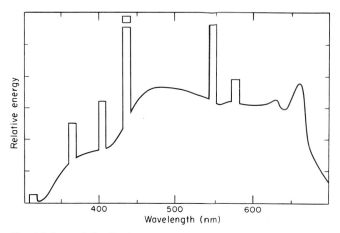

Fig. 6.3 Spectral distribution of power from a daylight fluorescent lamp

When spectral reflectance data can be obtained at the wavelengths of the lines, they can be multiplied by products of the heights of those bands times the values of $\bar{x}$, $\bar{y}$, and $\bar{z}$ at the actual wavelengths of the lines[35].

When spectral reflectance data are available only at integral multiples of 10 nm, the effect of linear interpolation for the reflectance at the wavelengths of the lines can be obtained with the weighted-ordinate calculation by revising the products $S_c\bar{x}$, $S_c\bar{y}$, $S_c\bar{z}$ at those 10 nm intervals, where S_c is the spectral distribution of the continuum. The nearest pair of those products should be revised by adding to them portions of the products f_λ of the height of the band for each line times the values of $\bar{x}$, $\bar{y}$, and $\bar{z}$ at its actual wavelength. Thus if a line at wavelength λ is between λ_1 and $\lambda_1 + 10$ nm, the revised values at λ_1 and $\lambda_1 + 10$ nm should be

$$f'_{\lambda_1} = f_{\lambda_1} + f_\lambda(\lambda_1 - \lambda + 10)/10$$
$$f'_{\lambda_1+10} = f_{\lambda_1+10} + f_\lambda(\lambda - \lambda_1)/10,$$

in these

$$f_\lambda = S_\lambda\bar{x}_\lambda, \quad S_\lambda\bar{y}_\lambda, \quad \text{or} \quad s_\lambda\bar{z}_\lambda,$$

where S_λ is the height of the band that represents the power in the line; f_{λ_1} and f_{λ_1+10} are the values of the products $S_c\bar{x}$, $S_c\bar{y}$ or $S_c\bar{z}$ at λ_1 and $\lambda_1 + 10$, respectively.

6.4 Color-Rendering Index

A practical light source, such as the daylight fluorescent lamp in Fig. 6.3, may have exactly the same chromaticity, i.e., correlated color temperature and departure from the blackbody locus, as some phase of natural daylight. However, because those sources have different spectral distributions of power, a colored material will usually have different chromaticities (i.e., x, y coordinates) when illuminated by them.

The average extent of such differences of chromaticities for a representative variety of colored materials, when calculated for the practical source and for a reference source, has been defined by the CIE as an inverse measure of the color-rendering quality of the light source[36]. Exact match of all of the chromaticities, i.e., zero differences, is defined as a color-rendering index of 100. Spectral reflectance data for a set of 8 moderately chromatic materials were provided by the CIE for use in calculations of the color-rendering index. They are given in Table 6.2.

For practical sources that have correlated color temperatures 5000 K or higher, the CIE recommends for use as the reference illuminant the spectral distribution of daylight given by the formulas in Sect. 6.1 for the correlated color temperature of the practical source. That correlated color temperature should be determined by preliminary calculations, as explained in Sect. 6.1.

The amount of each color difference is evaluated by use of a color-difference formula recommended by the CIE in 1964[37]. Denoting the average value of the color differences for the 8 test colors as ΔE_a, the CIE color-rendering index is $R_a = 100 - 4.6\,\Delta E_a$.

If the chromaticity coordinates of the practical source being evaluated are not very close to those of the reference source, the CIE recommends that the chromaticity coordinates calculated for the practical source should be corrected for chromatic adaptation, which is discussed in Chap. 11.

6.5 Luminous Efficiency of Light

The number of lumens per watt of light is called the luminous efficiency. The power (watts) involved is not the input power of the light source, but only the power of the radiated energy, of which the luminous flux (lumens) is the photometric evaluation. The excess of the input power over the radiant power is dissipated by thermal conduction in the structure that supports or contains the luminous material (e.g., filament, glowing gas, or fluorescing phosphor), by convection in the surrounding air, and by invisible, low-temperature radiation from filament supports and glass (or quartz) envelope. In the case of water-cooled lamps, considerable input energy is also removed by circulating water.

Table 6.2. Spectral reflectances of eight materials for calculation of color-rendering index

λ	1	2	3	4	5	6	7	8
360	0.116	0.053	0.058	0.057	0.143	0.079	0.150	0.075
370	0.159	0.059	0.061	0.062	0.233	0.089	0.218	0.084
380	0.219	0.070	0.065	0.074	0.295	0.151	0.378	0.104
390	0.252	0.089	0.070	0.093	0.310	0.265	0.524	0.170
400	0.256	0.111	0.073	0.116	0.313	0.410	0.551	0.319
410	0.252	0.118	0.074	0.124	0.319	0.492	0.559	0.462
420	0.244	0.121	0.074	0.128	0.326	0.517	0.561	0.490
430	0.237	0.122	0.073	0.135	0.334	0.531	0.556	0.482
440	0.230	0.123	0.073	0.144	0.346	0.544	0.544	0.462
450	0.225	0.127	0.074	0.161	0.360	0.556	0.522	0.439
460	0.220	0.131	0.077	0.186	0.381	0.554	0.488	0.413
470	0.216	0.138	0.085	0.229	0.403	0.541	0.448	0.382
480	0.214	0.150	0.109	0.281	0.415	0.519	0.408	0.352
490	0.216	0.174	0.148	0.332	0.419	0.488	0.363	0.325
500	0.223	0.207	0.198	0.370	0.413	0.450	0.324	0.299
510	0.226	0.242	0.241	0.390	0.403	0.414	0.301	0.283
520	0.225	0.260	0.278	0.395	0.389	0.377	0.283	0.270
530	0.227	0.267	0.339	0.385	0.372	0.341	0.265	0.256
540	0.236	0.272	0.392	0.367	0.353	0.309	0.257	0.250
550	0.253	0.282	0.400	0.341	0.331	0.279	0.259	0.254
560	0.272	0.299	0.380	0.312	0.308	0.253	0.260	0.264
570	0.298	0.322	0.349	0.280	0.284	0.234	0.256	0.272
580	0.341	0.335	0.315	0.247	0.260	0.225	0.254	0.278
590	0.390	0.341	0.285	0.214	0.232	0.221	0.270	0.295
600	0.424	0.342	0.264	0.185	0.210	0.220	0.302	0.348
610	0.442	0.342	0.252	0.169	0.194	0.220	0.344	0.434
620	0.450	0.341	0.241	0.160	0.185	0.223	0.377	0.528
630	0.451	0.339	0.229	0.154	0.180	0.233	0.400	0.604
640	0.451	0.338	0.220	0.151	0.176	0.244	0.420	0.648
650	0.450	0.336	0.216	0.148	0.175	0.258	0.438	0.676
660	0.451	0.334	0.219	0.148	0.175	0.268	0.452	0.693
670	0.453	0.332	0.230	0.151	0.180	0.278	0.462	0.705
680	0.455	0.331	0.251	0.158	0.186	0.283	0.468	0.712
690	0.458	0.329	0.288	0.165	0.192	0.291	0.473	0.717
700	0.462	0.328	0.340	0.170	0.199	0.302	0.483	0.721
710	0.464	0.326	0.390	0.170	0.199	0.325	0.496	0.719
720	0.466	0.324	0.431	0.166	0.196	0.351	0.511	0.725
730	0.466	0.324	0.460	0.164	0.195	0.376	0.525	0.729
740	0.467	0.322	0.481	0.168	0.197	0.401	0.539	0.730
750	0.467	0.320	0.493	0.177	0.203	0.425	0.553	0.730
760	0.467	0.316	0.500	0.185	0.208	0.447	0.565	0.730
770	0.467	0.315	0.505	0.192	0.215	0.469	0.575	0.730

The fundamentally correct way to evaluate the radiant power is to integrate the entire spectral power-density distribution measured by spectroradiometry. The spectral power density S_λ should be expressed in watts (or microwatts) per unit wavelength interval. It should be measured and integrated over the entire wavelength range in which significant amounts of power are detected, even though much of that range (e.g., in the infrared or ultraviolet) may be invisible. The integration may be performed by summation of the measured values of the power at discrete wavelengths. In that case, each value of spectral power density should be multiplied by half the difference between the nearest two other wavelengths for which spectral power densities are available and used in the summation (numerical integration). For equally spaced wavelengths, of course, this amounts to multiplying the spectral densities by the difference between successive wavelengths. The numerical integration of the radiant power can be represented by

$$P = \sum_{\lambda_1}^{\lambda_n} S_{\lambda_i}(\lambda_{i+1} - \lambda_{i-1})/2 .$$

The number of lumens is 683 times the value of the tristimulus value Y when S_λ is integrated as in Table 1.1. Then, the luminous efficiency of the light is 683 Y/P. Progress in lighting has been marked by increases of luminous efficiency, from about 10 lumens per watt for a candle, to 60 lumens per watt for a household incandescent lamp, to nearly 200 lumens per watt for mercury or sodium highway lights. Color-rendering index is sacrificed when lighting units are designed for highest luminous efficiency.

The luminous efficiency with which any chromaticity can be produced has an upper limit, which can be derived from the center-of-gravity and color-moment principles explained in Sect. 4.5. That limit is a function of chromaticity, as shown in Fig. 4.6. The maximum value for any chromaticity is 683 lumens per watt for spectrum light that has a wavelength of 555 nm, for which the luminosity function (which is identical to the $\bar{y}$ color-matching function) has its maximum value, 1.0.

The maximum luminous efficiency for a "white" light that matches D_{65} (daylight with correlated color temperature 6504 K) is 300 lumens per watt. That efficiency is obtained, however, only by using a suitable mixture of only two spectrally pure components, at 442 nm and 575 nm. Such a light would have a very low color-rendering index, probably less than zero! The luminous efficiency of D_{65} itself, for which the color-rendering index is 100, is 110 lumens per watt, if we assume that it has zero power density for wavelengths longer than 830 nm, which is the longest wavelength for which D_{65} was defined. All chromaticities can be produced at maximum luminous efficiency only by confining their power to two wavelengths, one of which, as mentioned in Sect. 4.5, must be blue, near 440 nm. For most purposes, such a restriction of spectral distribution is unacceptable. Consequently, luminous efficiencies are always less, and usually much less, than the values indicated in Fig. 4.6. Those values are useful, however, for judging progress in producing high-efficiency light and to combat unrealistic expectations and impossible requirements.

7. Colors of Objects

As with the colors of light, the colors of objects are relative, not absolute. Objects perceived to be as different as yellow and blue can have exactly the same chromaticities, when one is illuminated with a phase of daylight that has a higher correlated color temperature than the light that illuminates the other. The perceptions do not correspond in any absolute way to the chromaticities. The perceptions correspond, rather, to the locations of the chromaticities relative to the chromaticities of the illuminating lights. This is the basis of the practice in colorimetry of determining dominant wavelength by extending the straight line drawn from the illuminant point through the chromaticity (x, y) point of the sample when the latter is computed by use of the spectral distribution of the illuminant.

Although, as will be discussed in Sect. 8.3, the dominant wavelength does not correspond precisely to the perceived hue, it at least indicates that a blue object has a dominant wavelength less than 490 nm, whatever phase of daylight is used to illuminate it, and that a yellow object has a dominant wavelength in the range from 570 to 590 nm in any daylight.

That blue objects illuminated with daylight or any other usual quality of illumination always appear blue, yellow objects yellow, white objects white and other objects almost always appear to have the same hues as they do in daylight is called *color constancy*. It is a consequence of a property or behavior of color vision called *chromatic adaptation,* which is discussed in Chap. 11. Although hue is not exactly the same for all illuminations, it is nearly enough constant to justify the use of dominant wavelength determined relative to the illuminant chromaticity for colorimetry.

Chromatic adaptation and its corollary, color constancy, is of crucial benefit to mankind and to all other creatures that have color vision. By its action, objects, foods, prey, and predators are recognized by their colors despite enormous variations of quality of illumination, from firelight at correlated color temperatures as low as 1500 K, to skylight at 10,000 K or higher. To this trait can be largely credited the survival of the species. Color constancy does not hold for some modern illuminants that have low color-rendering indices, such as mercury or sodium street lights. How serious the consequences will be, in the long term, remains to be seen.

An analogy that indicates the seriousness of lack of chromatic adaptation is provided by color photography. Reversal color films, such as are used to make transparencies, or "slides" and "home movies" are designed differently according to whether they are intended for exposure in daylight or in incandescent tungsten light. If film designed for daylight is exposed in tungsten light, all colors in the resulting pictures are predominantly yellowish. Even blue objects in the scene are rendered yellowish, if only to the extent that they appear greenish or grayish. In the other case, when film designed for tungsten-light exposure is used in daylight, all colors in the scene are rendered bluish — what artists and photographers call "cold." Hardly any yellows or orange colors appear and even reds are rendered as purples. Such disastrous results would be common in everyday experience if human color vision were not characterized by chromatic adaptation.

Transparent color-correction filters are used in photography to simulate chromatic adaptation, but they provide only a few discrete levels of adaptation and must be selected appropriately and applied when the need for them is anticipated.

On the other hand, chromatic adaptation is continuous, rapid, fine-tuned, automatic, and nearly unconscious. If a person wears a pair of goggles fitted with one of the color-correction filters used for color photography, its initial effects on the appearances of colors in a scene rapidly fade as a consequence of chromatic adaptation. In a few seconds, the scene appears normal through the goggles. If the goggles are then removed, the effects of chromatic adaptation to them will be apparent (all colors will be tinted in the complementary sense) for the first second or two, but all colors will rapidly resume their normal appearance as chromatic adaptation returns to the condition appropriate for the ambient illumination.

7.1 Filter Colors

One of the most complete sets of available filters consists of the Wratten Light Filters. The chromaticities of those filters, when illuminated by illuminant A, are shown in Figs. 7.1, 2. In Fig. 7.2, the central portion of the chromaticity diagram is enlarged to show more clearly the distribution of color-correction filters and color-temperature conversion filters.

It is of interest and utility to note that a well-designed color-temperature conversion filter changes the reciprocal color temperature of the light from any blackbody by a constant amount within a rather wide range, regardless of the temperature of the blackbody. This is an example and quantitative expression of color constancy. Such a filter can be labelled with that conversion power, expressed in RMK (reciprocal megakelvins). A positive value increases the reciprocal color temperature of blackbody radiation that passes through the filter and consequently reduces the color temperature. The conversion power for correlated color temperature is nearly the same for incident light that has a reasonable approximation to the spectral distribution of a blackbody. For example, Wratten Light Filter number 85 in D_{65} incident

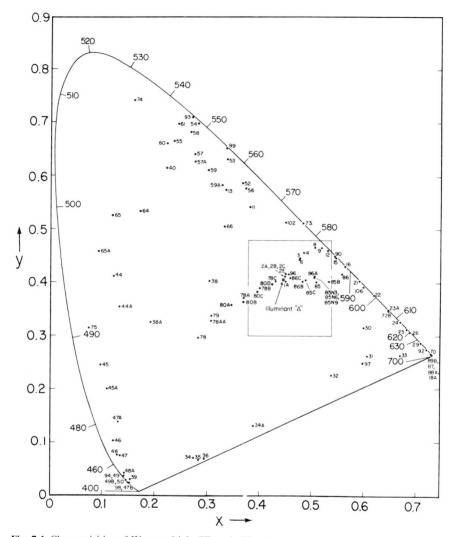

Fig. 7.1 Chromaticities of Wratten Light Filters in illuminant A

light transmits light that has a correlated color temperature of 3760 K, which indicates that its color-temperature conversion power is $10^6/3760 - 10^6/6500$ or 112 RMK. When the same filter is used with D_{55}, it transmits light that has a correlated color temperature of 3400 K. The power of a few Wratten filters useful for color-temperature conversion are

Filter number	80A	80B	80C	80D	81D	85C	85	85B
RMK power	−131	−112	−81	−56	42	81	112	131

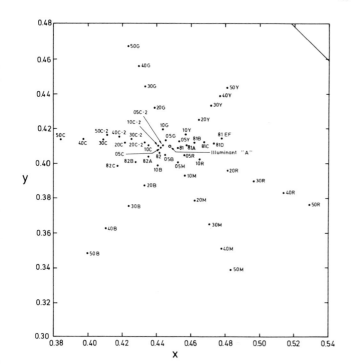

Fig. 7.2 Chromaticities of low-purity Wratten Light Filters in illuminant A

The chromaticities of the Wratten filters when illuminated by source C are shown in Fig. 7.3. The central region is enlarged in Fig. 7.4. The general resemblances of the configuration of the points in Fig. 7.3 to that in Fig. 7.1 and of the points in Fig. 7.4 to the configuration of points in Fig. 7.2 indicate the general and detailed character of color constancy. That some of the filters do not look exactly the same in daylight as they do in tungsten light will be discussed in connection with chromatic adaptation in Sect. 11.3, but the relative locations of points in Figs. 7.1 – 4 indicate moderately good first approximations to the appearances of the filters in the two illuminations.

If a straight line from the point in Fig. 7.1 that represents the chromaticity of one filter in D_{65} is drawn through the point that represents a second filter further to the right and extended until it intersects the spectrum locus, the wavelength that corresponds to that intersection is called the *conjunctive wavelength* of the second filter with respect to the first for D_{65}. The wavelength that corresponds to the intersection of the spectrum locus with the line drawn through the points that represent the same two filters in Fig. 7.3 is the conjunctive wavelength of the second with respect to the first for illuminant A. If those two conjunctive wavelengths are nearly the same, the two filters probably have nearly the same appearances in tungsten light as in daylight. If the conjunctive wavelengths are much different, the hue of at least one of the filters is different in tungsten light than in daylight. If the conjunctive

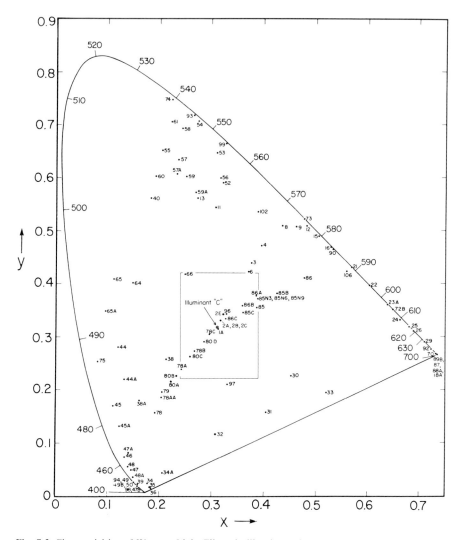

Fig. 7.3 Chromaticities of Wratten Light Filters in illuminant C

wavelength for illuminant A is longer than for D_{65}, then the second filter looks yellower or redder in illuminant A than it does in daylight, or the first filter looks bluer, or both changes may appear.

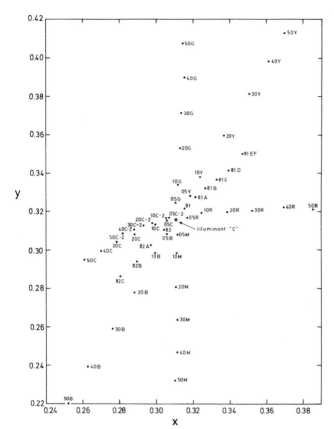

Fig. 7.4 Chromaticities of low-purity Wratten Light Filters in illuminant C

7.2 Absorptive Color Mixture

Spectrophotometric data for superimposed light filters or for solutions of mixtures of dyes that do not react with each other chemically or by change of acidity (pH) can be calculated in the ways described in Sect. 4.1.

When the three dyes, *AG, BF,* and *CC,* whose spectral transmittances are shown by the solid curves in Fig. 7.5 are mixed in the concentrations that resulted in those curves, the mixture has the spectrophotometric curve shown at the top of Fig. 7.6. That mixture has the same chromaticity as D_{65} when it is illuminated with that source. The ratio of the value of Y to that for the solvent alone, with zero concentrations of the dyes, is 0.1. The optical density of that gray mixture is 1.0. The solutions of the separate dyes whose spectral transmittance curves are drawn solid in Fig. 7.5 are said to have equivalent neutral densities of 1.0. In general, a concentration of any one of them such that a mixture of it with appropriate concentrations of the others produces a gray that has an optical density D is said to have D_e *equivalent neutral density,* END. The equivalent neutral densities of a dye are not exactly proportional to

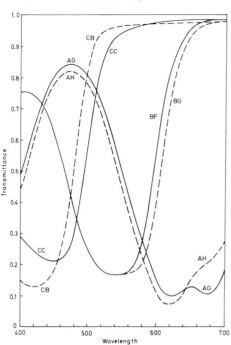

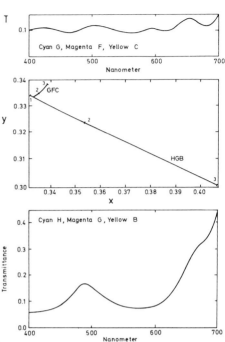

Fig. 7.5 Spectrophotometric curves of unit equivalent neutral densities of two yellow dyes *CB* and *CC*, two magenta dyes *BF* and *BH*, and two cyan dyes *AG* and *AH*

Fig. 7.6 *Top:* Spectrophotometric curve of combination of *CC*, *BF*, and *AG* dyes. *Bottom:* Spectrophotometric curve of combination of *CB*, *BG*, and *AH* dyes. *Middle:* Chromaticities in illuminant C of indicated combinations of dyes represented by curves in Fig. 7.5 and of double and triple concentrations of them

concentrations. The chromaticities produced by equal multiples of the concentrations for $D_e = 1$ are shown on the curve labeled *GFC* in the central section of Fig. 7.6. The concentration of a dye necessary to produce a neutral gray of any particular density depends on the other dyes with which it is combined and also on the source with which mixtures are illuminated.

A yellow dye produced curve *CC* in Fig. 7.5. A magenta dye produced curve *BF*. The dye that produced curve *AG* is called a *cyan*. Such dyes and mixtures are used in color photography. In transparencies, they behave in much the same manner as will be discussed for solutions. The terms cyan and equivalent neutral density originated in and are customarily used in color photography, in which the concentrations in terms of weights are almost never known.

Figure 7.7 shows, by the intersections of the curves, the chromaticities in D_{65} of combinations of the indicated multiples of the concentrations of the dyes represented by the solid curves in Fig. 7.5. Each curve is the locus of constant concentration of one of the dyes. The letters that appear near the center of each side of the triangular pattern in Fig. 7.7 identify the dye that

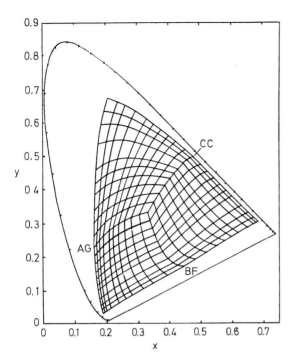

Fig. 7.7 Chromaticities in illuminant C of combinations of dyes *AG,* *BF,* and *CC*

has its maximum concentration on that curve. Every chromaticity shown in Fig. 7.7 is produced by a single dye or by combination of not more than two dyes. Thus, all of the chromaticities in the yellow-orange – red-magenta sector result from mixtures of the yellow and magenta dyes. The chromaticities represented in Fig. 7.7 are obtained with the maximum luminous transmittance Y possible with this set of dyes when the indicated pairs are used.

Use of some of the third dye with any of the indicated pairs would produce only a chromaticity already produced by some pair alone. The luminous transmittance of the 3-dye combination would in all cases be less than that of the 2-dye combination that has the same chromaticity. In this way, in color photography, all of the darker shades of all attainable chromaticities are produced by combinations of three dyes. The amounts of dyes in a 3-dye combination, as in a color photograph, can be measured in terms of END by use of specialized instruments, called *analytical densitometers,* or they can be computed from spectrophotometric data. To a very close approximation, the chromaticity of a 3-dye combination is the same as that indicated by such a network of loci as in Fig. 7.8 for the 2-dye combination that results by subtraction of the least of the three D_e values from the other two. The 3-dye combination is darker than that chromaticity by the amount of that least D_e, or by the luminous transmittance 10^{-D_e} of the neutral density formed by that END of all three of the dyes.

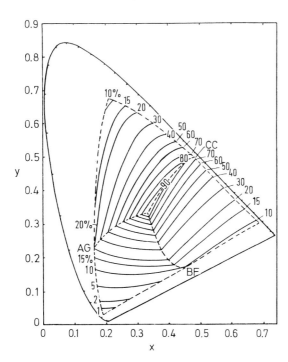

Fig. 7.8 Luminous transmittances of illuminant C of same combinations of pairs of dyes as in Fig. 7.7

The maximum values of luminous transmittance are shown for all chromaticities attainable with the *AG, BF,* and *CC* dyes, by the contours in Fig. 7.8. The indicated maximum values are the values of *Y* for the 2-dye combinations at the chromaticities shown in Fig. 7.7.

The outline of the contours in Fig. 7.8, which is the same as the outline of the loci in Fig. 7.7, shows the extent of the range of chromaticities producible with the three dyes represented by the solid curves in Fig. 7.5, used in concentrations not greater than three times the concentrations required for $D_e = 1$. Use of higher concentrations would not enlarge the range significantly.

The combined limits of chromaticity and luminous transmittance shown by the outline and contours in Fig. 7.8 is called the *gamut* of colors of the set of dyes represented by the solid curves in Fig. 7.5.

The distribution of chromaticities of the set of dyes represented by the broken curves in Fig. 7.5 is shown in Fig. 7.9. The maximum luminous transmittance producible with that set of dyes is shown in Fig. 7.10. The superiority of the first set of dyes, represented by the solid curves in Fig. 7.5, is evident from the greater gamut shown in Figs. 7.7, 8 than in Figs. 7.9, 10.

The lesser shift of chromaticity when the concentrations of a neutral gray combination are all increased by the same factor, shown by the curve *GFC* in the middle of Fig. 7.6 compared to the curve *HBG,* is another indication of the superiority of the first set of dyes. The shift of chromaticity of the $D = 1$

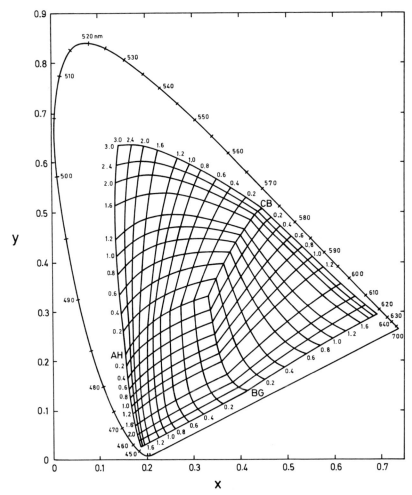

Fig. 7.9 Chromaticities in illuminant C of indicated combinations of dyes *AH, BG,* and *CB*

neutral at high concentrations indicates that dark colors in photographs made with the second set of dyes will appear too brownish. That shift is also associated with failure of color constancy, such that even middle-tone colors appear too warm or maroon when a light source such as illuminant A is used to view or project pictures made with the second set of dyes. The neutral combinations of the two sets of dyes shown in Fig. 7.6 and all chromaticities and luminous transmittances in Figs. 7.7–10 were computed for illuminant C.

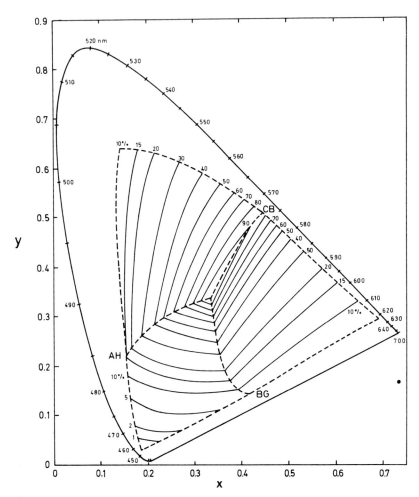

Fig. 7.10 Luminous transmittances in illuminant C of same combinations of pairs of dyes *AH*, *BG*, and *CB* as in Fig. 7.9

7.3 Scattering Absorbing Mixtures[38]

Substances that both scatter and absorb light do not obey Bouguer's (Lambert-Beer) law, which was used in Sect. 7.2. Analysis of the problem has led to use of the ratio of an absorption coefficient K to a scattering coefficient S. Those coefficients are, in general, functions of wavelength. For any particular scattering substance, for example, a pigment suspended in a medium such as paint oil or varnish, the values of K and S are practically independent of the amount of the pigment per unit thickness. In a mixture that contains two or more different scattering substances (e.g., pigments), the value of K at each wavelength for the mixture is the sum of the values of K for the constituent pigments, and the value of S is the sum of the values of S of the constituent pigments. When one of the constituent pigments has a much higher value of S (the scattering coefficient) than have the other pigments, or when a white pigment (such as titanium dioxide, TiO_2) that has a high value of S is predominant, the value of S is approximately the same for all mixtures and a single-constant approximation is often used. For low ratios of chromatic pigment to white pigment, the value of the ratio K/S at each visible wavelength is proportional to the concentration of the chromatic pigment, expressed as a dry-weight percentage of the total pigment content (chromatic plus white). For a mixture of two or more chromatic pigments in such a mixture with a white pigment, the value of K/S at each wavelength is approximately the sum of the values of K/S of the chromatic pigments. In that sum, the value of K/S at each wavelength for each chromatic pigment is equal to its concentration (percent) multiplied by the value of K/S for the mixture of one percent of that pigment alone with white.

The value of K/S for each chromatic pigment is calibrated by spectrophotometry of an opaque layer (film) of a 2 or 10 percent mixture of the pigment with the white (e.g., TiO_2). An opaque film is one that, at any wavelength, has a measured reflectance that is the same as would be measured for any thicker layer. The reflectance measured for an opaque layer is designated R'_∞. That value inevitably includes the effect of a small portion r (e.g., about 6%) of the incident light that is reflected from the surface of the paint film. Before K/S is calculated from it, R_∞ should be corrected for that reflection,

$$R_\infty = (R'_\infty - r)/(1 - r).$$

The first-surface reflectance can be evaluated directly by spectrophotometry of a black coating made with the same vehicle (oil or varnish). The black pigment used should have high absorption and tinting strength, so that the reflectance is as low as possible when 10 or 20 percent of the black is mixed with the white pigment that is to be used in chromatic mixtures. An alternative is to determine by iterative trials the value of r that gives, for any chromatic pigment, corrected K/S values that are as nearly as possible proportional to concentration, where

$$K/S = (1 - R_\infty)^2/2R_\infty.$$

If this method is used with all of the chromatic pigments that are to be used in mixture, the results averaged at various wavelengths for different pigments can give the dependence of r on wavelength.

The appropriate value of r should be used to correct all measured values of R'_∞ to R_∞. R_∞ should be determined at all wavelengths for a calibration concentration c_a (e.g., 2 or 10 percent) of each chromatic pigment with white.

Then, to compute the single-constant approximation of K/S at each wavelength for a mixture of two or more chromatic pigments with concentrations c_i in the white pigment, add the values of

$$\frac{c_i}{c_a} \left(\frac{K}{S} \right)_i$$

for the chromatic components. From the sum K/S of those values, the spectral reflectance R'_∞ of an opaque layer of the mixture can be calculated from

$$R'_\infty = R_\infty (1 - r) + r,$$

where

$$R_\infty = 1 + \frac{K}{S} - \sqrt{\left(\frac{K}{S} \right)^2 + 2 \left(\frac{K}{S} \right)}.$$

These formulas give satisfactory results for glossy or semi-glossy paints or for paper and textiles. They do not apply to matte or nearly matte paints or to metalized paints that contain flakes of metal (aluminum or bronze). Such flakes become oriented nearly parallel to the surface as the paint dries; thus oriented they interfere with complete diffusion of the light within the paint layer, which is assumed in the turbid-media theory.

Values of K/S for nine chromatic pigments mixed in the indicated dry-weight concentrations c_a with TiO_2 in opaque paint films are plotted on a logarithmic-versus-wavelength scale in Figs. 7.11 – 13. The curve of K/S for any multiple of the concentration c_a of any one of those pigments can be obtained by raising or lowering the curve by the amount $\log(c_a/c)$, for which purpose a relative-concentration scale is provided at the left sides of Figs. 7.11 – 13.

As in the case of the log-density curves of dyes, the shapes of the curves of $\log(K/S)$ do not depend on concentration. Therefore, the pigments present in an unknown mixture can be deduced by finding the pigments that have characteristic shapes that match those that appear in limited wavelength regions of the $\log(K/S)$ curve of the mixture.

Figures 7.14, 15 show $\log(K/S)$ curves for 24 mixtures of sets of three of the pigments represented in Figs. 7.11 – 13. The mixtures represented in Figs. 7.14, 15 all have the same chromaticity $x = 0.386$, $y = 0.3884$ in D_{65} for the 1964 observer.

The blue or black constituent in any mixture can be identified by search among the curves for the one that has the same shape as the mixture in the long-wavelength region, $600 - 700$ nm. This search is relatively easy because the K/S curves for the yellow, orange, and red pigments are nearly zero in that

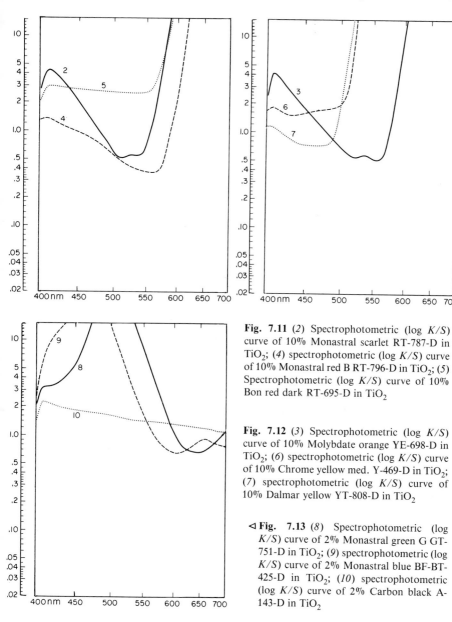

Fig. 7.11 (*2*) Spectrophotometric (log K/S) curve of 10% Monastral scarlet RT-787-D in TiO$_2$; (*4*) spectrophotometric (log K/S) curve of 10% Monastral red B RT-796-D in TiO$_2$; (*5*) Spectrophotometric (log K/S) curve of 10% Bon red dark RT-695-D in TiO$_2$

Fig. 7.12 (*3*) Spectrophotometric (log K/S) curve of 10% Molybdate orange YE-698-D in TiO$_2$; (*6*) spectrophotometric (log K/S) curve of 10% Chrome yellow med. Y-469-D in TiO$_2$; (*7*) spectrophotometric (log K/S) curve of 10% Dalmar yellow YT-808-D in TiO$_2$

◁ **Fig. 7.13** (*8*) Spectrophotometric (log K/S) curve of 2% Monastral green G GT-751-D in TiO$_2$; (*9*) spectrophotometric (log K/S) curve of 2% Monastral blue BF-BT-425-D in TiO$_2$; (*10*) spectrophotometric (log K/S) curve of 2% Carbon black A-143-D in TiO$_2$

region. Identification of the red, orange, or yellow constituent would be complicated by features of the K/S curves of the blue and black pigments in the middle (500 – 600 nm) and short (400 – 500 nm) regions which distort the K/S curve of the mixture in those regions and obscure the details of the K/S curves that are characteristic of the red, orange and yellow pigments.

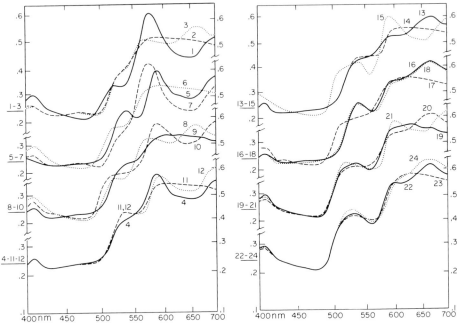

Fig. 7.14 Spectrophotometric (log K/S) curves of mixtures numbered 1 to 12 of 3 pigments in TiO$_2$

Fig. 7.15 Spectrophotometric (log K/S) curves of mixtures numbered 13 to 24 of 3 pigments in TiO$_2$

After the blue or black pigment has been identified, its concentration in the mixture can be determined from the displacement of the $\log(K/S)$ curve for that pigment that is necessary to make it coincident in the long-wavelength region with the $\log(K/S)$ curve of the mixture. The amount cK/S for that pigment can then be graphically subtracted from the $\log(K/S)$ curve of the mixture[39].

It is then relatively easy to identify the red or orange pigment in the mixture by searching among the $\log(K/S)$ curves of these pigments for the one that matches the shape of the reduced $\log(K/S)$ curve in the middle (500 – 600 nm) region. In that region, the yellow pigments do not have seriously interfering details. The concentration of the red or orange pigment can be determined from the displacement of the $\log(K/S)$ curve of that pigment that is necessary to make it coincide in the 500 – 600 nm region with the reduced $\log(K/S)$ curve of the mixture. The contribution of that pigment can then be subtracted from the previously reduced curve for the mixture.

The curve of the remainder should have the same shape as the $\log(K/S)$ curve for one of the yellow pigments. The amount of the yellow pigment in the mixture can be determined from the displacement of the $\log(K/S)$ curve of that pigment that is necessary in order to make it coincide with the curve of the remainder of the $\log(K/S)$ of the mixture. Determination of the pigments

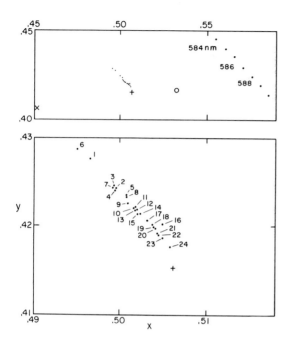

Fig. 7.16 Chromaticities in illuminant A for 1964 observer of mixtures 1 to 24

and their concentrations in the 24 mixtures represented in Figs. 7.14 and 7.15 by use of this method will be left as an exercise.

Although all of the mixtures represented in Figs. 7.14 and 7.15 have the same chromaticity in D_{65} for the 1964 observer, they do not match in illuminant A. Their chromaticities in illuminant A are shown in Fig. 7.16. Although the values of Y, the luminance factors for the mixtures, are also different for the various mixtures in illuminant A, little attention is usually paid to such differences. The chromatic differences are more noticeable and objectionable.

7.4 Metamerism

Lights from different sources or reflected from different samples having different spectral distributions yet looking alike, are called *metamers*. Thus, the varieties of light that are reflected from the mixtures represented by Figs. 7.14, 15 when they are illuminated by D_{65} are metamers. Because those mixtures look alike in D_{65}, the fact that the varieties of light they reflect are metamers cannot be detected visually in that illumination. It could be detected by spectrophotometry of the materials or by illumination of them by illuminant A for which their chromaticities are different, as indicated by Fig. 7.16. Illumination by many other sources significantly different than D_{65}

would also result in different chromaticities and reveal that the colors reflected in D_{65} are metamers. However, to recognize that they are metamers, it would be necessary to know and remember that the materials match in D_{65}. Then, when some other illuminant results in color difference, the presence of spectral reflectance (spectrophotometric) differences can be inferred. Materials that have different spectrophotometric curves yet match with some light source are said to be *metameric* for that light source and for the observer for whom the materials match. The amounts of the visual differences in some other illumination are taken to correspond to the amount of *metamerism,* that is, the importance of the spectral differences among the materials.

An index of metamerism has been devised and recommended by the CIE. It is the color difference between two samples illuminated with source A, provided that those samples match in D_{65}. The color difference in illuminant A is to be evaluated by use of one of the formulas for color difference recommended by the CIE. Those formulas will be discussed in Sect. 8.4.

7.5 Maximum Visual Efficiency of Colored Materials

The term *visual efficiency* will be used to refer to both the luminance factor Y of reflecting materials and the luminous transmittance Y of transparent materials. For any specified chromaticity O the maximum possible visual efficiency in illuminant I requires a spectrophotometric curve like Figs. 7.17 – 20. In general, the spectral reflectance or transmittance must be either zero or 100%, with not more than two transitions in the visible spectrum between these values. Those transitions must be abrupt; for example, if one occurs at wavelength λ_1, then τ or $\rho = 0$ for $\lambda < \lambda_1$ and τ or $\rho = 1$ for $\lambda \geq \lambda_1$, or the reverse.

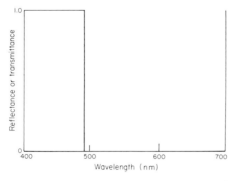

Fig. 7.17 Spectrophotometric curve of short-end type of optimal color

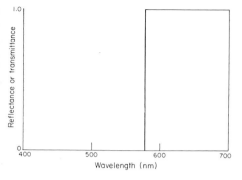

Fig. 7.18 Spectrophotometric curve of long-end type of optimal color

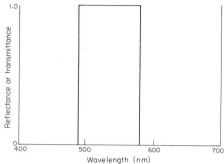

Fig. 7.19 Spectrophotometric curve of high-middle type of optimal color

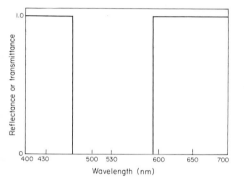

Fig. 7.20 Spectrophotometric curve of low-middle type of optimal color

The only possible deviations from the kind of curves shown in Fig. 7.17 are τ or ρ greater than 0 for some wavelengths greater than λ, and τ or ρ less than 1 for λ and some wavelengths less than λ, as indicated in Fig. 7.21. Similar deviations with respect to one or both transition wavelengths are the only changes possible for spectrophotometric curves of the types shown in Figs. 7.18 – 20.

Addition of transmittance or reflectance at wavelengths for which it was originally zero introduces mass whose center of gravity P must be separated from O by the straight line drawn between λ and I in Fig. 7.22 or by the line drawn through λ_1 and λ_2 in the case of colors like Figs. 7.19, 20. Reduction of transmittance or reflectance at wavelengths at which it was originally 1 subtracts mass whose center of gravity is at Q, which is on the same side as O of the line indicated in Fig. 7.22, for the corresponding type of ideal curve. Therefore Q is closer to O than is P.

In order to preserve the original chromaticity unchanged, the center of gravity of the net change must be coincident with O.[40] For the center of gravity of the net change to be coincident with O, the points O, Q, and P must

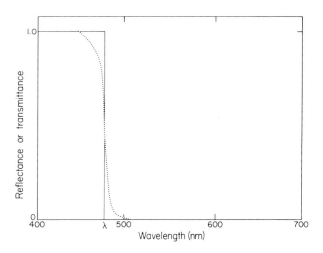

Fig. 7.21 Possible variation on spectrophotome-
tric curve of short-end
type of optimal color

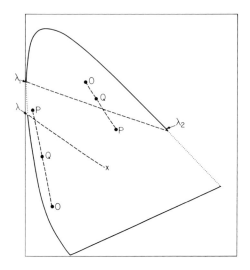

Fig. 7.22
Centers of gravity of differences
between optimal colors and typical
modifications

all be on a single straight line, and the moments of P and Q with respect to O must be equal. Because Q is closer to O than is P, the mass m_Q of the reduction of τ or ρ must be greater than m_P. If P and Q are lower than O, then y_P is less than y_Q; because both factors are less, the increase $\Delta Y_P = y_P m_P$ of visual efficiency is less than the decrease $\Delta Y_Q = y_Q m_Q$. Therefore, the visual efficiency is decreased by any modification of Figs. 7.17 – 19 whose net center of gravity is coincident with the original chromaticity. The same is true for colors of the type illustrated by Fig. 7.20, for which P and Q are higher than O. Then ΔY_P is again less than ΔP_Q *because the ratio* m_Q/m_P, which is equal to the ratio of the distances of P and Q from O, is greater than the ratio y_P/y_Q of their distances from the $y = 0$ axis.

The loci of chromaticities for which the maximum possible visual efficiencies in illuminant C have the indicated values are shown in Fig. 7.23. Similar loci for illuminant A are shown in Fig. 7.24.

A model prepared from Fig. 7.23 is shown by the stereoscopic pair of photographs in Fig. 7.25.[41] The values of λ_1 and λ_2 required in illuminant C for various visual efficiencies and dominant wavelengths are shown in Figs. 7.26, 27.[42]

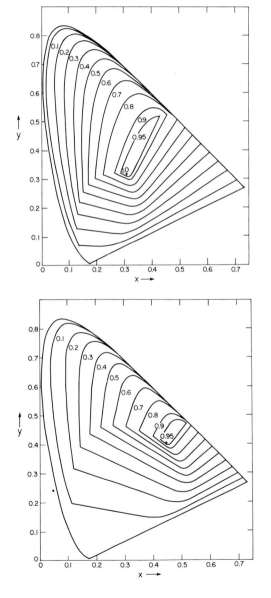

Fig. 7.23 Maximum visual efficiencies of transmitting or reflecting materials in illuminant C

Fig. 7.24 Maximum visual efficiencies of transmitting or reflecting materials in illuminant A

Fig. 7.25 Stereoscopic pair of photographs of model prepared from Fig. 7.23

Fig. 7.26 Dominant ▷ wavelengths λ of optimal colors for indicated transition wavelengths $λ_1$ and $λ_2$ in illuminant C

Fig. 7.27 Transition ▷ wavelengths of optimal colors for indicated visual efficiencies and dominant or complementary wavelengths in illuminant C

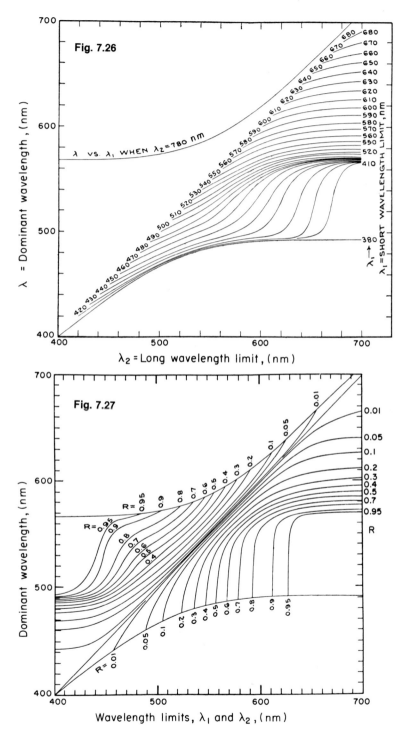

Fig. 7.26

λ vs. λ_1 WHEN $\lambda_2 = 780$ nm

λ = Dominant wavelength, (nm)

λ_1 = SHORT WAVELENGTH LIMIT, nm

λ_2 = Long wavelength limit, (nm)

Fig. 7.27

Dominant wavelength, (nm)

Wavelength limits, λ_1 and λ_2, (nm)

7.6 Linear Spectrophotometric Curves

Spectrophotometric curves of many natural materials exhibit almost linear relationships between transmittance or reflectance and wavelength. This characterizes most spectrophotometric curves for hair and many of wood, paper, pulp, minerals, and untinted papers and textiles. Such materials have dominant wavelengths in the neighborhood of 580 nm.

If the spectrophotometric data are assumed to be exactly linear with wavelength, for example,

$$\rho = c + d(\lambda - 400)/300,$$

then, for the 1931 observer and illuminant C,

$$
\begin{aligned}
X &= 0.9804c + 0.54d \\
Y &= c + 0.5243d \\
Z &= 1.1812c + 0.2172d \\
x &= (0.9804c + 0.54d)/(3.1616c + 1.2815d) \\
y &= (c + 0.5243)/(3.1616c + 1.2815d).
\end{aligned}
$$

The dominant wavelength of all colors for which d is positive is 580.1 nm. When d is negative, the dominant wavelength is 480.1 nm. When $c = 0$ and $d = 1$, the excitation purity is 54.9% and the visual efficiency is 52.4%. When $c = 0$ and $d = -1$, the excitation purity is 34.8% and the visual efficiency (Y) is 47.6%.

8. Color Differences

Analogous to Mercator charts and other kinds of maps of the world that misrepresent the ratios of distances, the chromaticity diagram does not represent perceptually equal color differences by equal distances between points that represent equally luminous colors. The noticeability of color differences was not considered − very few data were available − when the chromaticity diagram was devised and adopted. However, as soon as it came into use, anomalies were encountered in interpreting the configurations of points on the diagram. Inconsistencies between distances and perceived magnitudes of color differences were evident. The analogy with geographical maps was quickly noted and suggestions were made to change the representation so that equal distances would represent equally noticeable color differences. The hoped-for chromaticity diagram with such properties came to be called "uniform". The search for it has extended over 50 years and seems no nearer its goal than at the beginning. Much of the accumulated evidence indicates that the goal is unattainable − that a flat diagram cannot represent equal color differences by equal distances any more than a flat map of the world can represent equal geographical distances by equal distances on the map. Nevertheless, useful methods have been devised for evaluating color differences in terms of chromaticity differences.

8.1 Representations of Chromaticity Differences

An early example of the problem is represented in Fig. 8.1, which is an enlargement of a small portion of the CIE 1931 chromaticity diagram in the yellow region. The point labeled "standard" represents the chromaticity of a yellow material for which many attempted matches were made. Over a period of many years prior to 1931, four samples had been selected to illustrate the extreme variations of chromaticity that would be tolerated. When routine spectrophotometry and the associated colorimetric calculations became feasible, the tolerance samples were found to be represented by the points labeled "Red" for the reddish tolerance limit, "Green" for the greenish limit, "Strong" for the high-purity limit, and "Weak" for the low-purity limit. Thereafter, samples submitted for approval were measured spectrophotometrically and represented by points on the chromaticity diagram. The

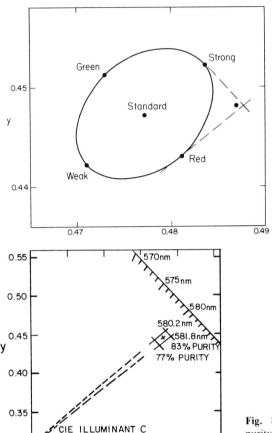

Fig. 8.1 Color tolerances in yellow portion of chromaticity diagram

Fig. 8.2 Dominant wavelengths and purity limits that express the tolerances indicated by the quadrilateral in Fig. 8.1

tolerances came to be expressed in terms of dominant wavelength 581 ± 0.8 nm and purity 80 ± 3%, as indicated in Fig. 8.2. Those numerical tolerances seemed to simplify the decision problem in cases of combined hue and strength (i.e., purity) deviations from the standard yellow. For a time, samples as far from the standard as that indicated in Fig. 8.1 near the red and strong were accepted. However, doubts began to be expressed concerning the acceptability of such samples. A visual study of the acceptability of a large variety of samples whose chromaticities were reasonably well distributed within and near the quadrilateral in Fig. 8.1 led to the conclusion that many samples whose chromaticities were near the corners of that quadrilateral were unacceptable. The decision was made to accept only samples whose chromaticities were within or on the ellipse inscribed in the quadrilateral. No difficulties or objections have ever been encountered with the use of that criterion.

In the meantime, many other colors were brought into the acceptance-control program and the advisability of generalizing the ellipse method was recognized.

As a result of a systematic experimental investigation, equal-noticeability ellipses were established around 25 standard chromaticities, as shown (10 times enlarged) in Fig. 8.3. Those ellipses were determined as results of over 20,000 separate color matches by a single young observer, PGN, who had normal color vision. For each match, the observer turned a knob that caused the chromaticity in one-half of a circular spot to vary along a straight line through one of the 25 standard chromaticities. The standard chromaticity was continuously visible in the other half of the spot, which subtended 2° and was surrounded by an extended (21° diameter) field of daylight (illuminant C) quality.

The luminance of the surrounding field was half that of the test spot[43]. The luminance of both halves of the test spot was about 50 candelas per square meter. The luminance of the variable half of the test field was kept at 50 cdm^{-2} by an optical system especially designed to keep the luminance constant while the chromaticity varied.

In Fig. 8.3, the radius in the direction of variation is ten times the standard deviation of 30 matches in a single observation session. Six to eight directions of variation through each standard were used, in different observation

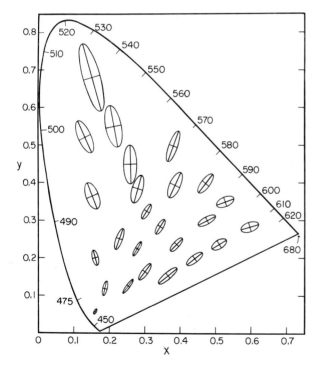

Fig. 8.3 Standard deviations (10 × enlarged) of color matches for 25 aim colors in CIE 1931 chromaticity diagram

sessions. The ellipse around each center was fitted as closely as possible to those radii. The ellipse whose center was nearest to the chromaticity of the standard yellow in Figs. 8.1, 2 has nearly the same shape and orientation as the ellipse in Fig. 8.2.

In a separate experiment, the observer determined that a just-noticeable difference of chromaticity is about twice the standard deviation of chromaticity difference in the same conditions – test-field size and luminance and surround quality, luminance and size. Therefore, the radii of the ellipses in Fig. 8.3 represent color differences about five times just-noticeable. The distribution of deviations was normal[44], so a just-noticeable deviation – about twice the standard deviation – would be expected about once in twenty matches.

Each ellipse in Fig. 8.3 provides good approximations for equally noticeable chromaticity differences around any chromaticity within it. For any reference-standard chromaticity that is represented by a point within it but not coincident with its center, the ellipse may be moved without change of orientation, so that its center is at the point that represents the new reference-standard chromaticity. Then, if a single other chromaticity is known that is just-noticeably or barely acceptably different from that reference chromaticity, any other chromaticity that is at the same multiple of the radius of the ellipse through it as the reference chromaticity will also be just-noticeably or barely acceptably different from the reference chromaticity.

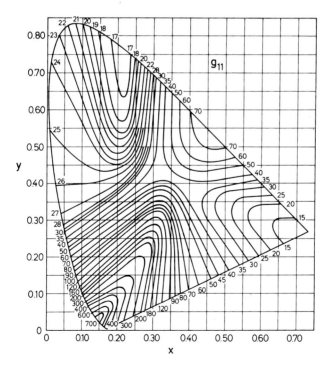

Fig. 8.4 Contours of g_{11} $\times 10^{-4}$ based on ellipses in Fig. 8.3

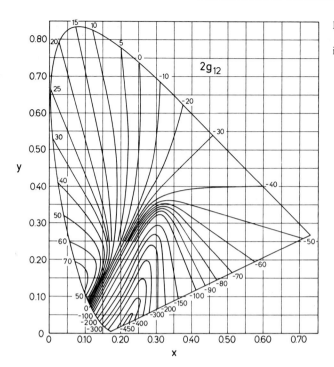

Fig. 8.5 Contours of $2g_{12}$ $\times\ 10^{-4}$ based on ellipses in Fig. 8.3

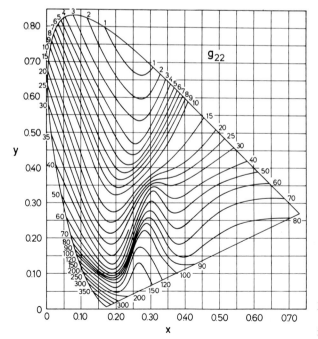

Fig. 8.6 Contours of g_{22} $\times\ 10^{-4}$ based on ellipses in Fig. 8.3

Similar procedures that employ the ellipses in Fig. 8.3 have been used with satisfactory results in many laboratories throughout the world for nearly four decades. During that period, there have been several other experimental investigations of color differences, but none have been more extensive and, even within restricted ranges, none are clearly more reliable than the results shown in Fig. 8.3.

For any reference chromaticity that is not inside any of the ellipses in Fig. 8.3, it is necessary to estimate an ellipse whose size, shape, and orientation are intermediate among those of the nearest ellipses in Fig. 8.3. Many people consider unaided estimation of such intermediate ellipses ambiguous and uncertain. Significantly different results are sometimes estimated by different people. Figures 8.4 – 6 make such estimations straightforward and unambiguous [45].

The unmagnified ellipse centered in any point x, y satisfies the equation

$$g_{11}(\Delta x)^2 + 2g_{12}(\Delta x)(\Delta y) + g_{22}(\Delta y)^2 = 1,$$

where g_{11} is 10,000 times the value interpolated for the point x, y between the nearest contours in Fig. 8.4, $2g_{12}$ is 10,000 times the value interpolated for the point x, y between the nearest contours in Fig. 8.5 (for many locations the value of $2g_{12}$ is negative), g_{22} is 10,000 times the value interpolated for the point x, y between the nearest contours in Fig. 8.6, Δx is the difference between the x coordinates of the center and any point on the ellipse, and Δy is the difference between the y coordinates of the center and that same point on the ellipse. The ellipse referred to here is the original ellipse whose radii are the standard deviations of chromaticity matching, not the 10-times-enlarged ellipses in Fig. 8.3.

The same coefficients, g_{11}, $2g_{12}$, and g_{22}, can be used to define a measure of chromaticity difference

$$\Delta C = \sqrt{g_{11}(\Delta x)^2 + 2g_{12}(\Delta x)(\Delta y) + g_{22}(\Delta y)^2},$$

where Δx is the difference between the x coordinate of any reference, or "standard" chromaticity and the x coordinate of any "sample" chromaticity, and Δy is the difference of their y coordinates.

If $\Delta C = 1$, then the chromaticity difference between the standard and sample is equal to the standard deviation of matching in that direction, by PGN. If $\Delta C = 2$, the chromaticity is just-noticeably different to such an observer. If in any application a standard differs from a just-acceptable sample that has exactly the same luminance factor by $\Delta C = A$, then any other sample that has that same luminance factor and also has $\Delta C = A$ will also be just acceptable. This is true so long as acceptable or tolerable differences depend on only the perceptibility of chromaticity differences. This seems to be the case for most consumers who are not involved with production of colors.

Persons concerned with production of colored materials are often influenced by the availability or costs of ingredients. Their criteria of acceptability of mismatches are also sometimes influenced by the criticalness of the dependence of some perceptual attribute of color, such as hue, on the difficulty and cost of close control of some production variable, such as colorant-concentration ratio or coating thickness. Production people may have, consequently, different or additional criteria for acceptability than perceptibility. For such persons, the ellipses in Fig. 8.3 and any based on Figs. 8.4 – 6 may not be sufficient indications of chromaticity tolerance. We will return to the distinction of acceptability from perceptibility in Sect. 8.4.

Although it is rarely necessary to draw ellipses, their parameters are easily determined from values of g_{11}, $2g_{12}$ and g_{22}. The inclination θ from the horizontal positive x direction of the major axis of the ellipse centered on any point x, y is

$$\theta = 0.5 \tan^{-1}[2g_{12}/(g_{11} - g_{22})] \quad \begin{array}{l} <90° \quad \text{when} \quad g_{12} < 0, \quad \text{or} \\ >90° \quad \text{when} \quad g_{12} > 0. \end{array}$$

The half lengths a and b of the major and minor axes are

$$a = 1/\sqrt{g_{22} + g_{12} \cot \theta} \quad \text{and}$$
$$b = 1/\sqrt{g_{11} - g_{12} \cot \theta}.$$

Note that g_{12} is one half of the value indicated in Fig. 8.5.

As an example of the evaluation of a chromaticity difference, consider the two yellow lines D_1 and D_2 in the spectrum of sodium at 589.00 and 589.59 nm. Their chromaticities are represented by the points $x = 0.5693$, $y = 0.4300$ and $x = 0.5728$, $y = 0.4265$, respectively. Although those points are outside the region covered by the experiments on which the ellipses and the contour maps in Fig. 8.4 – 6 were based, the trends of the contours were so well defined and regular that the extrapolations involved in this calculation are probably not seriously in error. From Fig. 8.4, $g_{11} = 42 \times 10^4$ in the neighborhood of the sodium D lines. From Fig. 8.5, $2g_{12} = -38 \times 10^4$, and from Fig. 8.6, $g_{22} = 37 \times 10^4$. From these and the value of $\Delta x = 0.0035$ and $\Delta y = -0.0035$ for the sodium D lines,

$$\Delta c = \sqrt{42 \times 0.1225 + 38 \times 0.1225 + 37 \times 0.1225} = 3.8.$$

This indicates that the chromaticity difference between the two D lines in the spectrum of sodium is 3.8 times as great as the standard deviations of chromaticity matching by PGN, or a little less than twice the just-noticeable difference.

A second example will indicate the general utility of the formula and will illustrate its use for comparing chromaticity differences. The chromaticity of the light from a blackbody at a temperature of 4000 K is represented by the point at $x = 0.3805$, $y = 0.3768$ and that of a blackbody at 3900 K is at $x = 0.3850$, $y = 0.3795$. For these $\Delta x = 0.0045$ and $\Delta y = 0.0027$. The coefficients for this region, indicated by Figs. 8.4–6 are $g_{11} = 39 \times 10^4$, $2g_{12} = -43 \times 10^4$, and $g_{22} = 25 \times 10^4$. Consequently

$$\Delta c = \sqrt{39 \times 0.45^2 - 43 \times 0.45 \times 0.27 + 25 \times 0.27^2} = \sqrt{4.5} = 2.1 \,.$$

This indicates that a difference of 100 K of color temperature near 4000 K is slightly more than twice the standard deviation of chromaticity matching by PGN. Therefore, it is just noticeable and slightly more than half as noticeable as the difference between the sodium D lines.

It is sometimes desirable to choose, from a continuous series of chromaticities that are represented by a smooth locus on the chromaticity diagram, the chromaticity that is least different from a certain chromaticity that is near, but not on that locus. Such a problem was discussed in connection with correlated color temperature in Sect. 6.1. The coefficients g_{11}, $2g_{12}$ and g_{22} are useful for the solution of such problems. For example, the point at $x = 0.384$, $y = 0.384$ is not on the blackbody locus, but is near to it at 4000 K. The chromaticity of the most nearly similar blackbody might be determined by constructing the ellipse centered on the point 0.384, 0.384 and drawing the tangent that is parallel to the nearest portion of the blackbody locus (Fig. 8.7). The intersection of the blackbody locus with the straight line drawn through the center of the ellipse and the point of tangency represents the chromaticity of the most nearly similar blackbody. In the neighborhood of 4000 K, the color-metric coefficients are those that were used in the preceding paragraph. For those values, the major axis of the ellipse is inclined 54.8°

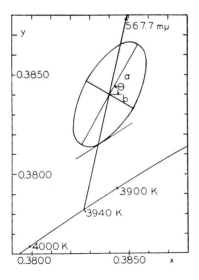

Fig. 8.7 Ellipse near 4000 K, illustrating method for determining correlated color temperature

counterclockwise from the horizontal. The cotangent of that angle is 0.5765 and the half lengths of the major and minor axes are 0.0029 and 0.0014. These values were used to construct the ellipse in Fig. 8.7.

That construction is, however, not necessary to get the result indicated in Fig. 8.7. The slope of the line drawn from the center to the point of tangency is $m' = -(g_{11} + g_{12}m)/(g_{12} + g_{22}m)$, where m is the slope of the nearest portion of the blackbody locus. The average slope m of the blackbody locus between 3900 and 4000 K is $0.0027/0.0045 = 0.6$, so the slope of the line from the center of the ellipse (the original off-locus chromaticity) to the point of tangency and to the nearest blackbody is

$$m' = -(39 - 21.5 \times 0.6)/(-21.5 + 25 \times 0.6) = 4.$$

The line with slope 4 is easily constructed through the point 0.384, 0.384. Its intersection with the blackbody locus is at $x = 0.3826$, $y = 0.3784$, which is the point that represents a blackbody at 3950 K. The amount of chromaticity difference between that point and the point at 0.384, 0.384 is

$$\sqrt{39 \times 0.14^2 - 43 \times 0.14 \times 0.56 + 25 \times 0.56^2} = 2.3 .$$

The kind of difference between the chromaticity represented by the point 0.384, 0.384 and the most nearly similar blackbody (3950 K) can be specified by its dominant wavelength with respect to that blackbody or, which is the same, by the conjunctive wavelength determined by continuing the line with slope m' until it intersects the spectrum locus. In the present instance, the dominant or conjunctive wavelength is 568.1 nm. Consequently, the chromaticity represented by the point $x = 0.384$, $y = 0.384$ has a color temperature of 3950 K and differs from a blackbody at that temperature by slightly more than one just-noticeable difference in the yellowish-green direction characterized by the dominant or conjunctive wavelength 568.1 nm.

If the series, analogous to the blackbodies, from which the selection is to be made, is represented by a nearly vertical locus, use of its reciprocal slope, $M = \Delta x/\Delta y$, to obtain the slope of the line between the off-locus point and the most similar member of the series should be calculated from

$$m' = -(g_{11}M + g_{12})/(g_{12}M + g_{22}).$$

It is frequently desirable to represent the chromaticity relationships among a large number of similar samples, one of which, for example, may be a standard to which all of the others may be attempted matches. Such distributions of chromaticities can, of course, be represented by plotting them in the x, y diagram. The standard-deviation ellipse for the standard or any appropriate enlargement of it can be drawn on the x, y diagram, as in Fig. 8.8. All points inside the ellipse represent chromaticities that are within the tolerance represented by the ellipse. Points outside the ellipse represent

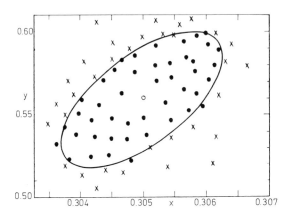

Fig. 8.8 Chromaticities of attempted matches, in relation to standard-deviation ellipse around aim color

chromaticities that differ from the standard by more than the tolerance. Graphical construction of diagrams such as Fig. 8.8 is inconvenient. Some simpler graphical representation is desirable.

A simpler graphical construction is facilitated by the coefficients g_{11}, g_{12}, g_{22} for the reference standard or the center of the expected distribution of chromaticities. The standard-deviation ellipse for PGN is transformed into a circle of unit radius when x and y are plotted with (usually) unequal scales along axes that are (usually) not at a right angle to each other. The cosine of angle w between those axes is

$$g_{12}/\sqrt{g_{11}g_{22}}.$$

The scale unit for x, measured along the horizontal axis, is $\sqrt{g_{11}}$. The scale unit for y, measured along the other axis above the horizontal at the angle w, is $\sqrt{g_{22}}$. Figure 8.9 shows such a diagram, which corresponds to Fig. 8.8. Unit distance in any direction, measured with the scale used to locate the lines that represent constant values of x and y in Fig. 8.9, represents PGN's standard deviation of color matching. The experimental results from which one of the ellipses in Fig. 8.3 was determined are plotted in the corresponding oblique-coordinate diagram in Fig. 8.9. In that region, $g_{11} = 102 \times 10^4$, $g_{12} = -50 \times 10^4$, and $g_{22} = 53 \times 10^4$. Therefore, the angle between the oblique-coordinate axes is

$$\cos^{-1}(-50/\sqrt{102 \times 53}) = \cos^{-1}(-0.679) = 132.8°.$$

The lengths of the graphed 0.001 increments of x and y were $0.001 \times \sqrt{102 \times 10^4} = 1.01$ cm and $0.001 \times \sqrt{53 \times 10^4} = 0.73$ cm in the original drawing. A circle of 1 cm radius was drawn around the point $x = 0.305$, $y = 0.323$ of the chromaticity that PGN attempted to match. The departures of the experimental points from that circle are not significantly greater than were the departures of the corresponding ellipse in Fig. 8.3 from the experimental results plotted in the CIE x,y diagram.

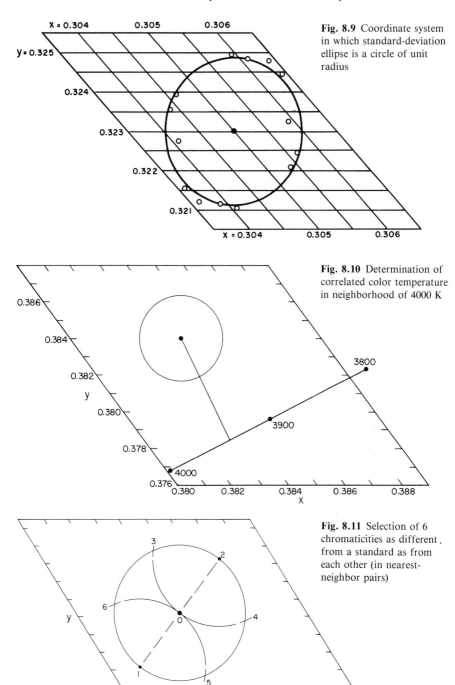

Fig. 8.9 Coordinate system in which standard-deviation ellipse is a circle of unit radius

Fig. 8.10 Determination of correlated color temperature in neighborhood of 4000 K

Fig. 8.11 Selection of 6 chromaticities as different . from a standard as from each other (in nearest-neighbor pairs)

Within the region for which the oblique-coordinate axes in Fig. 8.8 are appropriate, that is, within which g_{11}, g_{12}, g_{22} do not change by more than 25%, the ordinary metrical properties of plane geometry are applicable to the chromaticities represented. Thus, the closest match to a given chromaticity that can be found in a series represented by a smooth, continuous locus in that region is at the foot of the perpendicular to the locus, drawn from the given chromaticity. This is represented for the same case as in Fig. 8.7 by the diagram in Fig. 8.10. As another example, six chromaticities as noticeably different from a central chromaticity as from each other are indicated in Fig. 8.11 by the six corners of a regular hexagon inscribed in a circle whose radius represents the desired color difference.

The appropriate oblique coordinate system needs to be constructed for each region of interest. It should not be extended into regions in which any one of g_{11}, g_{12}, or g_{22} is 25% different than the values with which the coordinate system was designed. Several organizations have prepared and distributed sets of such charts that together cover the entire gamut of practical colors [46].

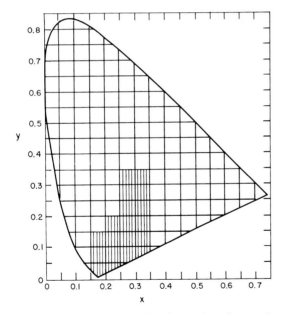

Fig. **8.12** Subdivision of CIE 1931 x, y diagram into rectangles that were converted into equal-noticeability quadrilaterals by use of Figs. 8.4 – 6

For study of the implications of such transformations the CIE x, y diagram was subdivided into horizontal and vertical strips of small rectangles, as shown in Fig. 8.12. Each of those rectangles was transformed into oblique quadrilaterals, by use of the values of g_{11}, g_{12}, and g_{22} from Figs. 8.4 – 6 for the center of each rectangle. Those quadrilaterals were then reassembled into strips in the same order in which they appear in the horizontal strips. When the corresponding edges of adjacent quadrilaterals had significantly different lengths, their centers were made to coincide. In general, the edges of the

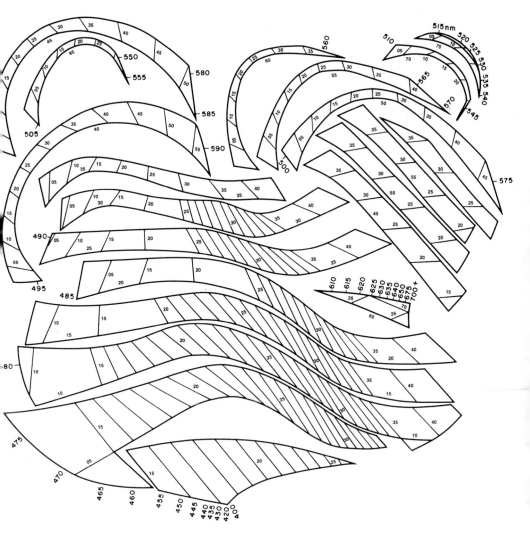

Fig. 8.13 Strips obtained by assembling equal-noticeability quadrilaterals in sequence of original rectangles in Fig. 8.12. Smooth curves have been drawn to replace stepped top and bottom edges. The little numerals on or under those curves indicate the corresponding values of the CIE y coordinates. The little numerals on the transverse lines indicate the values of the x coordinates. The decimal points before those numerals have been lost in reproduction

reassembled strips were slightly stepped. Drawing curves that smoothed the top and bottom edges of each strip produced the strips shown in Fig. 8.13.[47]

Finally, those curved strips were assembled by fitting together as nearly as possible the corresponding points that represented the same value of x on the

Fig. 8.14 Photograph of surface produced when strips shown in Fig. 8.13 were assembled so that corresponding points on edges were placed together (as nearly as possible)

top edge of one strip as on the bottom edge on the strip next above it. Because those edges had different curvatures, the adjacent strips could not be thus fitted together without allowing them to curl out of a plane. When all of the strips were thus assembled, smooth curves were drawn as nearly as possible through equal values of x. The surface shown in Fig. 8.14 was obtained. The curves seen on it are loci of constant x and y, as indicated by some labels on the surface. When plotted according to those coordinate loci on the surface portrayed, the ellipses in Fig. 8.3 and all other ellipses that represent the same multiples of PGN's standard deviations of chromaticity matching are equal-size circles.

Geodesics, that is, paths that consist of the smallest possible number of just-noticeable differences between pairs of chromaticities, can be found by stretching a thread or a broken rubber band between the points that represent the terminal chromaticities. At inflections, that is, where the center of curvature of the path changes from one side of the surface to the other, the thread or band should be put through a hole in the surface so that it remains everywhere snug against the curved surface. Its direction should be the same on both sides of the surface at the inflection point where it penetrates the surface. The x, y coordinates of a number of points along that path can be interpolated from the loci of constant x and y drawn on the surface. The curve drawn through the corresponding points in the CIE x, y diagram represents the geodesic on the CIE diagram. In general, it is curved − not a straight line as would be the locus of chromaticities produced by additive (light) mixtures of the terminal chromaticities. Geodesics between illuminant C and various spectrum chromaticities, determined by stretching threads on the curved surface shown in Fig. 8.14 are shown in Fig. 8.15.

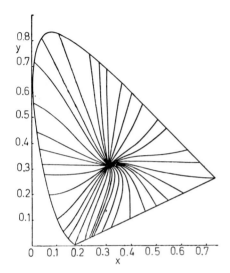

Fig. 8.15 Geodesics (loci of constant hue) between illuminant C and spectrum colors, obtained by stretching thread along surface shown in Fig. 8.14

In 1920, Schrödinger suggested that such geodesics would be loci of constant hue. It was known experimentally that additive mixtures of white with a spectrum light did not, in general, produce a series of colors that all have the same hue[48]. Schrödinger conjectured that by deviating from the series of chromaticities that exhibit the smallest number of just-noticeable differences between white and a spectrum color, the sequence of additive mixtures introduces some subjectively extraneous variation that is perceived as variation of hue. Because he did not have data adequate to determine geodesics, he used a formula (called a "line element") for color difference that had been suggested by Helmholtz several decades previously to show that geodesics were not the same as the results of additive mixture[49].

Helmholtz's line element has been modified by Stiles, on the basis of observations of color differences confined to the immediate neighborhood of the spectrum locus.

Stiles showed that Helmholtz's line element implies that the curvature of the surface represented in Fig. 8.14 should be negative (saddle shaped) everywhere[50]. However, the surface derived from PGN's data, shown in Fig. 8.14, is positive (dome shaped) in the central region and negative only towards the edges. Stiles's conclusion that it should be negative everywhere does not depend on his observational data. It is inherent in Helmholtz's line element. Stiles's modification does not alter that conclusion.

Available evidence indicates that Helmholtz's "line element" formula, even as modified by Stiles, is not adequate for evaluating the relative sizes of equally perceptible equal-luminance differences in the central region of the chromaticity diagram.

Because of its curvature, the surface shown in Fig. 8.14 is not practical for representation of chromaticities. The information in Figs. 8.3−6 is most conveniently employed by use of formulas that involve g_{11}, g_{12}, and g_{22} or by use of oblique-coordinate charts like Figs. 8.9, 10.

8.2 Projective Transformations of the Chromaticity Diagram

Efforts to modify chromaticity diagrams so that equal distances would represent equally noticeable chromaticity differences antedated adoption of the x, y diagram by the CIE in 1931. One such modification, defined in terms of the CIE x, y coordinates, was recommended by the CIE in 1960 despite the then-available evidence that such efforts were doomed to failure.

In general, every modification of the x, y diagram that was considered before 1960 could be represented by the bilinear formulas for two rectangular coordinates

$$u = (c_1 x + c_2 y + c_3)/(c_4 x + c_5 y + c_6)$$
$$v = (c_7 x + c_8 y + c_9)/(c_4 x + c_5 y + c_6).$$

Any diagram defined by such formulas is a projective transformation of the x, y diagram.

Every straight line in the x, y diagram is represented by a straight line in the u, v diagram. All lines in the x, y diagram that are parallel to any one line are represented in the u, v diagram by lines that converge to a single point in the u, v diagram. For different sets of parallel lines in the x, y diagram, the points of convergence are all on a single straight line in the u, v diagram. That line represents all points that are at infinity (where all parallel lines meet) in the x, y diagram. That line in the u, v diagram is called the *apeiron* of the x, y diagram. Conversely, there is a straight line (the apeiron of the u, v diagram) in the x, y diagram that corresponds to all points that are at infinity in the u, v diagram. The equation of that line (the apeiron) can be obtained by setting the common denominator of the formulas for u and v equal to zero,

$$c_4 x + c_5 y + c_6 = 0.$$

That line passes through the two points, $x = -c_6/c_4$, $y = 0$ and $x = 0$, $y = -c_6 c_5$.

For a uniform projective transformation to be possible, in which equally noticeably different chromaticities are represented by equally separated pairs of points, all curves (such as in Figs. 8.16 – 18) of the separations of just-noticeably different chromaticities of straight lines in the u, v diagram, plotted against distance along those lines, would have to be parabolas with vertical axes and zero minima. The locations of the zero minima along different straight lines in the x, y diagram would have to fall on a single straight line – the apeiron of the projective transformation. The separations of just-noticeably different pairs of chromaticities along any one of the lines in the x, y diagram would have to be proportional to the square of the distance of the nearest of each pair of chromaticities from the intersection of that line with the apeiron. Furthermore, the two common tangents of every pair of just-noticeable-difference ellipses in the x, y diagram would have to intersect on the apeiron. The left-hand side of the equation of the apeiron would be the denominator of the formulas for u and v.

None of those requirements for establishing the apeiron are fulfilled by experimental curves like Figs. 8.16 – 18 or by ellipses like those in Fig. 8.3. Every projective transformation of the x, y diagram implies such relations among data for just-noticeable color differences and among ellipses. The crucial significance of the apeiron is evident from this fact. The constants, c_1, c_2, c_3, c_6, c_7, c_8, in the numerators of the formulas for u and v govern merely the location, left or right, up or down, the rotation, and the relative scales, vertical and horizontal, of the chromaticity diagram. They have no influence on relative separations of chromaticities along any single lines in the diagram. Those are influenced only by the ratios C_4/C_6 and C_5/C_6, i.e., by the location of the apeiron.

The formulas recommended by the CIE in 1960 were

$$u = 4x/(12y - 2x + 3), \quad v = 6y/(12y - 2x + 3).$$

The spectrum locus and some of the lines of constant x and constant y are shown in the u, v diagram in Fig. 8.19. The x axis coincides with the horizontal u axis, but the lengths of equal increments of x are proportional to the squares of their distances from the point $u = -2, y = 0$ where all of the lines of constant y converge. In Fig. 8.17, the y axis coincides with the vertical v axis, but the lengths of equal increments of y are proportional to the squares of their distances from the point $u = 0, v = 0.5$ where all of the lines of constant x converge.

The line $u - 4v + 2 = 0$ between the points of convergence of the constant-x lines and the constant-y lines is the apeiron of the x, y diagram. The apeiron ($12y - 2x + 3 = 0$) of the u, v diagram passes through the points $x = 1.5, y = 0$ and $x = 0, y = -0.25$, as shown in Fig. 8.20. The lines across the x, y diagram that correspond to the curves in Figs. 8.16 to 8.18 are shown in Fig. 8.20. Parabolas with vertical axes and zero minima at the intersections

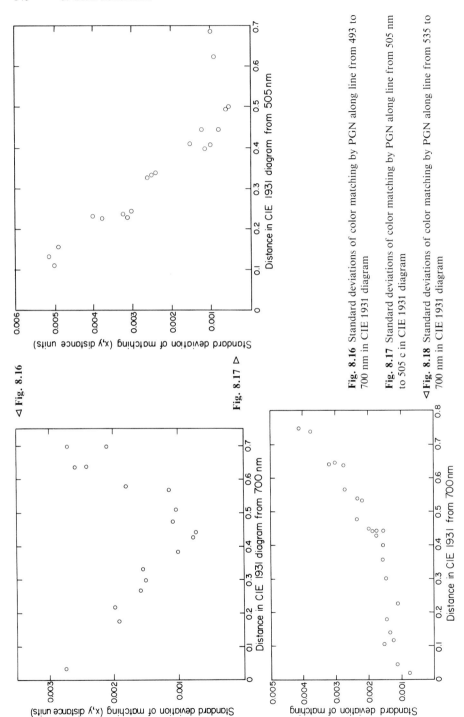

◁ **Fig. 8.16**

Fig. 8.17 ▷

Fig. 8.16 Standard deviations of color matching by PGN along line from 493 to 700 nm in CIE 1931 diagram

Fig. 8.17 Standard deviations of color matching by PGN along line from 505 nm to 505 c in CIE 1931 diagram

◁**Fig. 8.18** Standard deviations of color matching by PGN along line from 535 to 700 nm in CIE 1931 diagram

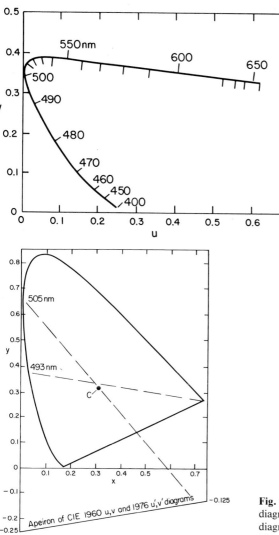

Fig. 8.19
CIE 1960 u, v diagram

Fig. 8.20 Apeiron of CIE 1960 u, v diagram, shown in CIE 1931 x, y diagram with lines corresponding to Figs. 8.16 – 18

of those lines with the apeiron in Fig. 8.20 are shown in Figs. 8.21 – 23, in comparison with the curves from Figs. 8.16 – 18. Those comparisons show how poorly the u, v diagram fits the observed data. The same is indicated by Fig. 8.24, where pairs of lines that converge at points on the apeiron are drawn tangent to a few ellipses selected from Fig. 8.3. In general, one line of each pair is not tangent to more than one ellipse.

The failure of the CIE 1960 u, v diagram to transform the ellipses from Fig. 8.3 into equal-size circles is shown in Fig. 8.25. The revision of the 1960 diagram that was recommended in 1976 by the CIE (which changed the

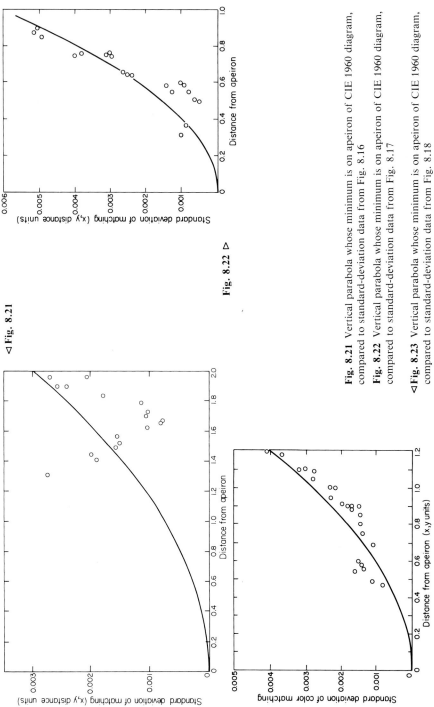

constant in the numerator of the formula for v from 6 to 9) merely expands the diagram 50% vertically, as shown in Fig. 8.26. The revision does not change the apeiron in the x, y diagram. It therefore does not change Figs. 8.21 – 24 in any way and does not make the ellipses in Fig. 8.25 significantly more circular, nor more nearly equal.

No experimental ellipses or line-segment curves like those in Figs. 5.16 – 18 were taken into account when the 1976 revision was proposed. The evidence relied upon was available prior to 1960.

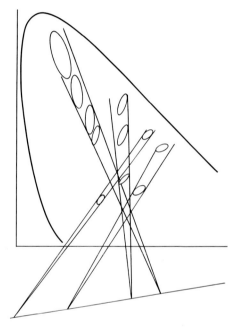

◁**Fig. 8.24** Pairs of lines that converge on apeiron of CIE 1960 diagram are not tangent to pairs of ellipses from Fig. 5.3

▽ **Fig. 8.25** Ellipses from Fig. 8.3 transformed to CIE 1960 u, v diagram

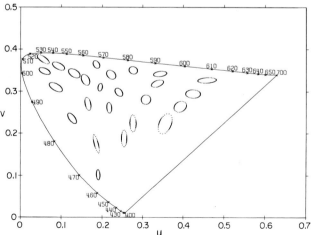

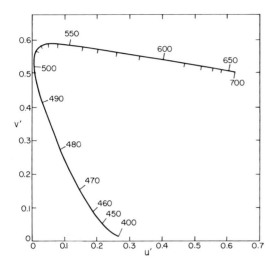

Fig. 8.26
CIE 1976 u', v' diagram

8.3 Nonlinear Transformations of the Chromaticity Diagram

Despite their indicated limitations, the 1960 and 1976 CIE diagrams are about as successful as any projective transform of the x, y diagram can be. Several efforts have been made to construct plane (flat) diagrams that, by allowing straight lines – in particular the lines of constant x and constant y – to be represented by curves, would transform just-noticeable-difference ellipses into nearly equal-size, nearly circular figures, and would represent all just noticeable chromaticity differences by nearly equal separations. Such transformations are called nonlinear.

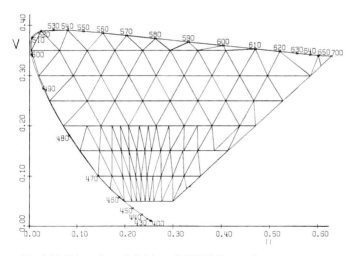

Fig. 8.27 Triangular subdivision of CIE 1960 u, v diagram

One example started from strips of triangles on the CIE 1960 diagram, as shown in Fig. 8.27. The x, y coordinates that correspond to the vertices of those triangles were computed from $x = 1.5 u/(u - 4v + 2)$ and $y = v/(u - 4v + 2)$. The noticeability of the chromaticity difference represented by each side of every triangle was computed as a multiple of the standard deviation of color matching, in that region and direction[51]. That calculation could have been done by use of values of g_{11}, g_{12}, g_{22} interpolated from Figs. 8.4–6. Actually, the chromaticity difference was computed by use of a formula devised by Friele and modified by MacAdam to represent the PGN data.

For use in that formula, the tristimulus values for each vertex were computed from the x, y coordinates for the luminance $Y = 50$ candelas per square meter that was common to all of the colors matched, by PGN, $X = 50x/y$, $Z = 50(1 - x - y)/y$. Then, for use in the Friele-MacAdam formula, those tristimulus values were transformed to

$$P = 0.7X + 0.27Y - 0.1Z$$

$$Q = -0.36X + 1.23Y + 0.1Z$$

$$S = 2.2Z.$$

The average values for the two ends of each side of each triangle were designated

$$P = (P_1 + P_2)/2, \quad Q = (Q_1 + Q_2)/2, \quad S = (S_1 + S_2)/2$$

and their differences were designated

$$\Delta P = P_1 - P_2, \quad \Delta Q = Q_1 - Q_2, \quad \Delta S = S_1 - S_2.$$

From P, Q, S were computed the parameters

$$A = (P^2 + Q^2)^4/(P^4 + Q^4)^2$$
$$T = 22/(S^2 + Q^2 + 2500)$$
$$C_{11} = 7000 (0.16 + A + TS^2)/P^2$$
$$C_{12} = 7000 (0.16 - A + TS^2)/PQ$$
$$C_{22} = C_{11} P^2/Q^2$$
$$C_{33} = 17700 T$$
$$C_{23} = -0.63 S C_{33}/Q$$
$$C_{13} = Q C_{23}/P,$$

then the color difference in units of standard deviation of matching by PGN is

$$\Delta C =$$
$$\sqrt{C_{11}(\Delta P)^2 + 2C_{12}(\Delta P\Delta Q + C_{22}(\Delta Q)^2 + 2C_{23}\Delta Q\Delta S + C_{33}(\Delta S)^2 + 2C_{13}\Delta S\Delta P}.$$

This formula for ΔC is applicable for the evaluation of colors whether equiluminous or not. Note, however, that the value of Y in candelas per square meter should be used in place of the constant 50 in the formulas for X and Z. Likewise, in the formula for T, the constant 2500 should be replaced by Y^2, where Y is the average of the values of Y for the two colors. If, as is often the case, Y is the luminance factor of an object color, that value should be multiplied by the illuminance, lumens per square meter, to convert Y to candelas per square meter. The ellipses (dashed) that correspond to this formula are compared with the PGN ellipses (solid) in Fig. 8.28.

Triangles whose side lengths were proportional to the color differences thus computed were assembled in strips, in the same order as their prototypes in Fig. 8.27. The several strips were placed together as nearly as possible on a plane, as shown in Fig. 8.29. The positions of successive strips relative to each other were adjusted so as to minimize the sum of the squares of the distances between vertices that represent identical points in Fig. 8.27. The midpoint of noncoincident representations of each original vertex was taken as the closest possible representation of it in a plane. Triangles homologous to those in Fig. 8.27 were drawn with those vertices to produce the analog of it, Fig. 8.29, in which standard deviations of chromaticity matching by PGN are most nearly represented by equal distances in a plane.

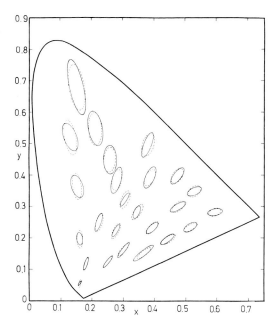

Fig. 8.28 Ellipses that correspond to $\Delta C = 10$, computed from Friele – MacAdam formula, compared to PGN standard-deviation-of-match ellipses in CIE 1931 x, y diagram

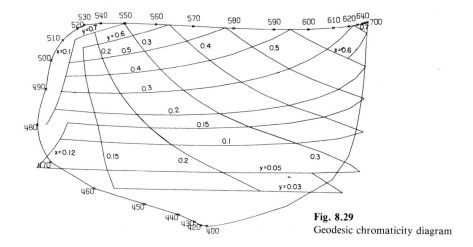

Fig. 8.29
Geodesic chromaticity diagram

Computer experiments with a step-wise linear-regression program yielded formulas for the horizontal ξ and vertical η coordinates of points in Fig. 8.29 in terms of

$$a_1 = 10x/(2.4x + 34y + 1), \quad b_1 = 10y/(2.4x + 34y + 1)$$

$$a_2 = 10x/(4.2y - x + 1), \quad b_2 = 10y/(4.2y - x + 1)$$

$$\xi = 3751\, a_1^2 - 10\, a_1^4 - 520\, b_1^2 + 13295\, b_1^3 + 32327\, a_1 b_1$$
$$\quad - 25492\, a_1^2 b_1 - 41672\, a_1 b_1^2 + 10\, a_1^3 b_1 - 5227\, a_1^{1/2} + 2952\, a_1^{1/4}$$

$$\eta = 404\, b_2 - 185\, b_2^2 + 52\, b_2^3 + 69\, a_2(1 - b_2^2) - 3\, a_2^2 b_2 + 30\, a_2 b_2^3.$$

The spectrum locus and portions of some loci of constant x and y values are shown in the ξ, η diagram in Fig. 8.29.[52] Figure 8.30 shows the results of transforming the PGN ellipses of Fig. 8.3 to the ξ, η diagrams. They are still not circles, but have approximately equal sizes. They are probably the closest approximations to equal-size circles that can represent the PGN data in a plane.

The ξ, η diagram has been called a geodesic diagram because straight lines in it are paths of the smallest number of just-noticeable chromaticity differences between colors represented by pairs of points on those lines. Loci of constant hue, determined by drawing straight lines from the point that represents D_{65} in the ξ, η diagram outward to the spectrum locus, and calculating the x, y coordinates of points that correspond to points on those lines, are shown in Fig. 8.31. Points on ovals that correspond to equal numbers of just-noticeable differences from D_{65} along constant-hue loci are also shown in Fig. 8.31. Those ovals are better indications of perceived saturation than are equal values of purity, such as are indicated by the spade-shaped loci in Fig. 1.16.

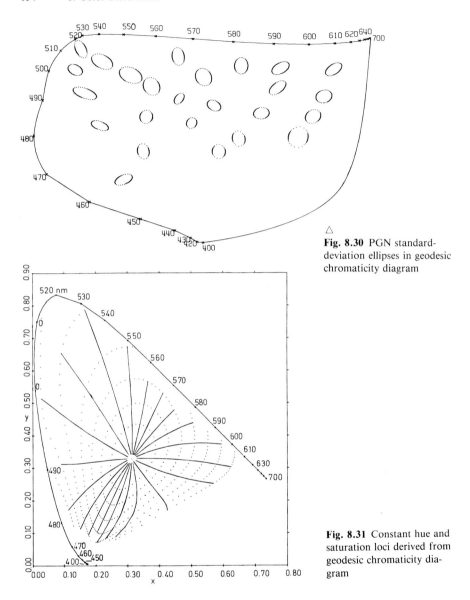

Fig. 8.30 PGN standard-deviation ellipses in geodesic chromaticity diagram

Fig. 8.31 Constant hue and saturation loci derived from geodesic chromaticity diagram

8.4 Noticeability of Combined Lightness and Chromaticity Differences

Conditions of observation, such as field size, separation of samples, sharpness of their edges, and size and luminance of the surrounding field, influence the relative noticeabilities of luminance and chromaticity differences. Such changes can be provided for by variation of the coefficient g_{33} of the term

$$g_{33} \left(\frac{\Delta Y}{Y} \right)^2$$

which is added when coefficients g_{11}, $2g_{12}$, g_{22} from Figs. 8.4 – 6 are used to evaluate the noticeability of combined lightness and chromaticity differences. Use of the relative increment $\Delta Y/Y$ is consistent with Weber's law, where Weber's fraction is $1/\sqrt{g_{33}}$. For a sharp dividing line and samples that subtend about $1°$, g_{33} is about 10^4. For less-well-defined dividing lines, g_{33} may be considerably less. For example, for $5°$ separation of samples that each subtend $5°$ or more, g_{33} is about 50. For perception of the shapes of extremely small samples in a background or surround of slightly different lightness and chromaticity, g_{33} is about 5000, and g_{11}, $2g_{12}$, g_{22} are reduced proportionately to about 1% of the values indicated in Figs. 8.4 – 6.

Use of the single added term $g_{33} (\Delta Y/Y)^2$ implies that all figures that represent just-noticeable color differences, including lightness and chromaticity differences, in the 3-dimensional rectangular coordinate system x, y, Y are ellipsoids that are symmetrical with respect to the planes for which Y is constant through their centers. In other words, one principal axis of each ellipsoid is vertical – parallel to the Y axis – and the other two principal axes are in the horizontal x, y plane, for which $Y = $ constant, through the ellipsoid center. The horizontal cross sections of the ellipsoids whose centers are indicated in Fig. 8.3 are the ellipses shown in that figure.

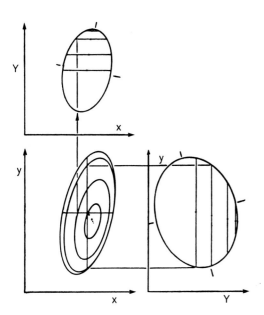

Fig. 8.32 Displacement of chromaticity of maximum point on noticeability ellipsoid

Because of the inclusion of X and Z in the definition of Q, and because of the inclusion of terms that involve the cross products $\Delta P \Delta Q$ and $\Delta Q \Delta S$ in the Friele – MacAdam formula for ΔC, the ellipsoids implied by that formula are slightly tipped. The maximum ΔY of any point on almost every ellipsoid defined by that formula occurs at a chromaticity that differs from the chromaticity of the center, that is, for $\Delta x \neq 0$ and/or $\Delta y \neq 0$, as indicated schematically in Fig. 8.32.

Experimental determinations of such ellipsoids indicated that few, if any, were significantly tipped[53]. The displacements of the chromaticities of their highest points from the chromaticities of their centers are shown in Fig. 8.33, together with their constant-luminance cross sections. The chromaticity displacements, showing the directions and magnitudes of tipping of the tops of all of the experimental ellipsoids are shown in Fig. 8.34 by arrows, 75 times enlarged, from the chromaticities of the centers. Figures 8.33, 34 indicate that the tippings of observed ellipsoids are so random in direction and insignificant

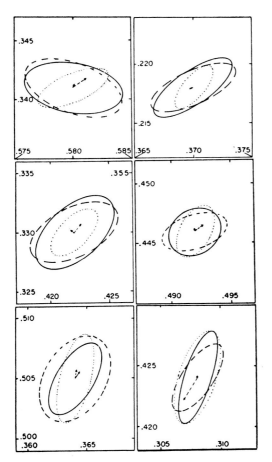

Fig. 8.33 Constant-luminance cross sections and chromaticities of points of highest luminance on ellipsoids of standard deviations of color matching. Dotted and dashed ellipses show results for two observers. Solid arrows refer to dotted ellipses. Solid ellipses were derived from Figs. 8.4 – 6

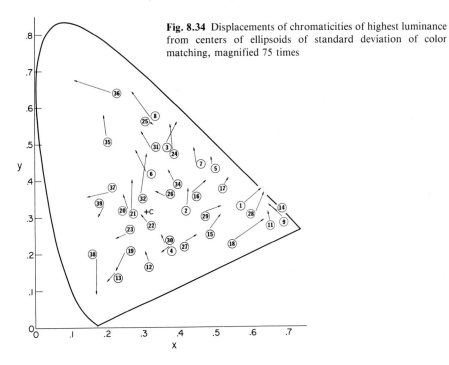

Fig. 8.34 Displacements of chromaticities of highest luminance from centers of ellipsoids of standard deviation of color matching, magnified 75 times

in magnitude that the slight tipping implied by the Friele – MacAdam formula cannot be confirmed or excluded.

Two mutually inconsistent color-difference formulas[54] recommended by the CIE in 1976, however, indicate much greater tippings; they are characterized schematically in Fig. 8.35. As indicated there, the tippings are all toward the illuminant (or "white") point. For each hue, they are proportional to the distance of the ellipsoid centers from the "white" point. These regularities of direction and growth of magnitude of tippings are not indicated by any experimental ellipsoids. Experiments designed especially to reveal such tipping led to the conclusion that if tipping occurs it must be much smaller than is implied by either of the CIE 1976 formulas[55].

One CIE formula, designated CIE Luv, employs the modified u, v diagram[56]. That formula is recommended by the CIE for calculation of metric hue angle, which corresponds to constant-hue lines that are straight on the x, y diagram[57]. The other CIE 1976 formula, designated CIE Lab, involves nonlinear, cube-root transformations of tristimulus values X, Y, Z.[58] Metric hue angle determined by use of that formula corresponds to constant-hue loci that are curved in the x, y diagram. However, they do not agree with experimentally determined constant-hue loci as well as do those in Figs. 8.15, 31. Ellipsoids derived from the CIE Lab formula in the high-purity-yellow region have constant-luminance cross sections whose major axes in the x, y diagram are almost at right angles to those in Fig. 8.3.

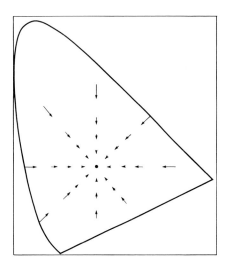

Fig. 8.35 Schematic diagram of displacements of chromaticities of highest luminance on ellipsoids determined by CIE Luv and CIE Lab formulas

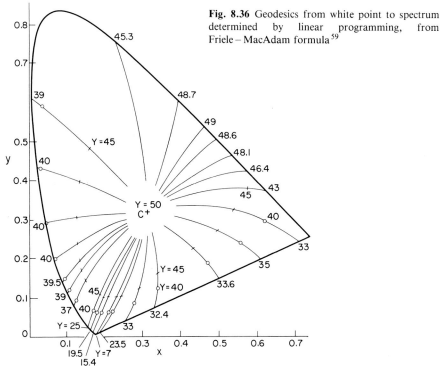

Fig. 8.36 Geodesics from white point to spectrum determined by linear programming, from Friele – MacAdam formula[59]

Dynamic programming was used by Muth and Persels[59] to determine some geodesics from white, D_{65}, to various points on the spectrum locus, according to the Friele – MacAdam formula. The geodesics obtained by Muth and Persels are shown in Fig. 8.36. They are in general agreement with observed constant-hue loci. Muth and Persels also noted the values of luminance Y for various points on the geodesics. In all cases, they assigned $Y = 50$ to the D_{65} point and adjusted the value of Y for the point on the spectrum locus so that the value of Y calculated for the second point on the geodesic, nearest to D_{65}, was 50. Schrödinger had suggested in 1920 that such a geodesic, with zero slope of luminance at its white end, would correspond to constant perceived brightness as well as constant hue. Schrödinger anticipated that, for equal perceived brightness, lesser values of luminance Y of colors of high purity would be required than for white or colors of low purity. This result, which has been confirmed many times by direct observation, is indicated by the values of Y that are written at the spectrum-locus ends of the geodesics in Fig. 8.36. The open circles on the geodesics indicate chromaticities that have 40 candelas per square meter luminance. According to Schrödinger's suggestion, they should appear as bright as 50 candelas per square meter of D_{65}. Solid dots on a few geodesics in the lower, blue-to-purple, region indicate chromaticities for which $Y = 30$.

Jain used the method of steepest descent, with the Friele – MacAdam formula, to determine geodesics between a few noncomplementary spectrum terminations of the Muth and Persels geodesics, Fig. 8.37.[60] Jain used the Muth and Persels terminal (spectrum) values of Y. He found that at the chromaticity intersections, his transverse geodesics had the same values of Y as Muth and Persels's geodesics from white to the spectrum. This consistency of Y over the surface that consists of geodesics that have zero slope at white was proposed by Schrödinger as a requirement for the definition of subjective, or perceived, brightness.

The general agreement of the geodesics in Fig. 8.36 with observed loci of constant hue and with the luminances of high purities that appear as bright as a white of higher luminance is a merit of the Friele – MacAdam formula; that merit is not possessed by any other formula for color difference.

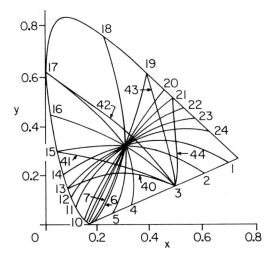

Fig. 8.37 Intersecting geodesics of constant brightness [60]

8.5 Nonlinear Relations of Psychometric Differences to Photometric and Colorimetric Differences

The umbrella-shaped surface of which the geodesics in Fig. 8.36 are ribs could be used to define a scale of subjective brightness or of lightness (for reflecting objects) for chromaticities much different than white. The luminance or luminance factor Y_w of white does not correspond well with perceived ratios of brightness or lightness. When illumination is doubled, for example, by use of two identical lamps shining on the same area that was initially illuminated by one, the brightness of the illuminated surface does not appear to be doubled. As mentioned in Chap. 7 as an aspect of color constancy, the lightness is changed hardly at all by the doubled illumination. Lightness depends almost exclusively on luminance factor, or reflectance of white and gray. But, like brightness, lightness is not perceived to be proportional to luminance factor or even to the reflectance of the equally light gray indicated by Fig. 8.37. For example, a gray that has 40% reflectance does not appear twice as light as a gray that has 20% reflectance.

Various mathematical functions have been proposed and used to define scales of brightness and lightness in terms of luminance and reflectance, respectively. Thus, Fechner defined (brightness) sensation as proportional to the logarithm of luminance[61]. Plateau suggested that it is proportional to the cube root of luminance[62]. Munsell first measured his value (lightness) as the square root of reflectance[63], but later provided printed papers whose reflectances, Y, were found by Judd to be closely related to the values V, with which the papers were labelled, by the quintic polynomial formula

$$Y = 1.2219\,V - 0.23111\,V^2 + 0.23951\,V^3 - 0.021009\,V^4 + 0.0008404\,V^5.$$

Determination of V for any particular value of Y requires either interpolation in a table of Y vs V that Newhall, Nickerson, and Judd published or iterative approximation with the quintic polynomial formula[64]. In 1976, for use in both the CIE Luv and CIE Lab formulas for color difference, the CIE recommended for lightness L^* the cube-root formula

$$L^* = 116(Y/Y_w)^{1/3} - 16.$$

The CIE did not make any provision for the decrease of Y required for constant lightness of high-purity colors. That subject is currently being studied by the CIE committee on colorimetry. As mentioned in Sect. 8.4, the effect is represented by the Friele – MacAdam formula.

The Committee on Uniform Color Scales of the Optical Society of America discovered that perceived ratios of nearly constant-luminance chromaticity differences are not proportional to ratios of chromaticity differences[65]. This was found to be the case even on transformations of small regions of the chromaticity diagram on which all chromaticity differences perceived to be equal to each other are represented by equal distances. For three different color centers and ratios as great as 1.69 of distances in the appropriate transformed chromaticity diagrams, the psychometric scale values of color differences were best fitted by curves that were proportional to the chromatic distances raised to powers that ranged from 0.37 to 0.8. This indicates that the cube-root relation does not give so close an approximation for perceived chromaticity differences as it does for lightness differences. Scale values for equiluminous chromaticity differences are nearly proportional to the square root of distances in a chromaticity diagram on which subjectively equal differences are represented by equal distances. Thus, a chromaticity difference represented on such a diagram by a distance twice as great as another would be judged to be only about 40% greater than the latter.

No studies have been made of the relation between psychometric scale values and combined differences of luminance and chromaticity. A square-root relation would probably not be seriously wrong. Thus, color differences with a ratio of 2 to 1, computed by use of the Friele – MacAdam formula or by either of the CIE 1976 formulas, would probably be judged subjectively to be in the ratio of about 1.4 to 1.

9. Color-Order Systems

At least two centuries before colorimetry attained widespread, routine use, efforts were made to arrange and display colors in orderly manners. I consider it probable that Leonardo da Vinci may have painted sequences in which closely related colors were near each other and contrasting colors were widely separated.

Sir Isaac Newton arranged all hues in a circle, with complementary colors – the most contrasted – at opposite ends of diameters, with similar colors close together on the circumference, and with white at the center.

Moses Harris in 1745 arranged colors of like hue but increasing saturation (colorimetry's purity) at increasing distances from the center along a radius, to the purest he could paint at the rim.

9.1 Ostwald System

Nobelist Wilhelm Ostwald, at the beginning of the 20th century, with almost modern understanding of spectrophotometric properties of dyes and

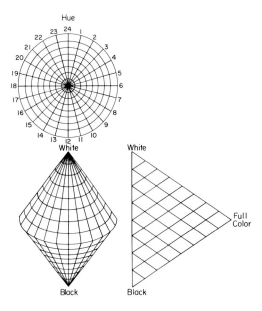

Fig. 9.1 Ostwald's double cone of colors. *Above:* top view, showing hue numbers. *Right:* vertical cross section from black-white axis to any full color. Every intersection in any view represents an Ostwald color

pigments, distributed grays between black and white along an axis perpendicular to the hue circle. He distributed the various tints of each hue from white to what he called the "full color" along a straight line from the apex of a double cone down along its surface to its rim; he put darker shades of the same tints on cones parallel to the top surface, with the darkest tone or shade of each tint on the concave-upward bottom surface of the double cone. This arrangement is indicated schematically in Fig. 9.1. Although he spaced the "pure" hues at various angles around the rim in accordance with his perception of the magnitudes of their differences, he distributed the grays on the axis in proportion to their reflectances and the tints and tones in proportion to physical parameters "color content," "white content", and "black content", which he based on his idealized generalization of spectrophotometric curves. Ostwald did not consider the relative perceptibilities of equal increments of color content or black content in his gray scale or along any of his isotone or isotint scales.

9.2 Munsell System

Contemporary with Ostwald, the artist Munsell painted cards that he presented in a cylindrical arrangement, Fig. 9.2. He prepared a gray series in which he judged the differences of all pairs of successive cards to be equal, from black to white. To extend horizontally outward from each gray, he prepared series of cards that he judged all had the same hue and lightness (which he called value) and equal perceived increases of saturation (which he

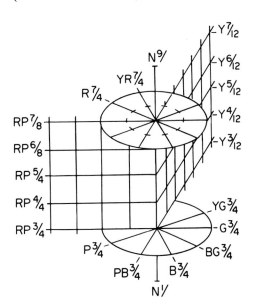

Fig. 9.2 Munsell's cylindrical arrangement of colors. Constant-value scales of chroma are shown on horizontal lines in radial planes of constant hue, RP and Y. Constant-chroma scales of value are shown on vertical lines

called chroma). He extended each of those series of constant hue and value to chromas as great as he could with available paints. Those series have come to be called chroma scales. He selected the colors in scales of like value and similar hues so that the steps of chroma in them appeared equally great. Because of the limitations of available pigments, some of the chroma scales have only two or three steps, whereas others have as many as eight or nine. Munsell assigned even numbers, 2, 4, 6, ... to chroma for the successive cards in his chroma scales. He provided scales of chroma for 10 hues (5 pairs of complementary hues) for each of 9 values numbered from 1 to 8, Fig. 9.2. Munsell chose the hues of his chroma scales so that at equal value and chroma, neighboring hues appeared equally different throughout the cycle of hues.

The Munsell system of colors has been available commercially since 1904. The colors of the cards have been modified many times in efforts to make them exemplify more perfectly the system conceived by Munsell. Additional chroma scales have been added to increase the number of hues to 40. Cards issued about 1934 were measured spectrophotometrically and the CIE color-matching data were used to specify them on the x, y chromaticity diagram. Further modifications, to make the CIE specifications more regular, and to embody subsequent judgments by many other observers, have continued to the present. The 1934 and subsequent measurements and specifications provided the first and, even currently, most complete data on loci of constant hue. Those measurements also show that Munsell value is uniquely related to the CIE tristimulus value Y, the same for all hues and chromas. Persistent reports by observers of variations of perceived lightness along constant-value chroma scales provided some of the earliest and most convincing evidence of the variation (increase) of lightness with saturation (chroma) of colors of constant Y (value). Judgments of the relative magnitudes of the difference between corresponding members (equal value and chroma) of chroma scales of neighboring hues confirm the geometrical necessity, e.g., Fig. 9.3, that equal nominal differences of hue are much more noticeable at high chroma

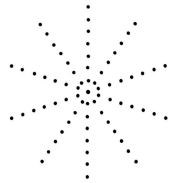

Fig. 9.3 Spacing of Munsell colors on constant-value plane

than at low − in proportion to chroma. This must be true of any system that stems from a scale of grays, such as those of Harris and Ostwald.

Artists, designers, and others concerned with selection of colors and color schemes have found color scales, such as those of Ostwald and Munsell, very suggestive and useful. Those of Munsell have been especially useful insofar as they are subjectively uniformly spaced, which is the case for the chroma scales (constant hue and value) and the lightness scales (black to white and constant hue and chroma).

9.3 Optical Society Uniform-Color-Scale Formula

A committee of the Optical Society of America undertook to review and supplement all available data on subjective magnitudes of color differences and to design a set of color cards that can be assembled to form uniform color scales of as many varieties as feasible[66]. The Munsell chroma scales and lightness scales were considered prototypes; uniform scales of essentially different types were sought. The committee enlisted the aid of 76 normal observers who each reported judgments of ratios of hundreds of pairs of color differences. As a result of thorough analysis of those data, the committee derived the following set of formulas for coordinates $\mathscr{L}$, j, g in a 3-dimensional euclidean space in which the ratios of separations of points that represent the pairs of colors judged by the committee's observers are as nearly as possible equal to the reported judgments:

$$\mathscr{L} = 5.9 \, [Y_0^{1/3} - \tfrac{2}{3} + 0.042 \, (Y_0 - 30)^{1/3}], \quad \text{where}$$

$Y_0 = Y(4.4934 \, x^2 + 4.3034 \, y^2 - 4.276 \, xy - 1.3744 \, x - 2.56439 \, y + 1.8103)$; Y is the CIE 1964 tristimulus value of a color in D_{65} on the basis of $Y = 100$ for white, and x, y are the 1964 CIE chromaticity coordinates;

$$j = C(1.7 \, R^{1/3} + 8 \, G^{1/3} - 9.7 \, B^{1/3})$$

$$g = C(-13.7 \, R^{1/3} + 17.7 \, G^{1/3} - 4 \, B^{1/3}), \quad \text{where}$$

$$C = \mathscr{L}/[5.9(Y_0^{1/3} - \tfrac{2}{3})] = 1 + 0.042 \, (Y_0 - 30)^{1/3}/(Y_0^{1/3} - \tfrac{2}{3}) \quad \text{and}$$

$$R = 0.799 \, X + 0.4194 \, Y - 0.1648 \, Z$$

$$G = -0.4493 \, X + 1.3265 \, Y + 0.0927 \, Z$$

$$B = -0.1149 \, X + 0.3394 \, Y + 0.717 \, Z,$$

where X, Y and Z are the 1964 CIE tristimulus values of a color in D_{65} on the basis of $Y = 100$ for white.

The term $0.042 \, (Y_0 - 30)^{1/3}$ in the formula for $\mathscr{L}$ represents a phenomenon called "crispening", which makes differences in a lightness scale appear

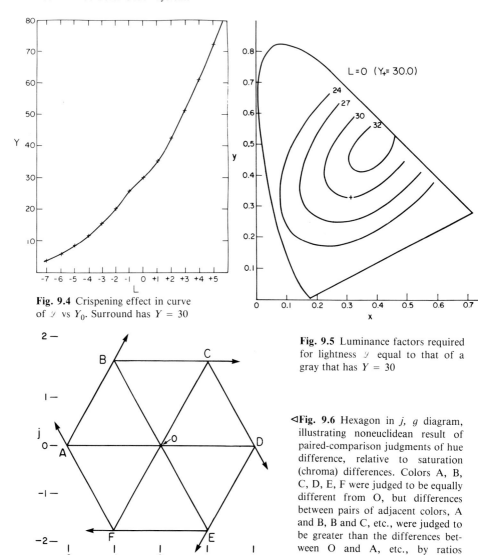

Fig. 9.4 Crispening effect in curve of y vs Y_0. Surround has $Y = 30$

Fig. 9.5 Luminance factors required for lightness y equal to that of a gray that has $Y = 30$

◁**Fig. 9.6** Hexagon in j, g diagram, illustrating noneuclidean result of paired-comparison judgments of hue difference, relative to saturation (chroma) differences. Colors A, B, C, D, E, F were judged to be equally different from O, but differences between pairs of adjacent colors, A and B, B and C, etc., were judged to be greater than the differences between O and A, etc., by ratios indicated by the lengths of the arrows

greater when the luminances compared are close to the luminance of the surrounding field than when they are much greater or less than the surround, as shown in Fig. 9.4. The surround used for all of the committee's comparisons was a medium gray that had 30% luminance factor. The dominant term in $\mathscr{L}$, $5.9[Y_0^{1/3} - \frac{2}{3}]$ is the committee's version of the relation between lightness and luminance factor. It was adopted prior to the 1976 adoption of the formula for L^* by the CIE. Even so, when we note that the maximum value of Y_0 for white is 100 whereas the maximum value of (Y/Y_w) used in the CIE formula for L^* is 1, we find that the subtracted constant $(\frac{2}{3})$ has only 4% greater effect, relative to the cube root, than has the subtracted constant (16) relative to the cube-root term $(116[Y/Y_w] Y^{1/3})$ in the formula for L^*.

The formula for Y_0 represents the effect of saturation in making a color appear lighter than a gray that has the same luminance factor Y. The values of Y required by that formula for colors of various chromaticities that have the same lightness L_0 as a gray that reflects 30%, are shown in Fig. 9.5.

The factor C in the formulas for j and g applies the same crispening to the perception of chromaticity differences as is applied to lightness differences. Use of transformed tristimulus values R, G, B in the formulas for j and g means that chromaticity differences of light colors appear greater than do the same chromaticity differences of dark colors.

The committee strongly recommended that its formula not be used to construct a formula for small color differences, because the color differences used by the committee were all about 20 times just-noticeable differences. Furthermore, multiplication of differences of chromaticity from gray by a function of Y, which is the effect of use of the tristimulus values R, G, B in the formulas for j and g, has the result that ellipsoids of equal noticeability are significantly tipped in CIE x, y, Y space. As discussed in Sect. 8.4, such tipping is not characteristic of perception of small color differences.

Strictly interpreted, the formulas for $\mathcal{L}, j,$ and g should not be used for evaluating large color differences either, because they represent only the committee's results for paired comparisons of large, separated hexagonal tiles on a medium gray background. Furthermore, the committee forced the data into an euclidean form, despite clear indications that the judgment data required noneuclidean representation. The clearest indication of this is that the total of the differences, judged around the perimeter of a hexagon (Fig. 9.6) formed by six colors of equal $\mathcal{L}$ that are all equally distant in the j, g diagram from a neutral gray (D_{65}), would be greater than six times their common judged differences from the gray. The percentage excess over six would probably increase with the size of the common difference from gray. It should increase in proportion with the square of that difference, if the truly representative space is riemannian. The available data are not sufficient for decision concerning this; euclidean representation, which the committee used in order to be able to define uniform color scales, is almost certainly an oversimplification.

The coordinates j and g are zero for grays. Positive values of j, especially when associated with small values of g, indicate yellow or brownish colors. Negative values of j, with nearly zero values of g, indicate blues. Positive values of g, with nearly zero values of j, indicate greens. Negative values of g, with nearly zero j, indicate magentas.

The values of g and j can be computed for spectrum colors. A specific value of Y must be assigned for each wavelength in order to determine the spectrum locus in the g, j diagram. Because, except for dominant wavelengths

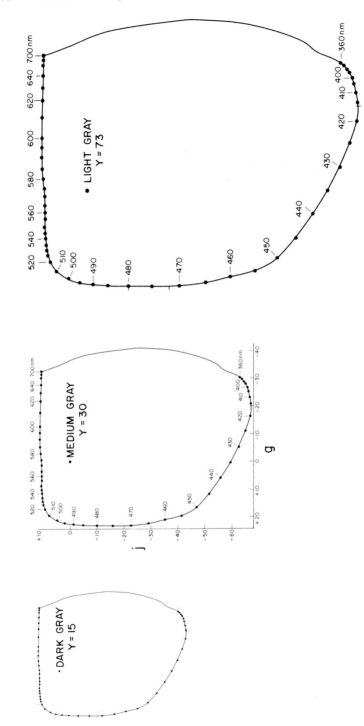

Fig. 9.7 Spectrum loci for $Y = 15$, 30, and 73, in j, g diagram

longer than 570 nm, materials that reflect sufficiently narrow wavelength bands to be represented by points on the spectrum locus have extremely low luminance factors, the spectrum locus for such materials would collapse on the $\mathscr{L}$ axis ($g = j = 0$) near black. Therefore, three values of Y, 15, 30, and 73, have been arbitrarily assigned. The corresponding spectrum loci, with the D_{65} point displaced so as to avoid overlap, are shown in Fig. 9.7. The same scale was used to plot those three spectrum loci. That the locus for $Y = 73$ is larger than that for $Y = 30$ and much larger than that for $Y = 15$ indicates that differences between light colors appear greater than differences between dark colors that have the same chromaticities. The boundary of purples, which is a straight line (between 380 and 700 nm) in Fig. 1.12, is distinctly curved in Fig. 9.7. It and the spectrum locus have identical shapes for all values of Y.

9.4 Uniform Color Scales

The Optical Society committee undertook to design a set of color cards that could be assembled in different ways to form the maximum number of uniform color scales, of as many different kinds as possible. To do this, the committee located about 500 equally spaced points in the $\mathscr{L}$, j, g coordinate system, according to the arrangement of atoms in a regular rhombohedral crystal. Each point in such an arrangement is equidistant from twelve other points. Because distances in the space defined by the $\mathscr{L}$, j, g system are, as nearly as possible in any euclidean space, proportional to the perceived differences of colors represented by pairs of points, the committee arranged for such colors to be made with glossy acrylic paints. They succeeded in obtaining 424 of the colors thus specified, all made with the most-permanent pigments available. Those colors can be arranged in 422 different color scales of three or more colors that correspond in the $\mathscr{L}$, j, g space to points equally separated along six different sets of equally separated parallel lines. Two of those sets of parallel lines identify series of equally light colors. All of the other uniform color scales range from dark colors to light, with novel variations of hue and saturation, for example, from deep green through pastel greenish yellow to bright orange. Only one of each set of eight to ten of each different kind of color scale includes gray. All of the other color scales, including the same proportion of the scales of colors of equal lightness, are chromatic throughout. In this feature, the Optical Society color scales differ from the color scales provided by the Ostwald and Munsell systems. Most of the OSA scales are of kinds that have never before been seen.

A few of the OSA uniform color scales are shown in Plates I to III.[67]

Although accuracy cannot be claimed for the color reproduction in Plates I to III, the variety and characteristics of the color sequences are well shown. Each line of colors that have sides adjacent to each other, in any direction in Plates I to III, is a uniform color scale. All of the differences of adjacent colors (including lightness-difference components) are subjectively equal in all scales. The over-all arrangement of the colors and scales is shown by the photograph of a model of the system in Plate IV. In the model, all colors and

scales of equal lightness are on horizontal layers. Plate I shows the arrangement of colors and scales in one of those layers. Vertical layers consist of scales that are aligned at 45° to the horizontal (in both senses) as shown in Plate II. Two mutually perpendicular sets of parallel vertical planes of that kind make up the model. Finally, four sets of slant planes that are parallel to the faces of a pyramid can also be traced in the photograph of the model (Plate IV). In each of those planes, colors are arranged hexagonally, as shown in Plate III.

Each color in the model is labeled with three integers, which are all either odd (positive or negative) or even (positive, zero, or negative). The first is L, which is related to $\mathscr{L}$ by $L = (\mathscr{L} - 14.4)/\sqrt{2}$. The value of L is zero for the medium gray ($Y = 30$) that was used as the background for the original judgments. Negative values of L represent colors darker than that background. Six colors as dark as $L = -7$ were made and seven colors as light as $L = 5$ were made. The other two numerals in the label of each color are j and g. The requirement that for any one color, all three numerals must be either odd or even, and the denominator $\sqrt{2}$ in the formula for L, established the crystal-lattice arrangement and the equal spacing of all points and colors.

When the 424 colors were made and studied, the committee decided to make 134 more in the medium-lightness and low-purity (grayish) region, so as to subdivide the color differences and to provide finer scales and greater choice of colors in the pastel range. Such colors were made for L from -1.5 to $+1.5$ (including ± 0.5) and for j and g from -2.5 to $+2.5$. The extra colors had labels that were either all fractional or all integers. The integer values of the extra colors were all mixed: even *and* odd.

9.5 Colorimetric Data for Uniform Color Scales

The chromaticities of the colors in the full-step uniform chromaticity scales at values of L from -7 to $+5$ are shown in Figs. 9.8 – 12.[68] Those of the half-step scales, for L from $-1\frac{1}{2}$ to 0 are shown in Figs. 9.13 – 16. The color cards actually made and distributed by the Optical Society of America had values of Y, x, y that inevitably differed from those intended. The color difference between any two colors, in terms of the committee's unit, is $\Delta C = \sqrt{2(\Delta L)^2 + (\Delta j)^2 + (\Delta g)^2}$. For the full-step scales, the average color difference is 2.0, as intended. The root-mean-square deviation of the differences for the 2058 nearest-neighbor pairs was 0.24 or 12% of the average. When the color differences were calculated by use of the 1976 CIE Luv formula, the average was 14.5 with an rms deviation of 3.1 or 21% of the average. The rms deviation of the color differences of the 740 nearest-neighbor pairs in the half-step scales was 0.17 or 16% of the average 1.03. When evaluated with the CIE Luv formula, the average was 7.43 and the rms deviation was 1.60 or 21%.

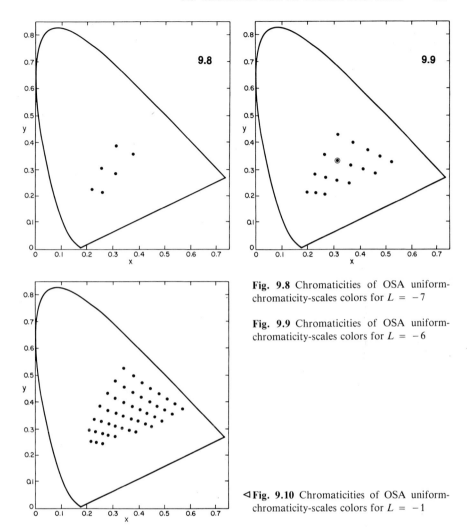

Fig. 9.8 Chromaticities of OSA uniform-chromaticity-scales colors for $L = -7$

Fig. 9.9 Chromaticities of OSA uniform-chromaticity-scales colors for $L = -6$

◁**Fig. 9.10** Chromaticities of OSA uniform-chromaticity-scales colors for $L = -1$

When evaluated by use of the Friele – MacAdam formula, the average color difference between nearest-neighbor pairs in the full-step scales is 20, which indicates that the differences between those nearest neighbors are about ten times just noticeable. To provide uniform color scales of the same types and ranges, but with just-noticeable differences, would therefore require 1000 times as many color cards, that is 424,000. To make them so that the rms deviation of color differences is not more than the 12% that characterizes the full-step scales, the accuracy of production would have to be increased 10 times.

Although the errors of production of the present colors are comparable to just-noticeable differences, they are in fact not noticed in the uniform color

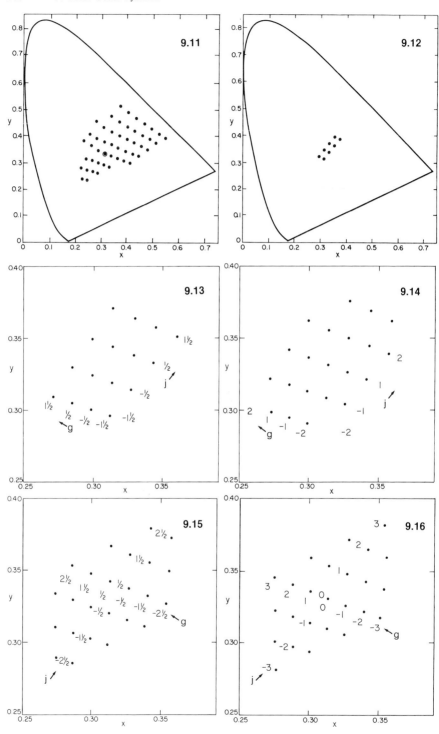

scales. That is because the errors are so small compared to the differences between adjacent colors. In order to make the errors noticeable, cards with errors of production only one-tenth as large as would have to be obtained and compared with the present cards. The present cards are sufficiently accurate for use in the scales for which they were designed. Higher accuracy, which would be required for scales with smaller steps, would increase the cost of production at least in proportion to the accuracy (inversely proportional to the allowed rms deviations).

Fig. 9.11 Chromaticities of OSA uniform-chromaticity-scales colors for $L = 0$

Fig. 9.12 Chromaticities of OSA uniform-chromaticity-scales colors for $L = 5$

Fig. 9.13 Chromaticities of OSA half-step uniform-chromaticity-scales colors for $L = -1\frac{1}{2}$

Fig. 9.14 Chromaticities of OSA half-step uniform-chromaticity-scales colors for $L = -1$

Fig. 9.15 Chromaticities of OSA half-step uniform-chromaticity-scales colors for $L = -\frac{1}{2}$

Fig. 9.16 Chromaticities of OSA half-step uniform-chromaticity-scales colors for $L = 0$

10. Color-Matching Functions

The amounts of any set of three primaries that are needed by the CIE observer to match any spectrum color can be computed by combination (addition or subtraction) of the same multiples of the CIE color-matching data $\bar{x}$, $\bar{y}$, $\bar{z}$ for all wavelengths. The amounts of those same primaries that the CIE observer would need to match any color, in general, are the same combinations of the tristimulus values X, Y, Z. Such combinations are called linear combinations because the tristimulus values themselves are used, not any nonlinear functions of them.

10.1 Chromaticities of Primaries

Linear combinations of tristimulus values were used in the Friele – MacAdam color-difference formula, Sect. 8.3, and in the formulas for the coordinate system of the OSA uniform color scales, Sect. 9.3. The corresponding color-

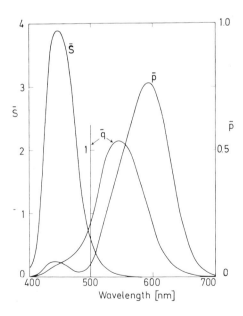

Fig. 10.1 Color-matching functions $\bar{p}$, $\bar{q}$, $\bar{s}$ for Friele – MacAdam color-difference formula

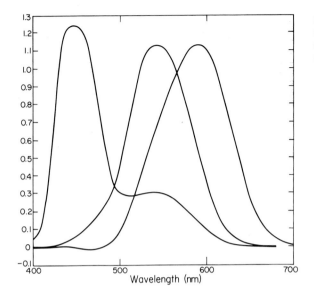

Fig. 10.2 Color-matching functions R, G, B for OSA uniform-chromaticity-scales formula

matching functions for the spectrum are shown in Figs. 10.1, 2, respectively. These are linear transformations of the CIE color-matching data.

The relative values of the coefficients used in the linear combinations depend upon the chromaticities of the primary colors for which the transformed color-matching data are appropriate. The chromaticity coordinates of those primaries can be found by setting R, G and B (or P, Q, S in the Friele – MacAdam formulas) separately equal to 1 (the other two being 0, in each case) in the inverse formulas. For example, from the formulas for P, Q, and S in Sect. 8.3, the inverse formulas for X, Y, and Z as linear combinations of P, Q, and S, obtained by solving the three simultaneous equations for X, Y, and Z, are

$$X = 1.284P - 0.282Q + 0.07S$$

$$Y = 0.376P + 0.73Q - 0.016S$$

$$Z = \qquad\qquad\qquad 0.455S.$$

When $P = 1$, $Q = 0$, and $S = 0$, those inverse formulas give $X_P = 1.284$, $Y_P = 0.376$, $Z_P = 0$, $x_P = 0.7735$, and $y_P = 0.2265$. Similarly, when $P = 0$, $Q = 1$, and $S = 0$, they give

$$x_Q = -0.63, \quad y_Q = 1.63;$$

and when $P = 0$, $Q = 0$, and $S = 1$, they give

$$x_S = 0.14, \quad y_S = -0.03.$$

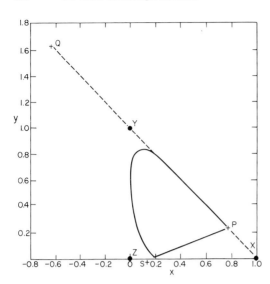

The chromaticities of these three primaries, which are implicit in the Friele – MacAdam formulas, are shown in Fig. 10.3. The color-matching functions for those primaries are shown in Fig. 10.1. For comparison, the primaries for the CIE color-matching data $\bar{x}$, $\bar{y}$, $\bar{z}$ are at $x_X = 1$, $y_X = 0$; $x_Y = 0$, $y_Y = 1$; and $x_Z = 0$, $y_Z = 0$. They are indicated by solid dots in Fig. 10.3.

The inverse formulas for the OSA color scales are

$$X = 1.06R + 0.41G + 0.3B$$

$$Y = 0.36R + 0.64G$$

$$Z = \qquad\quad -0.37G + 1.4B.$$

The chromaticity coordinates of the corresponding primaries are $x_R = 0.7465$, $y_R = 0.2535$; $x_G = 2.93$, $y_G = -4.57$; $x_B = 0.176$, $y_B = 0$. The chromaticities of these primaries are shown in Fig. 10.4.

At first, it may seem that the chromaticity of the green primary is unbelievable, because it is far below the x axis, in the region that might be imagined to represent unrealizably saturated purples. However, because it is on the side of the apeiron of the u, v diagram opposite to the spectrum locus, we are inspired to represent the R, G, and B primaries on the u, v diagram. When transformed to that diagram, the chromaticities are $u_R = 0.656$, $v_R = 0.334$; $u_G = -0.203$, $v_G = 0.4752$; $u_B = 0.266$, $v_B = 0$. These chromaticities are shown by $+$ on the u, v, diagram in Fig. 10.5. Although the G primary is rather far outside the spectrum locus, it is in a plausible direction relative to the green region of the spectrum. For comparison, the P, Q, and S primaries are also shown, and the CIE Y and Z primaries are also shown in Fig. 10.5.

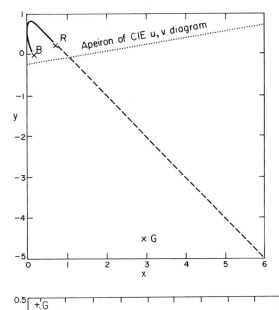

Fig. 10.4 Primaries implied by color-matching functions used in OSA uniform chromaticity scales

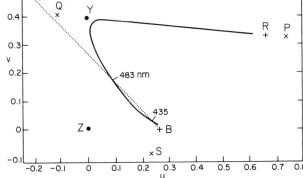

Fig. 10.5
Primaries of Figs. 10.3, 4 transformed to CIE 1960 *u, v* diagram

All of those primaries fall outside the gamut of realizable colors. That is necessary if none of the color-matching data are to be negative. It is also necessary for the three lines that connect any set of primaries to be entirely outside the spectrum locus. That condition is satisfied by the CIE (X, Y, Z) primaries and by the Friele – MacAdam (P, Q, S) primaries. As shown in Fig. 10.5, the line between the B and G primaries (extended, if necessary, as it would be in Fig. 10.4) intersects the spectrum locus at 443 nm and 480.2 nm. At those wavelengths, $\bar{r}$ is zero. Between those wavelengths, the $\bar{r}$ color-matching data are negative. Being negative at some wavelengths does not prevent use of the $\bar{r}$ data in the OSA color-scale formulas even as far as the spectrum, because cube roots of negative quantities are real, although negative.

10.2 Dependence of Color-Matching Functions on Chromaticities of Primaries

The relative values, or ratios, of the multipliers (called coefficients) of the CIE color-matching functions $\bar{x}$, $\bar{y}$, and $\bar{z}$ in the linear combination that defines the color-matching data for any primary of a set of three depend only upon the locations in the x, y chromaticity diagram of the straight line that is drawn between the other two primaries of the set. That means that color-matching data do not depend upon the color of the primary of which they are the amounts.

Only the relative values are determined by the primaries. All three coefficients of each formula can be adjusted by a common multiplier. This is usually done to make the totals of the three sets of color-mixture functions equal. However, that is not the only adjustment that might be made. For example, when they are based on the CIE 1931 color-matching data, the totals of $\bar{p}$, $\bar{q}$, and $\bar{s}$ used in the Friele – MacAdam color-difference formulas are in the ratios 0.9:1:2.27. When multiplied by S_c, the spectral distribution of illuminant C by use of which the Friele – MacAdam formula was obtained, the sums of $\bar{p}S_c$, $\bar{q}S_c$, and $\bar{s}S_c$ are in the ratios 0.854:1:2.66. Coefficients in the formulas for R, G, B used by the OSA Committee on Uniform Color Scales have been adjusted so that when the color-matching data for the CIE 1964 observer are multiplied by the spectral distribution of D_{65} their sums are all equal, i.e., in the ratios 1:1:1.

For use in the formulas for the ratios of the coefficients in the linear combination of $\bar{x}$, $\bar{y}$, and $\bar{z}$ for any primary U, V, or W, we define the slope m and y-axis intercept a of the other pair of primaries as in Fig. 10.6. When the absolute value of the slope m is much greater than 1, rounding errors can be minimized by using the reciprocal slope M and x-axis intercept A, as is also indicated in Fig. 10.6. The reciprocal slope M, and A, are usually appropriate for the color-matching function for the red primary,

$$\bar{r} = \bar{x} - \frac{(M + A)}{(1 - A)}\,\bar{y} - \frac{A}{(1 - A)}\,\bar{z}.$$

For the green primary,

$$\bar{g} = \bar{y} - \frac{(m + a)}{(1 - a)}\,\bar{x} - \frac{a}{(1 - a)}\,\bar{z}.$$

For the blue primary,

$$\bar{b} = \bar{z} - \frac{(1 - A)}{A}\,\bar{x} - \frac{(1 - a)}{a}\,\bar{y}.\ ^{69}$$

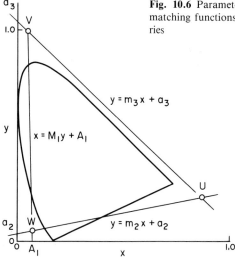

Fig. 10.6 Parameters of formulas for dependence of color-matching functions on chromaticities of corresponding primaries

To adjust the tristimulus values for white to any desired values, those expressions can be multiplied by different factors, as discussed previously.

Recall that for the color-matching data for any primary, the slope (or its reciprocal) and axis intercept must be those of the line through the other two primaries.

10.3 Zeros of Color-Matching Functions

For the elementary reason that every chromaticity represented by a point on the straight line between two primaries can be matched with a mixture of those two primaries, none of the primary whose color-matching data are determined by that line is needed to match the wavelengths at which that line intersects the spectrum locus. The color-matching data of that primary are therefore zero for the wavelengths of those intersections. For wavelengths represented on the spectrum locus by points that are on the opposite side of the line from that primary, its color-matching data are negative. For wavelengths represented by points on the same side as the primary, its color-matching data are positive.

When three wavelengths are used for primaries, as in the classic experiments of Wright on which the 1931 CIE data were partly based, and in those by Stiles that were used for the 1964 CIE data, the experimental color-matching data are zero for the other two primaries at the wavelengths of the primaries. The primaries used by Wright are indicated in Fig. 10.7. The color-matching functions computed for those primaries from the CIE 1931 data are shown in Fig. 10.8. Those are zero for both of the other primaries for each of the wavelengths that are used as primaries. For each primary, the curve

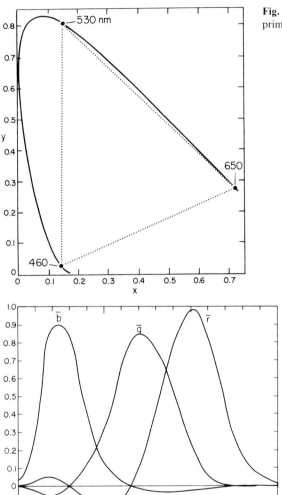

Fig. 10.7 Chromaticities of Wright's primaries

Fig. 10.8 Color-matching functions derived from CIE 1931 data for Wright's primaries

indicates negative values for wavelengths that are represented by spectrum-locus points that are on the opposite side of the line through the other two primaries. The same rule is followed by color-matching data for primaries (such as those produced by light filters and used by Guild in his contribution to the 1931 CIE data [70]) represented by points within the spectrum locus. In such cases, the three lines between the pairs of primaries do not intersect each other on the spectrum locus, so no two color-matching functions are zero for any wavelength. Rather, there are wavelengths that are opposite two of the primaries. For those wavelengths, the color-matching data for both of those

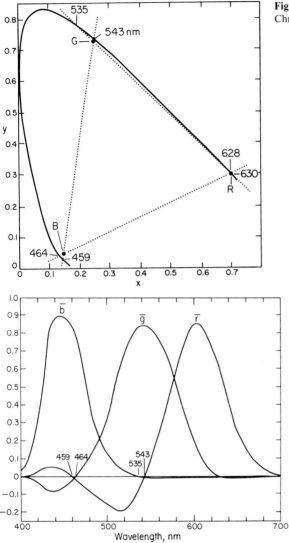

Fig. 10.9
Chromaticities of Guild's primaries

Fig. 10.10
Color-matching functions
derived from CIE 1931
data for Guild's
primaries

primaries are negative. The chromaticities of the primaries used by Guild are shown in Fig. 10.9. The corresponding color-matching functions (computed from the data recommended in 1931 by the CIE) are shown in Fig. 10.10, which indicates the overlapping wavelength ranges of negative color-matching data.

A third case, in which lines between primaries that are represented by points outside the spectrum locus nevertheless intersect the spectrum locus, has already been mentioned in connection with the OSA uniform color scales. The most general type of this case is represented in Fig. 10.11, where all three of the sides of the triangle formed by such primaries intersect the spectrum locus. In this case there are three ranges of wavelengths for which all three color-matching data are positive. The corresponding portions of the spectrum locus are drawn heavily in Fig. 10.11. For the other ranges of wavelength, two of the color-matching data are positive and the third negative. Again, as in general, the color-matching data are zero for the off-line primary at the wavelengths where each triangle side intersects the spectrum locus. The color-matching curves that correspond to Fig. 10.11 are shown in Fig. 10.12.

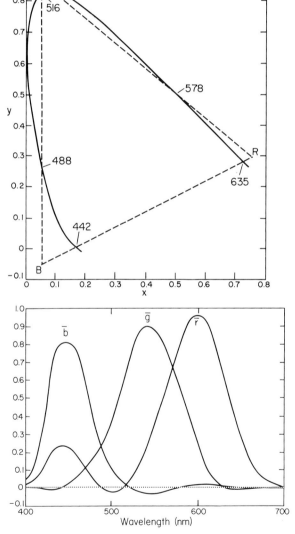

Fig. 10.11 Primary chromaticities outside spectrum-plus-purple boundary, but with triangle sides intersecting the spectrum locus

Fig. 10.12 Color-matching functions that correspond to primaries indicated in Fig. 10.11

Because the line between the X and Y primaries adopted in 1931 by the CIE is coincident with the spectrum locus for all wavelengths greater than 625 nm, the color-matching data $\bar{z}$ for the remaining primary are zero for all of those wavelengths. For the 1964 CIE data the XY line is coincident with the spectrum locus at all wavelengths greater than 555 nm; therefore, the 1964 $\bar{z}$ data are zero for all of those wavelengths.

Because the line between the Y and Z primaries is nearly tangent to the spectrum locus near 500 nm, but departs significantly from it at shorter wavelengths, the $\bar{x}$ data are small at 500 nm, but rise to a significant secondary maximum at shorter wavelengths. Like all of the color-matching data at both the long- and short-wavelength ends of the spectrum, the secondary maximum of the $\bar{x}$ data decreases for wavelengths shorter than 450 nm even though the spectrum locus continues to get further from the YZ line for all shorter wavelengths.

10.4 Elimination of Secondary Maximum of $\bar{x}$

For some purposes, such as designing of a photoelectric tristimulus colorimeter or preparation for use of gaussian quadrature, it would be desirable to eliminate the short-wave secondary maximum of the $\bar{x}$ data. This can be done by modifying the CIE Y and Z primaries so that the line from Y to Z becomes tangent to the spectrum locus near 450 nm, as shown for the 1931 data in Fig. 10.13. The line between the X and Y primaries can be kept unchanged, which retains the CIE $\bar{z}$ data. The revised $\bar{x}$ function for the 1931 data, which will be designated $\bar{x}'$, is shown in Fig. 10.14. Other than the elimination of the secondary lobe near 450 nm, the most notable change is the shift of the maximum to 570 nm from 607 nm, which characterizes the CIE $\bar{x}$ functions. In this connection, it is interesting to note that recent physiological results indicate that 570 nm is near the wavelength of maximum sensitivity of the long-wavelength receptors in human eyes.

The 1931 and 1964 data require quite different locations of the modified Y primary for maximum elimination of the secondary lobe of the $\bar{x}$ data. For the 1931 data it is at $x = 6.88$, $y = -5.88$ and the modified Z primary is at $x = 0.176$, $y = 0$. For the 1964 data the modified X primary is at infinity and the modified Z primary is at $x = 0.185$, $y = 0$; the line through the modified Y and Z primaries has a slope of -1, parallel to the long-wavelength end of the spectrum locus and the line through the X and Y primaries. The locations of the modified Y and Z primaries that eliminate the secondary lobe of the 1931 and 1964 $\bar{x}$ data are shown in the u, v diagram in Fig. 10.15. The modified data $\bar{x}'_{10}$ for the 1964 CIE observer are shown in Fig. 10.16.

The formula for the modified data for the 1931 CIE observer is $\bar{x}' = \bar{x} + 1.17\bar{y} - 0.214\bar{z}$. For the 1964 CIE observer $\bar{x}' = \bar{x}_{10} + \bar{y}_{10} - 0.22638\bar{z}_{10}$.

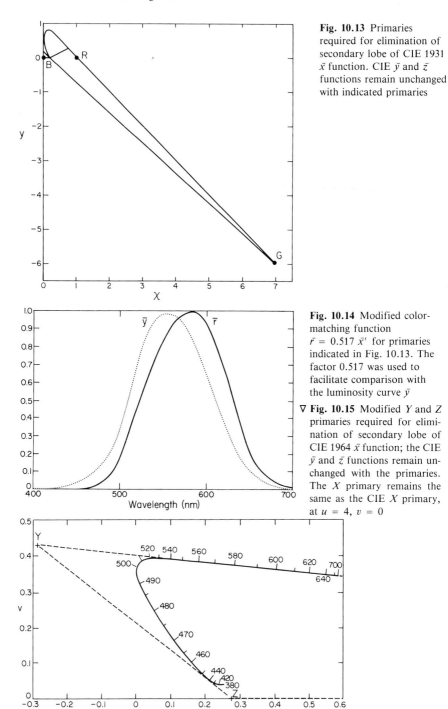

Fig. 10.13 Primaries required for elimination of secondary lobe of CIE 1931 $\bar{x}$ function. CIE $\bar{y}$ and $\bar{z}$ functions remain unchanged with indicated primaries

Fig. 10.14 Modified color-matching function $\bar{r} = 0.517\,\bar{x}'$ for primaries indicated in Fig. 10.13. The factor 0.517 was used to facilitate comparison with the luminosity curve $\bar{y}$

▽ **Fig. 10.15** Modified Y and Z primaries required for elimination of secondary lobe of CIE 1964 $\bar{x}$ function; the CIE $\bar{y}$ and $\bar{z}$ functions remain unchanged with the primaries. The X primary remains the same as the CIE X primary, at $u = 4$, $v = 0$

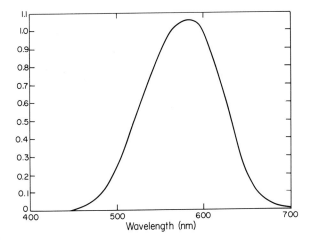

Fig. 10.16 Modified color-matching function $\bar{x}'$ for primaries indicated in Fig. 10.15

After a tristimulus value X' based on $\bar{x}'$ is determined by use of a colorimeter or any other means, the conventional 1931 tristimulus value can be determined from $X = X' - 1.17\,Y + 0.214\,Z$.

To get the conventional tristimulus value for the 1964 CIE observer, compute $X_{10} = X'_{10} - Y_{10} + 0.22638\,Z_{10}$. Wavelengths and weights for gaussian quadrature with $\bar{x}'_2$ and $\bar{x}'_{10}$ are given in Tables 10.1, 2.

10.5 Alychne

The line between the X and Z primaries can also be kept unchanged, which preserves $\bar{y}$. In the case of the 1931 data, $\bar{y}$ are luminosities. In that case, all points on the line between the X and Z primaries represent colors that have zero luminosities. Therefore that line is called the *alychne,* which is Greek for "line without light" or "lightless line." Because that line is entirely outside the spectrum – purple boundary, no colors represented by points on the alychne are physically realizable. The alychne is nevertheless frequently referred to. It is well defined in the 1931 x, y diagram and in the 1960 u, v diagram. The alychne is not defined in the 1964, x, y diagram because the luminosity function is not a linear combination of the 1964 CIE "supplementary" color-matching data.

10.6 Orthogonal Color-Matching Functions

Negative values of color-matching data, which are commonly shunned, have one possible use – for constructing sets of orthogonal color-matching functions. Such functions were mentioned briefly in Sect. 5.6 in the discussion

Table 10.1. Wavelengths and weights for gaussian quadrature with $\bar{x}_2'$ and illuminants A, C, D_{65}, for orders 7 to 10

Order	A		C		D_{65}	
	$\lambda(\bar{x})$ [nm]	$\omega(\lambda)$	$\lambda(\bar{y})$ [nm]	$\omega(\lambda)$	$\lambda(\bar{z})$ [nm]	$\omega(\lambda)$
7	434.4	0.0004	421.8	0.0004	418.8	0.0004
	500.0	0.0810	490.4	0.0820	490.4	0.0783
	543.2	0.5450	533.3	0.5132	532.5	0.5270
	588.9	0.9580	578.1	0.8184	577.6	0.7979
	632.7	0.5541	623.6	0.4345	622.8	0.4365
	680.0	0.0535	670.4	0.0490	670.0	0.0473
	737.0	0.0004	739.9	0.0001	729.9	0.0001
8	416.7	0.0000	412.4	0.0002	409.9	0.0001
	487.4	0.0278	477.6	0.0272	477.1	0.0245
	526.5	0.3003	515.9	0.2808	515.9	0.2920
	567.7	0.7791	556.9	0.7176	556.0	0.7012
	609.2	0.8029	599.3	0.6365	598.9	0.6381
	649.8	0.2683	641.2	0.2219	640.4	0.2184
	695.9	0.0135	686.6	0.0133	686.3	0.0128
	744.9	0.0002	740.1	0.0001	739.4	0.0001
9	408.6	0.0000	406.5	0.0001	404.5	0.0001
	473.2	0.0062	458.2	0.0041	457.0	0.0034
	510.5	0.1334	498.9	0.1216	499.0	0.1199
	547.8	0.5136	537.4	0.4933	536.4	0.5053
	587.3	0.8366	576.7	0.7221	576.2	0.7024
	625.4	0.5792	616.5	0.4524	615.8	0.4560
	664.2	0.1204	655.9	0.1009	655.4	0.0971
	708.4	0.0028	700.2	0.0032	700.2	0.0031
	749.7	0.0001	746.5	0.0001	745.4	0.0001
10	402.7	0.0000	400.5	0.0000	399.0	0.0000
	450.9	0.0006	436.3	0.0007	434.6	0.0006
	494.9	0.0455	486.6	0.0521	486.4	0.0495
	530.2	0.3122	521.6	0.3031	521.3	0.3243
	567.0	0.6881	557.9	0.6216	557.2	0.6246
	603.9	0.7469	595.2	0.6092	594.9	0.5747
	639.4	0.3468	632.0	0.2696	631.3	0.2734
	677.0	0.0519	669.6	0.0407	669.2	0.0397
	718.1	0.0001	711.8	0.0005	712.0	0.0005
	752.8	0.0000	750.9	0.0000	749.7	0.0000

of the propagation of spectrophotometric errors into chromaticity coordinates.

Orthogonal color-matching functions should also be used in discussions of the colorimetric theory of mosaic-screen-plate additive color photography, such as plates and films produced and sold for color photography fifty or more years ago by Lumière, Agfa, Dufay, Ansco, and DuPont. Even the lenticular Kodacolor film sold for amateur motion pictures in the 1920s used

Table 10.2. Wavelengths and weights for gaussian quadrature with $\bar{x}'_{10}$ and illuminants A, C, D_{65}, for orders 7 to 10

Order	A		C		D_{65}	
	$\lambda(\bar{x})$ [nm]	$\omega(\lambda)$	$\lambda(\bar{y})$ [nm]	$\omega(\lambda)$	$\lambda(\bar{z})$ [nm]	$\omega(\lambda)$
7	417.6	0.0004	412.5	0.0011	410.8	0.0011
	488.8	0.0565	479.0	0.0672	478.7	0.0632
	536.3	0.4434	525.3	0.4054	524.9	0.407
	583.8	0.8976	572.6	0.7494	572.1	0.7401
	628.3	0.5728	619.0	0.4332	618.4	0.4419
	675.4	0.0609	666.0	0.0537	665.6	0.0519
	734.8	0.0002	726.6	0.0000	726.9	0.0000
8	409.8	0.0002	408.2	0.0007	406.8	0.0007
	475.8	0.0208	465.3	0.0235	464.3	0.0214
	518.7	0.2219	506.3	0.2147	506.3	0.2221
	562.1	0.6924	550.7	0.6130	549.6	0.5896
	604.7	0.7865	594.3	0.6131	593.8	0.6234
	645.6	0.2936	636.7	0.2296	635.8	0.2328
	691.5	0.0163	682.1	0.0153	681.7	0.0151
	743.5	0.0002	738.2	0.0001	737.7	0.0000
9	406.0	0.0001	404.9	0.0006	403.7	0.0005
	460.1	0.0048	445.2	0.0045	443.1	0.0038
	500.9	0.0951	488.7	0.1002	488.4	0.0966
	541.4	0.4277	530.4	0.3942	529.5	0.3920
	582.4	0.7789	571.5	0.6572	570.8	0.6485
	621.1	0.5889	612.1	0.4441	611.5	0.4561
	660.1	0.1325	651.8	0.1054	651.2	0.1037
	704.3	0.0038	695.9	0.0039	695.8	0.0039
	748.6	0.0001	745.3	0.0000	744.3	0.0000
10	402.3	0.0001	400.4	0.0002	399.3	0.0003
	437.4	0.0007	425.5	0.0015	423.5	0.0013
	484.8	0.0353	476.6	0.0483	476.2	0.0445
	523.4	0.2363	513.8	0.2309	513.9	0.2404
	561.9	0.6083	552.6	0.5383	551.8	0.5356
	599.6	0.7167	590.8	0.5781	590.5	0.5711
	635.6	0.3773	628.1	0.2686	627.4	0.2698
	673.2	0.0567	665.8	0.0434	665.5	0.0415
	714.8	0.0005	708.1	0.0008	708.4	0.0007
	751.8	0.0000	749.8	0.0000	748.7	0.0000

the same principle. Those plates and films used the same color filters for final display, by additive light combination, as were used for the original camera exposure that recorded the pictures. If photographic material that had constant spectral sensitivity were used for such a process, then for exact color reproduction the three filters should have spectral transmittances that are orthogonal color-matching functions. Because at least two of three orthogonal functions must have negative values of significant magnitude, whereas light filters cannot have negative transmittances, the requirement for exact color reproduction cannot be fulfilled by any additive, mosaic-screen or lenticular process.

Orthogonal functions, such as U, V, W, are defined by the relations $\Sigma UVF\Delta\lambda = \Sigma VWF\Delta\lambda = \Sigma UWF\Delta\lambda = 0$, where F can be any non-negative function of wavelength. The function F may be thought of as the spectral distribution of the illumination or that distribution multiplied by the spectral sensitivity of the film. In the following, $F\Delta\lambda$ is assumed to be constant and independent of wavelength, which would be the case if F were the spectral distribution of a so-called equal-energy source, if the film were uniformly sensitive from 380 to 770 nm, and if $\Delta\lambda$ were constant.

The following set of orthogonal color-matching functions is defined in terms of the 1931 CIE data,

$$U = 0.5657\bar{x} - 0.3965\bar{y} - 0.169193\bar{z}$$

$$V = \qquad\qquad 0.3598\bar{y}$$

$$W = 0.203231\bar{x} - 0.1738\bar{y} + 0.224559\bar{z}.$$

This set of functions, shown in Fig. 10.17, is also normalized so that the sums of the squares of their values at 10 nm intervals throughout the visible spectrum are unity,

$$\Sigma U^2 = \Sigma V^2 = \Sigma W^2 = 1.$$

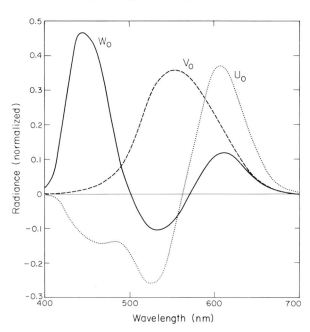

Fig. 10.17 Normal and orthogonal color-matching functions. V_0 is proportional to CIE 1931 $\bar{y}$ function

This set also fulfills two additional requirements: V is proportional to the luminosity function $\bar{y}$, and $\Sigma U = 0$, so that the value of U for an "equal-energy" white is zero. The additional feature, $\Sigma W = 0$ for white, which would simplify some theoretical work, cannot be obtained with any set of orthogonal color-matching functions of which one (like V) is positive at all wavelengths.

All other sets of orthogonal color-matching functions based on the 1931 CIE data can be derived from U, V, W by use of

$$U' = \lambda_1 U + \mu_1 V + \nu_1 W$$

$$V' = \lambda_2 U + \mu_2 V + \nu_2 W$$

$$W' = \lambda_3 U + \mu_3 V + \nu_3 W,$$

where the coefficients are independent of wavelength and are subjected to the restrictions

$$\lambda_1 \lambda_2 + \mu_1 \mu_2 + \nu_1 \nu_2 = \lambda_2 \lambda_3 + \mu_2 \mu_3 + \nu_2 \nu_3 = \lambda_3 \lambda_1 + \mu_3 \mu_1 + \nu_3 \nu_1 = 0.$$

If these coefficients also satisfy the conditions

$$\lambda_1^2 + \mu_1^2 + \nu_1^2 = \lambda_2^2 + \mu_2^2 + \nu_2^2 = \lambda_3^2 + \mu_3^2 + \nu_3^2 = 1,$$

then U', V', and W' are normalized and can also be used to calculate other sets of orthogonal functions by use of the same formulas, subject to the same restrictions on the coefficients.

Orthogonal color-matching functions can correspond to physically producible primaries. Producible primaries, which must be represented by points on the spectrum locus or within the area enclosed by it and the straight line drawn between its extremities (380 and 770 nm), are often called "real" primaries, whereas primaries represented by points outside that area are often called "unreal" or "imaginary" primaries. Those names suggest a distinction among primaries that is pointless; primaries outside the spectrum − purple boundary are just as well defined and usable as primaries within it.

It is rarely necessary to actually use primaries in experiments. When such experiments are necessary, negative quantities, such as are indicated by negative values of color-matching data, can easily be handled by use of ordinary arithmetic. Primaries represented by points outside the spectrum − purple boundary offer the advantage that (subject to further conditions that were discussed in Sect. 10.3) use of them results in color-matching data and tristimulus values that are always positive (or zero), which simplifies thinking about color problems. They will not be called "unreal" or "imaginary" in this book. Primaries that can be produced physically, which lie on or within the spectrum − purple boundary, will be called "producible" colors, merely for brevity. For example, the producible spectrum colors 557 and 654 nm, used with 463 nm (dominant wavelength) with 93% purity as a set of primaries, yield orthogonal color-matching functions.

There is an infinite variety of pairs of orthogonal functions that are orthogonal to the V function. They correspond to an infinite variety of pairs of primaries that are all confined to the alychne, the $y = 0$ axis. For all sets of orthogonal color-matching functions that include V, the third primary, which corresponds to the V function, is uniquely determined by the function F that is used in the normalization. In the present example, for which $F\Delta\lambda$ is assumed constant throughout the visible spectrum, the coordinates of the primary V are $x = 0.398$, $y = 0.542$.

When the V primary has those coordinates and the W primary is assigned the coordinates x_w, 0, then the chromaticity of the U primary for the orthogonal set is completely determined,

$$x_u = 0.2383 + 0.0889/(0.2383 - x_w).$$

For the original functions U, V, W, $x_W = 0.2301$ and $x_U = 11.08$. Because both are on the alychne, $y_U = y_W = 0$.

In general, when one primary of a set that corresponds to orthogonal color-matching functions based on the 1931 CIE data is fixed, the other two are confirmed to a specific line in the chromaticity diagram. The slope m of that line, its y-axis intercept a, and its x-axis intercept A are

$$m = (3.3945x - y - 0.8091)/(x - 2.1343y + 0.3182),$$

$$a = -(0.8091x + 0.3182y - 0.4930)/(x - 2.1343y + 0.3182)$$

$$A = (0.8091x + 0.3182y - 0.4930)/(3.34945 - y - 0.8091),$$

where x and y are the chromaticity coordinates of the fixed primary. Therefore, the shape of any orthogonal color-matching function U is determined by the chromaticity x_U, y_U, of the corresponding primary,

$$U = C[(1 - A^{-1})\bar{x} + (1 - a^{-1})\bar{y} + \bar{z}].$$

The preceding formulas for a and A may be substituted. Fractions may be cleared and the coefficient of the first or any other term may be reduced to unity, because C is an arbitrary adjustment factor. Thus, $U = C[(x_U - 0.51y_U - 0.1224)\bar{x} - (0.7x_U - 0.7025y_U - 0.676)\bar{y} - (0.313x_U + 0.1231y_U - 0.1906)\bar{z}]$, where C is, in general, numerically different than it was originally.

A *horizontal* line joins two primaries that, when used with a third, have an orthogonal set of color-matching functions if the third primary lies anywhere on the line L defined by setting the numerator of the formula for m equal to zero:

$$3.3945x - y - 0.8091 = 0.$$

A *vertical* line joins two primaries that, when used with a third, have an orthogonal set of color-matching functions if the third primary lies anywhere on the line L_2 defined by setting the *denominator* of the formula for m equal to zero:

$$x - 2.1343y + 0.3182 = 0.$$

The intersection of the two lines L_1 and L_2 can be located by solving the equations for those lines simultaneously,

$$x = 0.3275, \quad y = 0.3025.$$

That point P_1 is also the intersection of all lines along which lie primaries that correspond to constant values of m. A set of such lines and the corresponding values of m are shown in Fig. 10.18.

The line that joins two primaries, which (when used with a third) have an orthogonal set of color-matching functions, passes through the origin ($a = 0$) if the third primary is anywhere on the line L_3 defined by setting the numerator of the formula for a equal to zero:

$$-0.8091x - 0.3182y + 0.4930 = 0.$$

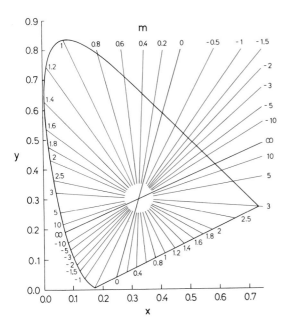

Fig. 10.18 Lines that show locations of all primaries for which lines with slope m connect the other two primaries of every set that has orthogonal color-matching functions for CIE 1931 observer

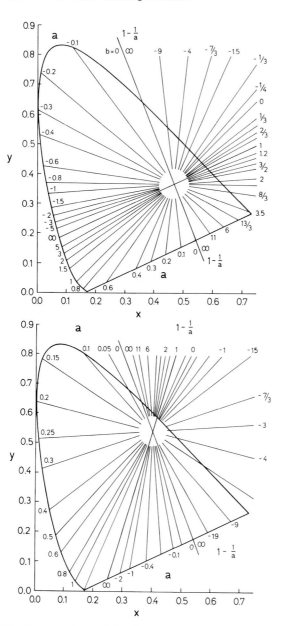

Fig. 10.19 Lines that show locations of all primaries for which lines with y-axis intercept *a* connect the other two primaries of every set that has orthogonal color-matching functions for the CIE 1931 observer

Fig. 10.20 Lines that show locations of all primaries for which lines with x-axis intercept *A* connect the other two primaries of every set that has orthogonal color-matching functions for CIE 1931 observer

The intersection of the lines L_2 and L_3 ($x = 0.4651$, $y = 0.3670$) is also the intersection P_2 of all lines along which lie primaries that correspond to constant values of *a*. The coefficient $(1 - a^{-1})$ of $\bar{y}$ in the formula for *U* is, of course, also constant for all primaries that lie along any straight line passing through P_2. A set of such lines and the corresponding values of *a* and of $(1 - a^{-1})$ are shown in Fig. 10.19.

The intersection of the lines L_1 and L_3 ($x = 0.398$, $y = 0.5422$) is also the intersection of all lines along which lie primaries that correspond to constant values of A and of $(1 - A^{-1})$. The latter is the coefficient of $\bar{x}$ in the formula for U. A set of lines for which A is constant and the corresponding values of A and $(1 - A^{-1})$ are shown in Fig. 10.20. When $F\Delta\lambda$ is independent of wavelength, a spectral-power distribution that is proportional to any orthogonal color-matching function has the same chromaticity as the corresponding primary of any set that has that as one of its color-matching functions.

10.7 Self-Conjugate Primaries

Figures 10.18 and 10.19, or the formulas for m and a from which they were derived, can be used to locate the region in the chromaticity diagram within which can be found a special class of colors that will be called self-conjugate primaries. They have a property that has, in superficial discussions of colorimetry, often been mistakenly attributed to additive primaries in general. The mistake is to say that a color-matching function "is the primary". Because the color-matching function is a function of wavelength, that statement inevitably leads the auditor, and even the speaker, to think that the curve represents the spectral distribution of power in the primary, or even the spectral transmittance of a color filter used to produce the primary. In general, as illustrated by the examples in Figs. 10.9, 10, the presumption is false.

However, some primaries can be produced with illumination function F by use of filters that have spectral transmittances proportional to their color-matching functions when they are used with pairs of other primaries with which they have orthogonal color-matching functions. We have already had one example, the V primary of the original orthogonal set, which can be produced with a spectral transmittance that is proportional to the CIE 1931 $\bar{y}$ or luminosity function. Of course, the same chromaticity could also be produced with other spectral distributions. The special feature in this case is that it can be produced with a spectral transmittance proportional to its color-matching function.

As mentioned at the beginning of this chapter, the color-matching function of a primary does not, in general, depend upon its chromaticity. The same color-matching function could be obtained with any primary, regardless of either its spectral distribution or chromaticity. The only condition necessary to obtain the color-matching function V is that the chromaticities of the *other two* primaries be represented by points on the x axis ($y = 0$), the alychne. Figures 10.18, 19 show that this condition is fulfilled by all pairs of primaries with which the primary at $x = 0.398$, $y = 0.542$ can be used to produce orthogonal color-matching functions of which V is one. Because of the conditions by which orthogonal color-matching functions were defined, the tristimulus value of the spectral distribution VF is a positive number for the V primary, whereas both tristimulus values for the U and W primaries are zero. The chromaticity produced in illumination F by use of the spectral transmittance V is therefore identical with the chromaticity of the V primary for which the color-matching function in any orthogonal set is proportional to V.

The problem is, can another chromaticity be selected that can be produced by use of a spectral transmittance that is proportional to its color-matching function when it is used with all pairs of primaries with which it produces sets of orthogonal color-matching functions?

Because spectral transmittances cannot be negative at any wavelength, the line indicated by Figs. 10.18, 19 for the primary we are seeking must not intersect the spectrum locus. By rotating tangents around the spectrum – purple boundary in the CIE 1931 x, y diagram, the limiting combinations of m and a, shown in Fig. 10.21, were determined. Pairs of values of m and a that correspond to points between the two curves in Fig. 10.21 give lines that intersect the spectrum locus. The self-conjugate primaries that we are seeking must therefore give pairs of values that correspond to points below or above those curves. The region within which self-conjugate primaries must be confined is therefore within the boundary in Fig. 10.22 that corresponds to the points on the curves in Fig. 10.21. The points on the boundary in Fig. 10.22

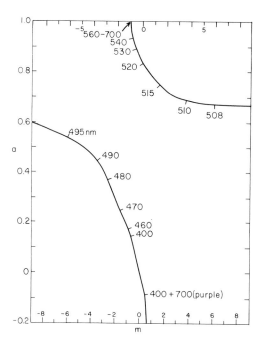

Fig. 10.21 Limiting combinations of slopes, m, and y-axis intercepts, a, for lines that determine self-conjugate primaries and color-matching functions for CIE 1931 observer. Allowed combinations are above top curve and below the bottom curve

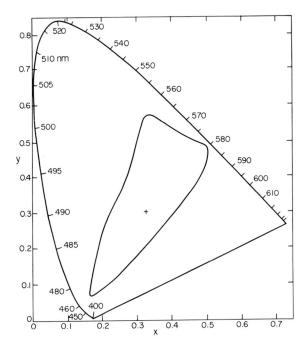

Fig. 10.22 Boundary of self-conjugate primaries for CIE 1931 observer

were determined by use of Figs. 10.18, 19 and the formulas for *m* and *a* that were used to construct them.

The chromaticity of the first-found self-conjugate primary V is indicated on Fig. 10.22, which shows that it barely scratched the surface of the possibilities. Recall that a self-conjugate primary has a color-matching curve proportional to its spectral transmittance only when it is used with two other primaries that are both outside the gamut of producible colors. Because the lines that connect them with the self-conjugate primary cross the spectrum locus, the color-matching functions for those other primaries are necessarily significantly negative for some wavelengths. Therefore, a set of primaries correct in principle for processes of color reproduction like mosaic-screen plates and lenticular films is not possible.

Whether any uses will be found for self-conjugate primaries is not known. At least their existence and restrictions demonstrate the fallacy of saying that a color-matching function "is a primary". The result found by use of them provides warning concerning attempts to develop high-quality mosaic or lenticular processes for color reproduction: the same filters cannot be used for both taking and display.

11. Chromatic Adaptation

Monochrome television screens seen through windows from outdoors at night seem very blue, although when viewed indoors at normal distances their blueness is rarely remarked. This is caused by rapid, nearly complete adaptation of the observer, such that the quality of the illumination that prevails in the observer's field of view seems colorless and is his criterion for white. Outdoors at night, the prevailing illumination from street lamps or interior lighting seen through windows determines his adaptation and criterion for white. Relative to that criterion, the television screen, seen as a small, distant object, is definitely bluish. But viewed close up, the TV screen dominates our field of view, governs our adaptation, becomes our criterion for white, and (if it is a monochrome set) appears nearly colorless.

One of the earliest triumphs of colorimetry was a fairly accurate accounting for the facts of chromatic adaptation. The coefficient law enunciated by *von Kries* in 1878 still provides the simplest good first approximation to the effect[71]. It postulates that visual responses are proportional to the physical stimulation of each of three sets of spectrally differently sensitive receptors in the eye and that only the ratios of the coefficients of proportionality change from one chromatic adaptation to another. According to the von Kries law, the relative spectral sensitivities of any class of receptors do not change as a result of adaptation. So far as is yet known, that is true for ordinary levels of illumination.

Investigations since 1878 have concentrated on determining the relative spectral sensitivities of the three classes of receptors. The predictions of the coefficient law are dependent on those functions. Those functions are, in principle, color-matching functions for a particular set of primaries. Therefore, a major aim of chromatic-adaptation research from its beginning has been to identify the effective primaries. Because spectral sensitivities must be non-negative, primaries appropriate for use in the von Kries law must all be represented by points outside the spectrum − purple boundary.

A more recent aim of chromatic-adaptation research has been to confirm, if possible, the postulated proportionality between the responses and the physical stimulations (tristimulus values for the appropriate primaries). When evidence was found that indicated failure of proportionality between responses and stimulations, nonlinear relations, such as cube-root dependence of response on stimulation, were tried.

11.1 Linear Adaptation Formula (von Kries Coefficient Law)

Several experimental procedures have been used to determine the tristimulus values of colors that when viewed by an observer adapted to one illumination, have the same appearances as other colors (whose tristimulus values are known) viewed by the same observer adapted to a second illumination. Such pairs are called corresponding colors. Examples for adaptations to illuminants A and C are shown in Fig. 11.1. For test of the coefficient law, the known tristimulus values of one of the colors viewed with adaptation to the second illumination are designated X, Y, Z. The tristimulus values of the corresponding color observed to have the same appearance with adaptation to the first illumination are designated X', Y', Z'. The tristimulus values, when expressed in terms of an assumed set of primaries, are designated R, G, B, R', G', B'. Then the von Kries coefficient law is

$$R' = K_R R, \quad G' = K_G G, \quad \text{and} \quad B' = K_B B,$$

where K_R, K_G, and K_B are the same for all pairs of corresponding colors.

For several assumed sets of primaries and optimized values of K_R, K_G, and K_B, values of R', G', and B' were computed. From those, by the inverse linear combinations, computed values of X'_c, Y'_c, and Z'_c were obtained for comparison with the observed values. The differences

$$\Delta X = X'_c - X'$$
$$\Delta Y = Y'_c - Y'$$
$$\Delta Z = Z'_c - Z'$$
$$\Delta S = \Delta X + \Delta Y + \Delta Z$$

were computed. The values of K_R, K_G, and K_B were adjusted to minimize the average square of the relative discrepancy $\Delta S/S$. The dependence of the rms value of $\Delta S/S$ on the choice of primaries was then minimized. The chromaticities of the most successful red and blue primaries [72] were found to be the Judd P and T points,

$$x_R = 0.747, \quad y_R = 0.253$$
$$x_B = 0.1785, \quad y_B = 0.$$

With those primaries, the chromaticities of the most successful green primaries, for various observers and pairs of adaptations, were distributed along the straight line $y = 1 - x$ that is tangent to the long-wavelength end of the spectrum locus. The x coordinates of the most successful green primaries, for various cases, ranged from 1.0 to infinity. The dependence of the rms

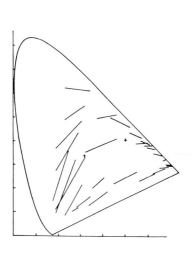

Fig. 11.1 Corresponding chromaticities for adaptations to CIE illuminants A and C. The chromaticity indicated by the right-hand end of each line has the same appearance when the observer is adapted to illuminant A (indicated by the right-hand +) as has the chromaticity indicated by the left-hand end of that line when the observer is adapted to illuminant C (left-hand +)

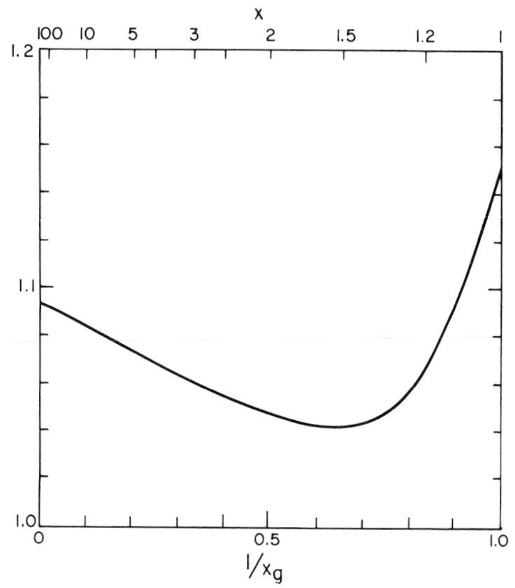

Fig. 11.2 Dependence of average relative error (σ_S/S) on x coordinate of G primary for von Kries coefficient law of chromatic adaptation (y coordinate of G primary is assumed to be $y_G = 1 - x_G$)

value of $\Delta S/S$ on $1/x_G$ for two observers and five pairs of adaptations is shown in Fig. 11.2. The minimum of this shallow dependence is at about $x_G = 1.5$.

Systematic behaviors of the discrepancies were found by plotting the chromaticities of the differences,

$$x_d = \Delta X/\Delta S, \quad y_d = \Delta Y/\Delta S.$$

The chromaticity of the average discrepancy and the covariance matrix

$$\begin{pmatrix} \Sigma x_d^2 & \Sigma x_d y_d \\ \Sigma x_d y_d & \Sigma y_d^2 \end{pmatrix}$$

were computed for each pair of adaptations and for each observer, separately. From each covariance matrix, the length of the major axis of the covariance ellipse that represents the distribution of discrepancy chromaticities around the average, the angle of inclination of that axis, and the ratio of the major to the minor axis were computed.

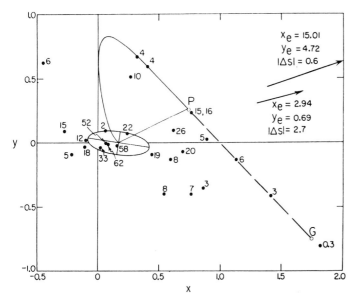

Fig. 11.3 Discrepancy chromaticities and covariance ellipse for predictions of corresponding colors in Fig. 11.1 by use of von Kries coefficient law with $x_G = 1.75$, $y_G = -0.75$. The absolute values of $\Delta S = \Delta X + \Delta Y + \Delta Z$ are indicated for each discrepancy chromaticity ($x_e = \Delta X/\Delta S$, $y_e = \Delta Y/\Delta S$). Two discrepancy chromaticities are coincident at $x_e = 0.76$, $y_e = 0.24$. Two others lie outside the diagram; they are indicated by arrows

Figure 11.3 shows an example for one observer and a pair of adaptations. The location of the optimum green primary is shown at G. The value of x_G for this case is indicated in Fig. 11.2. The values of ΔS are written beside the points that represent the chromaticities of the discrepancies of prediction of corresponding colors by the linear coefficient law. Two points lie outside the figure. Their coordinates and ΔS values (very small) are shown in the upper right-hand corner. The ellipse at the left is the covariance ellipse for this particular observer and pair of adaptations.

The discrepancy-covariance ellipses indicate in four ways the likelihood that the discrepancies arise from inadequacies of the linear coefficient law rather than from random experimental errors. The first is the length of the major axis: concentrated discrepancies and hence short major axes indicate systematic errors of the law. The second is the magnitude of the ratio of the major to minor axis: nearly equal axes (small ratio) would indicate nearly equal probability of errors in all directions, hence merely random observation errors. The third indication of inadequacy of the linear coefficient hypothesis is near parallelism of the major axes for different observers and pairs of adaptations. The fourth is the closeness together of the centers of the major axes (average chromaticities of discrepancies) for various observers and pairs of adaptations.

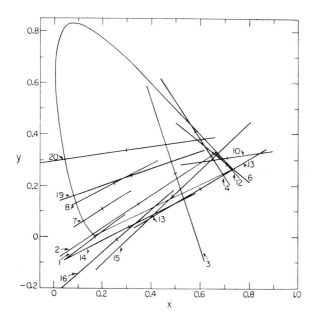

Fig. 11.4 Major axes of discrepancy-covariance ellipses for which axis ratio exceeds 2:1 for von Kries predictions of results of two observers for 5 pairs of adaptations

Figure 11.4 shows the major axes of the covariance ellipses for all of the observers and pairs of adaptations for which the major-to-minor-axis ratios were greater than 2. The tendency to parallelism of the major axes of those distinctly elongated ellipses is evident, as is also the concentration of the center points in the blue-to-purple region.

11.2 Nonlinear Adaptation Formula

The discrepancies between calculated and observed corresponding colors are reduced by applying the coefficient law to nonlinear transformations of the R, G, B and R', G', B' values. The resulting values are designated

ρ, γ, β, ρ', γ', β',   where

$\rho = a_1 + b_1 R^{p_1}$

$\gamma = a_2 + b_2 G^{p_2}$

$\beta = a_3 + b_3 B^{p_3}$

$\rho' = a_4 + b_4 (R')^{p_4}$

$\gamma' = a_5 + b_5 (G')^{p_5}$

$\beta' = a_6 + b_6 (B')^{p_6}$.

The values of the exponents $p_1 - p_6$ depend upon the chromaticities of the adaptations. The values of the coefficients $a_1 - a_6$, $b_1 - b_6$ are unique functions of the associated p's. For the results that will be shown, the Judd P and T primaries will be used, the same as were used with the linear formula. The G primary will be at $x_G = 1.75$, $y_G = -0.75$. The corresponding linear combinations are

$$R = c(0.32X + 0.75 Y - 0.07Z),$$

$$G = c(-0.46X + 1.36 Y + 0.1 Z)$$

$$B = cZ.$$

The coefficient c is a constant that is selected for each group of data so that the greatest value of R, G, B, R', G', or B' is 80. The predicted tristimulus values X_c', Y_c', Z_c' of the corresponding colors are computed from the inverse formulas,

$$X' = 1.74 R'/c - 0.96 G'/c + 0.22 B'/c$$

$$Y' = 0.59 R'/c + 0.41 G'/c$$

$$Z' = B'/c.$$

The coefficients K_R, K_G, K_B in the nonlinear coefficient law for adaptation

$$\rho' = K_R \rho$$

$$\gamma' = K_G \gamma$$

$$\beta' = K_B \beta$$

were adjusted to minimize the average square of the relative discrepancies of the tristimulus sums, $\Delta S/S$, where $S = X + Y + Z$ and $\Delta S = \Delta X + \Delta Y + \Delta Z$. The values of R', G', B' were calculated from the inverse formulas

$$R' = [(\rho' - a_4)/b_4]^{1/p_4}$$

$$G' = [(\gamma' - a_5)/b_5]^{1/p_5}$$

$$B' = [(\beta' - a_6)/b_6]^{1/p_6}.$$

The values of the exponents $p_1 - p_6$ that minimized the average square of the relative discrepancies were found to depend upon the chromaticities of the adaptations, as indicated in Figs. 11.5–7.[73] The exponents p_1 and p_4, for ρ and ρ', respectively, are indicated in Fig. 11.5, for the chromaticities of the corresponding adaptations ("second" and "first" as defined in the first paragraph of Sect. 11.1). The exponents p_2 and p_5, for γ and γ' are indicated

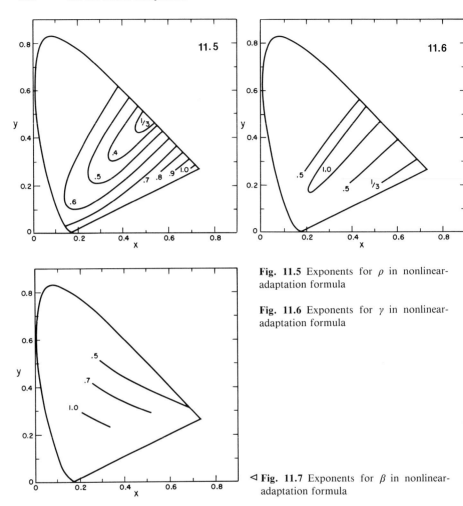

Fig. 11.5 Exponents for ρ in nonlinear-adaptation formula

Fig. 11.6 Exponents for γ in nonlinear-adaptation formula

◁ **Fig. 11.7** Exponents for β in nonlinear-adaptation formula

in Fig. 11.6 for the same two adaptations in the same order. The exponents p_3 and p_6 for β and β' are indicated in Fig. 11.7 for those same adaptations. The heads of the arrows indicate results obtained by similar optimization by use of data obtained by other experimenters, who used an entirely different experimental method and different observers[74].

The locations and lengths of major axes of the discrepancy ellipses, for comparison with those in Fig. 11.4, are shown for the nonlinear coefficient formula in Fig. 11.8. The axes in Fig. 11.8 are longer in general, and much less regularity of locations of centers or of directions is apparent than in Fig. 11.4. Therefore, because it reduces the alignments of discrepancy chromaticities and clustering of their averages, the nonlinear formula is superior to the linear formula. Furthermore, the nonlinear formula gave smaller ratios of major to

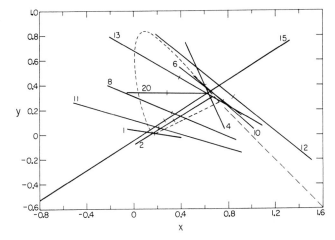

Fig. 11.8 Major axes of discrepancy-covariance ellipses for which axis ratio exceeds 2:1 for predictions of nonlinear adaptation formula

minor axes for 13 of the 20 covariance ellipses. The rms relative discrepancy was reduced from 5% with the linear formula to 3% with the nonlinear formula.

11.3 Color Constancy

The most notable consequence of chromatic adaptation is that each object appears to have nearly the same color whatever its illumination. White paper "looks white" in both tungsten light and daylight. After sufficient time for adaptation, it appears white even in such extreme illuminations as the red light of a photographic darkroom or the nearly spectral blue-green of mercury-arc factory or street lighting. The appearances of chromatic materials, such as yellow paper, red paint, or blue cloth, are not so resistant to changes of illuminant, but are remarkably constant for moderate changes, such as from tungsten light to daylight. This effect, which results from chromatic adaptation, is called color constancy.

That color constancy cannot be exact, i.e., within a just-noticeable difference, is evident from the fact that metameric materials that are exactly matched in daylight can differ by many times the just-noticeable difference of chromaticity in tungsten light. At most, only one of them can have the same appearance as they both have in daylight.

Figure 7.25 shows the chromaticities in illuminant A of the 24 paint samples that have the different spectral-reflectance curves shown in Figs. 7.23, 24. As explained in Sect. 7.3, those samples were made with mixtures of different sets of pigments. Those mixtures were adjusted so that the paint samples all had the same chromaticity and luminance factor in D_{65} (for the 1964 observer). If, as a result of chromatic adaptation, one of them has the same appearance in illuminant A as it has in D_{65}, then none of the others that are noticeably different from it can have the same appearance as it has in D_{65}. The problem is to identify which sample, if any, has exact color constancy.

The colorimetric specifications of all 24 samples when illuminated by D_{65} (for the CIE 1964 observer) are $X = 43.10$, $Y = 43.37$, $Z = 25.17$, $x = 0.3860$, $y = 0.3884$. For D_{65}, the values of the coefficients in the formulas for ρ, γ, β, ρ', γ', β', for illuminants A and D_{65} and the CIE 1964 observer, are given in[73]. If we assume that the observer is in illuminant A sufficiently long for complete chromatic adaptation so that a perfectly reflecting white object has the same appearance as it has in D_{65}, then

$$K_R = \rho'_w/\rho_w, \quad K_G = \gamma'_w/\gamma_w, \quad K_B = \beta'_w/\beta_w,$$

where ρ_w, γ_w, β_w are the values computed from the values of X, Y, Z for a perfect white in D_{65}, and ρ'_w, γ'_w, β'_w are the values computed with P_4, P_5, P_6, a_4, a_5, a_6, b_4, b_5, b_6 from the values of X, Y, Z for a perfect white in illuminant A. The constant c was such as to make $R'_w = 80$.

With the foregoing values of the exponents and coefficients, the chromaticity in illuminant A that corresponds to the matched metameric samples in D_{65} is at $x'_c = 0.5322$, $y'_c = 0.4165$. That chromaticity is represented by the open circle in the small-scale diagram at the top of Fig. 7.25. Its location indicates that none of the 24 samples have the same appearance in illuminant A as in D_{65}: color constancy fails for all of them! By reference to the chromaticity of illuminant A, shown by the $\times$, and the appropriate part of the spectrum locus, dominant wavelengths between 584.4 and 585.7 nm are found for the 24 samples; according to the nonlinear adaptation formula, the color that has the same appearance in illuminant A, as have all of the samples in D_{65}, has dominant wavelength 587.4 nm. Furthermore, its purity, 64.6%, is more than one-third greater than the purity, 48%, of the most nearly similar sample, number 24.

The chromaticity required for color constancy by the von Kries formula, using the same primaries as the nonlinear formula, is indicated by the $+$ in both parts of Fig. 7.19. It again indicates that color constancy fails for all of the samples. However, it indicates that sample 24 is much closer to exhibiting color constancy than is indicated by the nonlinear formula. The dominant wavelength of the color required by the von Kries formula for constancy is 586.5 nm and its purity is 46%. Although the von Kries formula indicates that color constancy is much more nearly characteristic of sample 24 than is indicated by the nonlinear formula, that indication is not conclusive nor is it an indication of the superiority of the linear over the nonlinear formula. Rather, it offers a possibility for an experimental test and comparison of the two formulas, for investigation of color constancy, and for a critical evaluation of the suggested procedure for prediction of constancy.

Appendix Notes and Sources

Chapters 1 – 3 and Sect. 4.1 – 3, 5.1 – 3 are abridgments (with revisions and additions) of text in the *Handbook of Colorimetry,* which was prepared by the staff of the Color Measurement Laboratory of the Massachusetts Institute of Technology under the direction of Professor Arthur C. Hardy. I participated in its preparation. The handbook was published in 1936 by The Technology Press. It is kept in print by the MIT Press. It contains extensive tables and charts that are uniquely useful, especially for colorimetry with the CIE 1931 color-matching data and illuminant C. The abridgments, Figs. 1.1 – 4.1, 5.1, and Tables 1.1 – 5.3, 5.6 have been revised and are included in this book by permission of the MIT Press.

1 For a discussion of operational definitions, see
P. W. Bridgman: *The Logic of Modern Physics* (Macmillan, New York 1927).

2 Reflectance can depend on intensity of the incident beam in the case of *photochromic* materials, or when the intensity is so great that it burns or otherwise irreversibly changes the sample. Long periods of exposure to light can also cause irreversible changes of reflectance, which are usually referred to as *fading.* Fading is rarely encountered in modern spectrophotometric practice, because the measuring beams are not very intense. Fading is usually accelerated, or even occurs in the absence of light, by high temperatures and/or high humidity, or exposure to other vapors. Photochromic changes are temporary; the rapidity and magnitudes of photochromic changes and the time required for recovery from them are proportional to the intensity of the exposing beam. The intensities and durations of exposure to the measuring beams in modern spectrophotometers are so low and short that appreciable photochromic effects are rare in spectrophotometry of materials ordinarily encountered. Photochromic glass is used in some sunglasses, and in industrial and military goggles. Those sunglasses darken on continued exposure to sunlight. The goggles darken rapidly on exposure to extremely intense light, as from nuclear explosions or lasers. An increasingly common example of photochromic change of color occurs in house paint that contains the rutile variety of titanium dioxide. Normally, being exposed continually to daylight, the paint is an untinted white, but paint fresh out of the can has a more or less distinct ivory or cream tint. That tint fades or bleaches in daylight to the white. But storm sash stored in the dark may revert to the cream or ivory over the summer and exhibit a dismaying mismatch when reinstalled. A few days in daylight restores the match by *photochromism*. A more expensive variety of titanium dioxide, anatase, is always white; it is not photochromic.

3   For use in double-beam spectrophotometers, or for calibrating single-beam spectrophotometers, actual white materials are used as working standards. Around 1930, freshly scraped blocks of magnesium carbonate were used. Later, the fresh surface of such blocks was coated with a 1 or 2 mm-thick layer of magnesium oxide, deposited as smoke from freely burning metallic chips or ribbon of magnesium. More recently, such a layer of MgO deposited in a 2 mm cavity machined in an aluminum plate has been widely used, because it is more durable and has constant reflectance as high as MgO on $MgCO_3$ throughout the visible spectrum. More durable and more easily prepared working standards of purified barium sulfate have also been used recently, in the form of disks prepared under pressure and a paint made with polyvinyl alcohol. A proprietary material named Halon® (Allied Chemical Corp.) has recently become available, with which very durable and high-reflectance working standards can be prepared very conveniently. Disks of beryllium oxide are available; they are extremely durable and easily cleaned to assure constant reflectance, although their reflectance is not quite so high as MgO, $BaSO_4$, or Halon® .

Whatever working standard is used should be calibrated by absolute reflectometry. Spectrophotometers determine the ratios of spectral reflectances of samples to the reflectance of the working standard. That ratio should be divided by the absolute reflectance of the working standard, to determine the absolute spectral reflectances of the sample. Because most laboratories lack means for determination of absolute reflectances of working standards, it is necessary to use very durable, accurately replaceable, and easily cleaned working standards of a type whose absolute reflectance has been determined in some standardizing laboratory, such as the US National Bureau of Standards, the National Physical Laboratory in Teddington, England, the National Research Council in Ottawa, Canada, or the Bundesanstalt für Materialprüfung in Berlin. Durability and precise interchangeability are more-desirable attributes of such working standards than highest-possible or constant reflectance.

In the most-recent spectrophotometers, which incorporate computers, the absolute spectral reflectances can be stored and automatically divided into the measured ratios of the reflectances of samples and the working standard.

4   That a surface illuminated by a single wavelength will reflect light of only that wavelength is not true of fluorescent materials. In general, they also emit wavelengths longer than the illuminating wavelength. Such materials greatly complicate the concept and measurement of spectral reflectance. Those complications will not be discussed in this book. The problem is dealt with by F. Grum, C. J. Bartleson (eds.): *Optical Radiation Measurements, Vol. 2: Color Measurements* (Academic, New York 1980). Here, it is sufficient to state that the method presented in this book may be used to evaluate the color of the light received by the eye from any material, whether or not it is fluorescent.

5 The wavelengths indicated by the dashed vertical lines in Figs. 1.1 – 5 are the dominant wavelengths, which will be defined in Sect. 1.10. The dashed line in Fig. 1.6 indicates the complementary wavelength, which will also be defined in Sect. 1.10.

6 The initials (ICI) of the English translation of the name of the Commission Internationale de l'Eclairage are frequent in the literature of colorimetry from 1932 until about 1950. The initials (CIE) of the official French name have generally been used more recently, although IBK (the initials of the German name) and MKO (the initials of the Russian name) are still encountered. The initials CIE will be used in this book.

7 This account of the fundamental experiments of colorimetry is schematic and greatly simplified. It is valid in principle and adequate for this discussion. Complicating details of procedure and results, some of which will be mentioned later, are of more concern in relation to the psychology and physiology of color vision than for colorimetry.

8 J. C. Maxwell: On the theory of compound colors and the relations of the colours of the spectrum. Proc. Roy. Soc. London **10**, 404, 484 (1860); Phil. Mag. (4) **21**, 141 (1860); *Scientific Papers* (Cambridge Univ., Cambridge 1890) pp. 149, 410.

9 A. König, C. Dieterici: Die Grundempfindungen in normalen und anomalen Farbensystemen und ihre Intensitätsverteilungen im Spektrum. Z. Psychol. Physiol. Sinnesorg. **4**, 231 (1892); A. König: *Gesammelte Abhandlungen* (Barth, Leipzig 1903) p. 214.

10 W. deW. Abney: The colour sensations in terms of luminosity. Phil. Trans. Roy. Soc. London **193**, 259 (1905).

11 L. T. Troland: Report of Committee on Colorimetry for 1920 – 21. J. Opt. Soc. Am. **6**, 527 – 596 (1922).

12 W. D. Wright: A redetermination of the trichromatic coefficients of the spectral colours. Trans. Opt. Soc. London **30**, 141 – 164 (1928 – 29).

13 J. Guild: The colorimetric properties of the spectrum. Phil. Trans. Roy. Soc. London **A230**, 149 – 187 (1931).

14 CIE *Proceedings 1931* (Cambridge Univ., Cambridge 1932) p. 19.

15 W. S. Stiles, J. M. Burch: NPL colour-matching investigation, final report. Opt. Acta **6**, 1 – 26 (1959).

16 N. I. Speranskaya: Determination of spectrum color coordinates for twenty-seven normal observers. Opt. Spectrosc. (USSR) **7**, 424 – 428 (1959).

17 CIE *Proceedings 1963,* Bureau Central de la CIE, 52, Boulevard Malesherbes, 75008 Paris, France. If copies are available, they may be obtained from J. L. Tech. Secretary USNC/CIE, National Bureau of Standards, Washington, D.C. 20234.

18   Specification of hue in terms of wavelength is not strictly correct, as discussed in Sects. 5.2, 3. The wavelengths mentioned here are dominant wavelengths, which are defined in Sect. 1.10. In the present instances, the straight lines drawn from the white (illuminant C) point to the points on the spectrum locus of the wavelengths mentioned are extended beyond the spectrum locus to the points that represent the green and the blue primaries (at $x = 0, y = 1$ and $x = y = 0$, respectively). The "red" primary, at $x = 1, y = 0$ does not have a dominant wavelength. It has the complementary wavelength 496 nm.

19   Simultaneous color contrast is discussed in G. A. Agoston: *Color Theory and Its Application in Art and Design,* Springer Series in Optical Sciences, Vol. 19 (Springer, Berlin, Heidelberg, New York 1979) pp. 5, 61.

20   Gloss and other appearance characteristics are discussed by Richard S. Hunter: *The Measurement of Appearance* (Wiley, New York 1975).

21   Light that does not originate from atoms comes from electrons, in such unusual phenomena as synchroton radiation and Čerenkhov radiation.

22   Tables of spectral power of blackbodies at various temperatures have been published in many books. Various values of c_2 are used in those tables. The value currently recommended by the Conférence Générale du Poids et Mèsures (CGPM) is 0.014388 m K. To conform to that standard, the temperatures T in the tables in any compilation should be revised to $T' = 0.014388\ T/c_2'$, where c_2' is the value used for the compilation, expressed in meter Kelvins (m K). However, it is expressed in "centimeter degrees" (cm K) in some and in "micron degrees" (μK) in others. The "degrees" referred to in older publications are the same as the Kelvin units of absolute temperature used by the CGPM. In the now generally used SI system of symbols, both the word "degree" and the superscript ° sign are omitted for Kelvin temperatures. The CGPM value of c_2 is equivalent to 1.4388 cm K and 14,388 μK.

Various values of c_1 are also used in different compilations. Those variations are of little or no consequence for colorimetry because only relative values of spectral radiance are used. Adjustment of tables based on values of c_1 other than 3.7415×10^{23} to that basis requires simple proportional modifications, independent of temperature and wavelength. For example, Table 2.1, which was copied from the *Handbook of Colorimetry,* was based on $c_1 = 3.703 \times 10^{23}$ and $c_2 = 1.433 \times 10^7$. The easiest way to revise Table 2.1 to conform to the constants currently recommended by the CGPM would be to increase the values of power by 1% and to specify that they are for the spectral band from 561.74 to 562.24 nm. Tables of relative spectral distribution are most easily revised by changing the temperature specifications in proportion to c_2. For example, illuminant A was originally specified as 2848 K, when c_2 was assumed to be 1.435×10^7. Currently, when 1.4388×10^7 is the accepted value of c_2, the nominal temperature of illuminant A is

2856 K. Similarly, Judd and Wyszecki, in *Color in Business, Science, and Industry* (see [7.1]), point out that on the basis of $c_2 = 1.4388 \times 10^7$, the color temperature of D_{65} is 6504 K. The temperature 6500 K, originally intended, was based on $c_2 = 1.438 \times 10^7$.

23 Sections 4.4, 5 are the first of the "variations" mentioned in the subtitle of this book — new material that was not in the *Handbook of Colorimetry*. Further details are available in D. L. MacAdam: Photometric relationships between complementary colors. J. Opt. Soc. Am. **28**, 103 – 111 (1938).

24 The effectiveness of various wavelengths in white mixtures with the most effective combinations of short and long wavelengths has been discussed by Ralph W. Pridmore: Complementary colors: composition and effectiveness in producing various whites. J. Opt. Soc. Am. **70**, 248 – 249 (1980).

25 Tables of the products of $\bar{x}S$, $\bar{z}S$, and $\bar{z}S$ at 10 nm intervals from 380 to 770 nm for both the 1931 and 1964 CIE observers and for illuminants A, C, D_{65} and three other less frequently used illuminants are included in D. B. Judd, G. Wyszecki: *Color in Business, Science, and Industry*, 3rd ed. (Wiley, New York 1975). The values in each of those tables have been multiplied by a common factor such that the sum of $\bar{y}S$ values is 100. Therefore, when the values in those tables are multiplied by decimal values of transmittance (or reflectance) the totals of the products are tristimulus values expressed as percent. No division is necessary, provided that values of transmittance (or reflectance) at 10 nm intervals over the entire range from 380 to 770 nm were used. However, if only values at 20 nm intervals are used, the sums of the products should be divided by the sum of $\bar{y}S$ at only those intervals. That sum is, in general, somewhat different than 50. The result of the divisions must be multiplied by 100 to get the tristimulus values in percent. To guard against forgetting division by the total of $\bar{y}S$ for the utilized wavelength range and intervals, the products $\bar{x}S$, $\bar{y}S$, and $\bar{z}S$ are given without any adjustments in Tables 5.2 – 4. For convenience, the totals for all values given are printed at the bottoms of the corresponding columns in Tables 5.2 – 4, 8 – 10.

26 The symbol Δ indicates a small change or difference of the quantity represented by the symbol that follows Δ. In the present case, $\Delta\lambda$ indicates the difference between successive values of λ.

27 Some of the values of f'' in Table 5.12 are negative. If negative values cannot be used, linear combinations of f' and f'' can be used, where a in the formula $(1 - a)f' + af''$ has the value for which the linear combination for 410 nm is zero for the least of $S\bar{x}$, $S\bar{y}$, or $S\bar{z}$. A different value of a can be used for the long-wavelength combinations, such that the minimum value of $S\bar{x}$ or $S\bar{y}$ is zero at 690 nm. These adjustments correspond to using weighted averages of linear and parabolic extensions of spectrophotometric data to unmeasured wavelengths shorter than 400 nm and longer than 700 nm. If the indicated adjustments seem too troublesome and if negative $S\bar{x}$, $S\bar{y}$, $S\bar{z}$ values are not usable, the values of f' alone in Table 5.12 are recommended. Use of them, which assumes linear extensions of spectrophotometric curves to unmeasured wavelengths shorter than 400 nm and longer than 700 nm, is superior to the usual practice of ignoring the color-matching data and illuminant distributions outside those limits or merely adding their products to the values at 400 and 700 nm.

28   The symbol $\sum$ indicates that all quantities of the kind represented by the succeeding expression are to be summed (added together). Numerals (or symbols) placed under and over $\sum$ identify the first and last (respectively) quantities to be included in the sum.

The symbol $\int$ is the integral sign. The process indicated by it, called integration, consists of summation but with intervals (indicated here by $d\lambda$) so small that the result of the integration would not be changed if they were made smaller.

29   The numbers of ordinates are multiples of 9. For X and Z they are different from 99 in order to keep the multiplying factors as nearly as possible equal to those for Y. However, for illuminant A the factors for Z, for the 1931 and 1964 observer data, are only about $\frac{1}{3}$ as much as for Y when 99 ordinates are used for both Z and Y, but 99 wavelengths are listed in the tables. If factors for Z nearly as great as those for X and Y are desired, the abridged set of 33 wavelengths marked by asterisks can be used, with the corresponding factors. Greater accuracy is obtained, however, by using the full list of 99 wavelengths with the smaller factors.

30   A. C. Hardy: History of the design of the recording spectro-photometer. J. Opt. Soc. Am. **28**, 360 – 364 (1938);

D. L. MacAdam, W. E. White: Universal, digital tristimulus integrator. J. Opt. Soc. Am. **47**, 605 – 611 (1957).

31   If the coefficients of correlation between the pairs of weights used for determination of the indicated tristimulus values with the weighted-ordinate method are represented by ρ_{XY}, ρ_{YX}, and ρ_{XZ}; if S is expressed in units such that

$$\sum_{1}^{n} \bar{y}S = 1$$

and the sums

$$\sum_{1}^{n} \bar{x}S \quad \text{and} \quad \sum_{1}^{n} \bar{z}S$$

are designated C_X and C_Z, respectively; and if F_X, F_Y and F_Z represent the factors defined in Sect. 5.6, then, for the weighted-ordinate method,

$$r_{XY} = C_X(\sigma_{XY} \sqrt{(F_X^2 - 1)(F_Y^2 - 1)} + 1)$$

$$r_{YZ} = C_Z(\sigma_{YZ} \sqrt{(F_Y^2 - 1)(F_Z^2 - 1)} + 1)$$

and

$$r_{XY} = C_X C_Z(\sigma_{YZ} \sqrt{(F_X^2 - 1)(F_Z^2 - 1)} + 1).$$

The symbol δ indicates the change of the quantity specified by the letter that follows δ in the numerator, caused by a small change of only the quantity specified by the letter that follows δ in the denominator. All other quantities are kept unchanged. The term "partial derivative" is the name for the ratio of the change indicated by the numerator divided by the amount of the change that causes it, that is, the quantity indicated by the denominator.

32   The wavelengths and weights by which the ordinates for gaussian quadrature should be multiplied can be calculated by the method published by Robert Wallis: Fast computation of tristimulus values by use of gaussian quadrature. J. Opt. Soc. Am. **65**, 91 – 94 (1975). Wallis included wavelengths and weights for orders 3 to 6 for illuminants A and C for the CIE 1931 observer. 5 nm intervals from 380 to 770 nm were used for the results given in Tables 5.20 – 25.

33   The rms errors of fit for 3 typical spectrophotometric curves (from 380 to 770 nm) with polynomials of orders 6 to 10 are shown in this table.

Color # Order	76	96	105
6	2.7%	0.8%	1.2%
7	2.1%	0.5%	0.9%
8	1.6%	0.3%	0.7%
9	1.4%	0.2%	0.5%
10	1.2%	0.1%	0.3%

34   H. R. Condit, Franc Grum: Spectral energy distribution of daylight. J. Opt. Soc. Am. **54**, 937 – 944 (1964). According to the CIE formula, the phase of daylight most nearly like illuminant C has a color temperature of 6680 K. Figure 1.16 indicates for that phase of daylight a dominant wavelength of 550 nm and 2.5% purity.

35   Values of $\bar{x}$, $\bar{y}$ and $\bar{z}$ at every nanometer from 380 to 770 nm are listed in CIE Publication 15, *Colorimetry: Official Recommendations*. It can be obtained from the Bureau Central de la CIE, 52, Boulevard Malesherbes, 75008 Paris, France or from J. L. Tech, Secretary USNC/CIE, National Bureau of Standards, Washington, D.C. 20234.

36   Commission Internationale de l'Eclairage: *Method of Measuring and Specifying Colour Rendering Properties of Light Sources,* Publ. CIE No. 13.2 (E-1.3.2) 1974. Bureau Central de la CIE, 52, Boulevard Malesherbes, 75008 Paris, France or from J. L. Tech, Secretary USNC/CIE, National Bureau of Standards, Washington, D.C. 20234.

CIE publication 13.2 gives spectral reflectance data for 14 test samples, of which only the first 8 are used for the general color-rendering index. The remaining 6, like the first 8, are recommended for determination of special indices for applications in which specific ranges of colors are of major interest or importance. One or more of the 14 test samples are probably close to any such range. The corresponding special index is then more appropriate than the general index. Only the first 8 test colors, for the general index, are included in Table 6.2. CIE publication 13.2 gives the spectral reflectance data at 5 nm intervals from 360 to 795 nm. The data for the 8 samples are abridged in Table 6.2, at 10 nm intervals from 400 to 700 nm. The values given in CIE publication 13.2 at the intermediate 5-nm intervals rarely differ more than 0.001 from the values linearly interpolated between the values in Table 6.2. The differences of tristimulus values, between the 5-nm-interval integrations recommended by the CIE and the 10-nm interval integrations provided for by Table 6.2 do not have significant effects on color-rendering indices.

37   Use of the 1976 CIE Luv formula, rather than the color-difference formula recommended by the CIE in 1964, would give substantially the same color-rendering indices. The 1976 CIE Luv formula will be given and discussed in Sect. 8.1.

38   Further information on the Kubelka and Munk theory and applications is in D. B. Judd, G. Wyszecki: *Color in Business, Science, and Industry,* 3rd ed. (Wiley, New York 1975) pp. 420 – 460. For applications, see Rolf G. Kuehni: *Computer Colorant Formulation* (D. C. Heath, Lexington, MA 1975).

39   To avoid confusion with the other curves in Figs. 7.14, 15, trace the curve of interest on a piece of translucent paper. Include the left and right boundary lines for 400 and 700 nm. Mark on the 400 nm line the location of the horizontal stroke labeled with the number of the curve traced. Place the tracing over the curve for the Monastral Blue with the 400 and 700 nm lines coincident, and slide the tracing up or down until the right-hand portion of the traced curve is as nearly as possible coincident with the curve for the pigment. If the traced curve does not nearly fit the right-hand end of the pigment curve, try fitting it to the curve for Monastral Green or Carbon Black. When the right-hand end of the traced curve nearly fits one of the pigment curves, make a note of the name of that pigment and record the location of the horizontal stroke (on the 400 nm boundary) on the concentration scale on the pigment-curve chart. That is the ratio of the concentration of the pigment in the mixture represented by the curve for the pigment alone. For example, if the stroke on the tracing is at 0.4 on the scale of the curve for 2% Monastral Blue, then the amount of Monastral Blue in the mixture is $0.4 \times 2\% = 0.8\%$. To subtract the contributions of that pigment from the values of K/S for the mixture, tape the tracing to the pigment curve with the right-hand ends of the curves coincident and also the 400 and 700 nm lines. At every 20 nm (or 10 nm where changes are rapid), measure the separations between the traced curve and the pigment curve. At each of those wavelengths, find the value of the scale that is at that distance below 1. Subtract that value from 1. Find the distance from 1 on the concentration scale to the result of that subtraction. Mark a point at that distance above the traced curve at the corresponding wavelength. Draw a curve through the points thus determined. Try to fit the pigment curves for Monastral Scarlet, Monastral Red, Bon Red and Molybdate Orange to the resulting curve. Using the pigment curve that fits best, determine its concentration in the mixture in the manner explained previously. Subtract its contributions to K/S in the way explained above. The curve obtained represents K/S for the yellow constituent of the mixture. Find which of Medium Chrome Yellow or Dalmar Yellow best fits that curve. Determine its concentration in the mixture by the method described previously.

40   An apparent exception, to the effect that the chromaticity of the net change need not be coincident with O if the change of mass is zero, is fallacious because the change of mass is the denominator of the expression for each of its chromaticity coordinates. If the net change of Y is other than zero when the net change of m is zero, the chromaticity coordinate y of the change is infinite. The moment of the change, which then seems indeterminate, is merely the net change of Y. If that is other than zero, the y coordinate of the modified color is different than that of the original color, because the numerator of that fraction is changed, whereas its denominator is not changed.

41   Tables of data from which Figs. 7.23 – 25 were prepared are in D. L. MacAdam: Maximum visual efficiencies of colored materials. J. Opt. Soc. Am. **25**, 361 – 367 (1935).

42   To determine the transition wavelengths for a desired dominant wavelength and maximum reflectance (or transmittance) $R,$ draw a horizontal line in Fig. 7.27 through the dominant wavelength indicated on the left-hand margin. Through the points where that line intersects the two curves for R, draw vertical lines. They indicate the transition wavelengths on the horizontal axis. If a purple is desired, substitute the complementary wavelength in place of the dominant wavelength in the foregoing instructions. Short-end optimal colors have the dominant wavelengths indicated by the intersections of the R curves with the left-hand margin. The single transition wavelength for each is indicated by the intersection of the corresponding horizontal line with the other curve labelled with that same value of R. Long-end optimal colors have the dominant wavelengths indicated by the intersections of the R curves with the right-hand axis. The transitional wavelength for each is indicated by the intersection of the corresponding horizontal line with the other curve labelled with the same value of R.

43 A description of the apparatus used and complete results are in D. L. MacAdam: Visual sensitivities to color differences in daylight. J. Opt. Soc. Am. **32**, 247 – 274 (1942).

44 The statistical distributions of the data from which the ellipses were determined are discussed in L. Silberstein, D. L. MacAdam: Distribution of color matchings around a color center. J. Opt. Soc. Am. **35**, 32 – 39 (1945). For other studies of the normality of distributions of color matches, see:
W. R. J. Brown: Statistics of color-matching data. J. Opt. Soc. Am. **42**, 252 – 256 (1952);
W. R. J. Brown, W. G. Howe, J. E. Jackson, R. H. Morris: Multivariate normality of the color-matching process. J. Opt. Soc. Am. **46,** 46 – 49 (1956).

45 The derivation of g_{11}, $2g_{12}$ and g_{22}, Figs. 8.4 – 6, and various uses of them are explained in D. L. MacAdam: Specification of small chromaticity differences. J. Opt. Soc. Am. **33,** 18 – 26 (1943).

46 The charts mentioned have, in the past, been available as follows.
"Color speed computing charts"; Color Laboratory, Columbus Coated Fabrics Co. (Div. of the Borden Co.) P.O. Box 208, Columbus, OH 43216.
J. J. Hanlon: "Charts for rapid calculation of color difference"; Mohawk Carpet Mills, Inc., Amsterdam, NY 12010.
F. T. Simon and W. J. Goodwin: "Rapid graphical computation of small color differences"; Circulation Section, Advertising and Public Relations Dept., Bakelite Co. (Div. of Union Carbide Corp.) 420 Lexington Av., New York, NY 10017. These are now available, as Part Number 100019 P001, from Diano Corporation, Woburn, MA 01801

47 D. L. MacAdam: On the geometry of color space. J. Franklin Inst. **238**, 195 – 210 (1944).

48 E. Schrödinger: Grundlinien einer Theorie der Farbmetrik in Tagessehen. Ann. Phys. (Leipzig) (IV) **63**, 397 – 447, 481 – 520 (1920); translated and abridged by D. L. MacAdam: *Sources of Color Science* (MIT Press, Cambridge, MA 1970) pp. 134 – 182.
E. Schrödinger: in Müller-Pouillets *Lehrbuch der Physik,* 2nd ed., Vol. 2, Part 1 (1926); translated and abridged by D. L. MacAdam: *Sources of Color Science* (MIT Press, Cambridge, MA 1970) pp. 183 – 193.

49 H. v. Helmholtz: *Handbuch der Physiologischen Optik,* 2nd ed. (Vos, Hamburg 1896).

50 W. S. Stiles: A modified Helmholtz line element in brightness-colour space. Proc. Phys. Soc. London **58**, 41 – 65 (1946).

51 D. L. MacAdam: Color measurement and tolerances. J. Paint Technol. **37**, 1487 – 1531 (1965);
D. L. MacAdam: Geodesic chromaticity diagram: Farbe **18**, 77 – 84 (1969);

D. L. MacAdam, Geodesic chromaticity diagram, II. Derived directly from observational data. Farbe **19**, (1/6), 38 – 42 (1970);

D. L. MacAdam: Geodesic chromaticity diagram based on variances of color matching by 14 normal observers. Appl. Opt. **10**, 1 – 7 (1971).

52   D. L. MacAdam: Specification of color differences. Acta Chromatica **1**, 147 – 156 (1965).

53   D. L. MacAdam, W. R. J. Brown: Visual sensitivities to combined chromaticity and luminance differences. J. Opt. Soc. Am. **39**, 808 – 834 (1949).

D. L. MacAdam: Role of luminance increments in small color differences. In *Color Metrics,* ed. by J. J. Vos, L. F. C. Friele, P. L. Walraven, AIC/Holland (Institute for Perception TNO, Soesterberg, Holland 1972) pp. 160 – 170.

54   For contour diagrams that show values of the maximum and minimum ratios of color differences evaluated by use of the two 1976 CIE formulas, as functions of chromaticity, see Noboru Ohta: Correspondence between color differences calculated by the two CIE 1976 color-differences formulae. In *AIC Color 77* (Hilger, Bristol 1978) pp. 485 – 487.

55   W. Schultze, L. Gall: Experimentelle Überprüfung mehrerer Farbabstandsformeln bezüglich der Helligkeits- und Sättigungsdifferenzen bei gesättigten Farben. Farbe **18**, 131 – 148 (1969).

56   The CIE Luv formula for color difference is

$$\Delta E(L^*, u^*, v^*) = [(\Delta L^*)^2 + (\Delta u^*)^2 + (\Delta v^*)^2]^{1/2},$$

where $L^* = 116 \, (Y/Y_0)^{1/3} - 16$

$u^* = 13 L^* (u' - u_0')$

$v^* = 13 L^* (v' - v_0')$

in which $u' = 4X/(X + 15 Y + 3Z), \quad v' = 9Y/(X + 15 Y + 3Z)$

$u_0' = 4X_0/(X_0 + 15 Y_0 + 3Z_0), \quad v_0' = 9 Y_0/(X_0 + 15 Y_0 + 3Z).$

The constants X_0, Y_0, Z_0 are the tristimulus values of the material adopted as the standard white for each application, illuminated by the source appropriate for that application. The variables X, Y, Z are the tristimulus values of the samples whose color difference is to be evaluated, illuminated by that same source. The differences between their values of L^*, u^*, and v^* are designated ΔL^*, Δu^*, and Δv^*.

57   In terms of the CIE Luv formula, the metric hue angle $H_{uv}^0 = \tan^{-1}(v^*/u^*)$.

58   The CIE Lab formula for color differences is written in terms of the same constants X_0, Y_0, Z_0, variables X, Y, Z, and L^*,

$$E(L^*, a^*, b^*) = [(\Delta L^*)^2 + (\Delta a^*)^2 + (\Delta b^*)^2]^{1/2},$$

where $a^* = 500 \left[\left(\dfrac{X}{X_0} \right)^{1/3} - \left(\dfrac{Y}{Y_0} \right)^{1/3} \right]$

$\quad\quad b^* = 200 \left[\left(\dfrac{Y}{Y_0} \right)^{1/3} - \left(\dfrac{Z}{Z_0} \right)^{1/3} \right].$

In terms of the CIE Lab formula, the metric hue angle $H^0_{ab} = \tan^{-1}(b^*/a^*).$

59   E. J. Muth, C. G. Persels: Constant-brightness surfaces generated by several color-difference formulas. J. Opt. Soc. Am. **61**, 1152–1154 (1971).

60   A. K. Jain: Color distance and geodesics in color 3-space. J. Opt. Soc. Am. **62**, 1287–1291 (1972);

A. K. Jain: Role of geodesics in Schrödinger's theory of color vision. J. Opt. Soc. Am. **63**, 934–939 (1973).

The FMC1 formula used by Muth and Persels, and by Jain, is given by K. D. Chickering: Optimization of the MacAdam-modified 1965 Friele color-difference formula. J. Opt. Soc. Am. **57**, 537–541 (1967).

61   G. Fechner: *Elemente der Psychophysik* (Leipzig 1866).

62   J. Plateau: Über die Messung physischer Empfindungen und das Gesetz, welches die Stärke dieser Empfindungen mit der erregenden Ursache verknüpft. Ann. Phys. (Leipzig) **150**, 465–476 (1873).

63   A. H. Munsell: *A Color Notation* (Elis, Boston 1970) Chapt. 7;

A. H. Munsell: *An Atlas of the Munsell System* (Wadsworth-Howland, Malden, MA 1915);

John E. Tyler, Arthur C. Hardy: An analysis of the original Munsell color system. J. Opt. Soc. Am. **30**, 587–590 (1940);

K. S. Gibson, D. Nickerson: Analysis of the Munsell color system. J. Opt. Soc. Am. **30**, 591–608 (1940).

64   S. M. Newhall, D. Nickerson, D. B. Judd: Final report of the O.S.A. Subcommittee on the spacing of the Munsell colors. J. Opt. Soc. Am. **33**, 385–422 (1943);

D. B. Judd, G. Wyszecki: *Color in Business, Science, and Industry,* 3rd ed. (Wiley, New York 1975) pp. 483–486.

65   D. L. MacAdam: Nonlinear relations of psychometric scale values to chromaticity differences. J. Opt. Soc. Am. **53**, 754–757 (1963).

66   D. L. MacAdam: Uniform color scales. J. Opt. Soc. Am. **64**, 1691–1702 (1974).

67   See also Dorothy Nickerson: Gleichabständige OSA-Farbreihen. Ein einzigartiges Farbmustersortiment. Farbe + Design **12**, 16–24 (1979).

68 The specified and actual values for one set of cards were published in D. L. MacAdam: Colorimetric data for samples of OSA uniform color scales. J. Opt. Soc. Am. **68**, 121 – 130 (1978). The color differences between all nearest-neighbor pairs of those color cards, in terms of the committee's unit, are also tabulated in that article.

69 These formulas provide an easy way to determine the chromaticities of the primaries implied by any set of linear combinations of the CIE color-matching data. The axis intercept(s) and slope (or reciprocal slope) of the line that connects the chromaticities of the other two primaries can be determined directly from the formula

$$f = C\bar{x} + D\bar{y} + E\bar{z}$$

for the color-matching data for any primary.
The y-axis intercept a is $E/(E - D)$.
The x-axis intercept A is $E/(E - C)$.
The slope m is $C/(E - D) - A$.
The easiest way to draw the line that connects the chromaticities of the red and green primaries is to connect the two axis intercepts. Better accuracy is obtained for the line that connects the blue and red primaries by drawing a line with slope m through the y-axis intercept a. The line that connects the blue and green primaries is best drawn with the reciprocal slope M, through the x-axis intercept A. The primaries implied by any set of three formulas for color-matching data, in terms of the CIE data, $\bar{x}$, $\bar{y}$, $\bar{z}$, are at the three intersections of those three lines. This method of determining their chromaticities avoids inversion of the matrix of the coefficients of the formulas for the color-matching data or solution of three pairs of simultaneous equations, which are otherwise necessary and have been customary.

70 The chromaticities of the primaries used by Guild have never been explicitly published. For the preparation of Fig. 10.10 they were determined by interpolating the wavelengths at which the mean (average) trichromatic coefficients of the seven subjects tested by Guild were zero. Those coefficients, which are zero where the color-matching data are zero, were published by Guild in Table II on pp. 180 and 181 of his paper "The colorimetric properties of the spectrum," Phil. Trans. Roy. Soc. **A230**, 149 – 187 (1931). As indicated on Fig. 10.9, the zeros of the coefficients for the red primary were at 459 and 543 nm. For the green primary, the zeros occurred at 464 and 630 nm. For the blue primary, they were at 535 and 628 nm. The intersections of the three lines drawn on the CIE 1931 chromaticity diagram through those wavelengths on the spectrum locus are at $x = 0.7080$, $y = 0.2921$ for the red primary; $x = 0.2500$, $y = 0.7274$ for the green primary; and $x = 0.1475$, $y = 0.0419$ for the blue primary. The axis intercepts for the line between the red and green primaries are $a = 0.96494$ and $A = 1.01532$; its slope is $m = -0.95038$. The y-axis intercept of the line between the blue and red primaries is $a = -0.02391$ and its slope is 0.44629. The x-axis intercept of the line between the blue and green primaries is $A = 0.14127$ and its reciprocal slope is $M = 0.14946$. The formulas derived from these values were multiplied by arbitrary normalizing factors for graphical convenience in the preparation of Fig. 10.10.

71 Johannes von Kries: Contribution to the physiology of visual sensations. Arch. Anat. Physiol., Physiol. Abt. **2**, 505 – 524 (1878);

Johannes von Kries, "Chromatic adaptation", in *Festschrift der Albrecht-Ludwigs-Universität,* Fribourg (1902), pp. 145 – 158;

Johannes von Kries: "Influence of adaptation on the effects produced by luminous stimuli", in *Handbuch der Physiologie des Menschens,* Vol. 3 (Vieweg, Braunschweig 1905) pp. 109 – 282.

These are translated and abridged in D. L. MacAdam: *Sources of Color Science* (MIT Press, Cambridge, MA 1970) pp. 101 – 126.

72 H. Helson, D. B. Judd, M. H. Warren: Object-color changes from daylight to incandescent filament illumination. Illum. Eng. (NY) **47**, 221 – 223 (1952); reprinted in Deane B. Judd, *Contributions to Color Science,* NBS Spec. Publ. 545 (1979), pp. 382 – 395. Order from Supt. of Documents, US Govt. Printing Office, Washington, D.C. 20402. SD Stock No. SN 003-003-02126-I ($14.00).

73 Values of p_1 and p_4 may be computed with sufficient accuracy from the chromaticity coordinates x, y of the "second" and "first" adaptations, respectively, by use of the formula

$$p(R) = 6.2(x^2 + y^2) - 11xy - 1.1x - 0.61y + 0.82.$$

Whenever a value of p greater than 1.0 results from use of this or the following formulas for $p(G)$ or $p(B)$, the value $p = 1$ should be used instead. Values of p_2 and p_5 may be computed with sufficient accuracy by use of the formula

$$p(G) = 1 - 23(x - y)^2 + 2.3(x - y).$$

Values of p_3 and p_6 may be computed with sufficient accuracy by use of the formula

$$p(B) = 1.8 - x - 2y.$$

The constants b and a to be used with any value of p are

$$b = 6.1/(55.63^p - 2.422^p)$$
$$a = 7.8 - b(55.63^p).$$

Thus, for the 1964 observer and the indicated illuminants

	$p(R)$	$a(R)$	$b(R)$	$p(G)$	$a(G)$	$b(G)$	$p(B)$	$a(B)$	$b(B)$
A	0.35	-1.36	2.25	1.0	1.42	0.115	0.54	0.30	0.87
C	0.42	-0.51	1.52	0.98	1.40	0.126	0.85	1.25	0.21
D_{65}	0.42	-0.53	1.54	0.95	1.39	0.138	0.82	1.20	0.24

The corresponding values for the 1931 observer are within one unit in the last digit shown.

74 R. W. Burnham, R. M. Evans, S. M. Newhall: Influence on color perception of adaptation to illumination. J. Opt. Soc. Am. **42**, 597 – 603 (1952).

Subject Index

Author Index

G. A. Agoston

Color Theory and Its Application in Art and Design

1979. 55 figures, 6 color plates, 12 tables.
XI, 137 pages
(Springer Series in Optical Sciences, Vol. 19)
ISBN 3-540-09654-X

Contents: Introduction. – Color: Two Concepts. – Perceived Colors. – Light and Color. – Colored Materials. – Color Specification CIE). – Diverse Applications of the CIE Chromaticity Diagram. – Color Systems. – Appendix. – Color Plates I–VI. – References. – Author and Subject Index.

"...This book is an introductory text including topics of interest to artists and designers. It may be read and understood by anyone: no previous training in physics, mathematics, or color science is presumed. Equations are completely avoided in the body of the text. However, graphs and tables are included that give many specific details, for example, a table to convert Munsell designations to ISCC-NBS color names... The major strengths of clear, accurate writing on a wide variety of up-to-date topics and extensive references outweigh the deficiencies. The book provides an excellent overall perspective on color theory and is condescending to neither artist nor scientist. Practically anyone interested in color would benefit from reading Color Theory and its Application in art and design."

Applied Optics

Springer-Verlag
Berlin
Heidelberg
New York

W. Schultze

Farbenlehre und Farbenmessung

Eine kurze Einführung

3., überarbeitete Auflage. 1975. 57 Abbildungen, davon 4 in Farbe, 3 Tabellen. VII, 97 Seiten
ISBN 3-540-07214-4

Inhaltsübersicht: Das Wesen der Farbe. Die Grundlagen der Farbmetrik und die Normvalenz-systeme. Die Methoden der Farbmessung und Farbbewertung. Beziehungen zwischen spektraler Energieverteilung und farbmetrischer Bewertung. Farbsammlungen, Farbordnungen und die Bewertung des Farbabstandes. Besondere Einflüsse bei der Farbbetrachtung. Fluoreszenzfarben. Praktische Anwendung der Farbmetrik.Zur Frage der ästhetischen Farbbewertung.

Dye Lasers

Editor: F. P. Schäfer

2nd revised edition. 1977. 114 figures.
XI, 299 pages
(Topics in Applied Physics, Volume 1)
ISBN 3-540-08470-3

Contents: *F. P. Schäfer:* Principles of Dye Laser Operation. – *B. B. Snavely:* Continuous-Wave Dye Lasers. – *C. V. Shank, E. P. Ippen:* Mode-Locking of Dye Lasers. – *K. H. Drexhage:* Structure and Properties of Laser Dyes. – *T. W. Hänsch:* Applications of Dye Lasers. – *F. P. Schäfer:* Progress in Dye Lasers: September 1973 till March 1977.

Springer-Verlag
Berlin
Heidelberg
New York